Buried But Not Quite Dead

Anthony Daniels

Buried But Not Quite Dead

Forgotten Writers of Père Lachaise

Criterion
Books

First American edition published in 2024 by Criterion Books,
an activity of Encounter for Culture and Education,,
a nonprofit, tax exempt corporation.

Encounter Books website: *www.encounterbooks.com*

Manufactured in the United States and printed on acid-free paper.
The paper used in this publication meets the minimum requirements
of ANSI/NISO Z39.48–1992 (R 1997) (*Permanence of Paper*).

FIRST AMERICAN EDITION

LIBRRARY OF CONGRESS
CATALOGING-IN-PUBLICATION DATA IS AVAILABLE

Information for this title can be found
at the Library of Congress website under the following
ISBN 9781641773676 and LCCN 2023055001

Contents

If the fate of the living is sometimes strange, the fate of the dead is no less capricious.

Eugène-Melchior de Vogüé, Mazeppa, *1879*

FOR FAMILY REASONS, we bought a flat in Paris, near the entrance to the most famous cemetery in the world, Père Lachaise. I have always loved cemeteries and find them almost as irresistible as bookshops.

I took many walks in Père Lachaise, and one day the not very startling idea came to my mind, that if there were many famous writers – Balzac, Proust, Oscar Wilde – buried there, it was likely that there were also writers, many more of them in fact, buried there who had been completely forgotten, not necessarily because they were not good but because cultural memory is necessarily limited.

And so it proved. In an afternoon, without much difficulty, I assembled the names of at least twenty writers. I checked that they were unknown to the educated and literate French and British people of my acquaintance, and even when their names rang a faint bell, which was rarely, my acquaintances' knowledge of them never went further.

I have chosen eight such authors more or less at random. By the miracle of modern technology, I was able, through my telephone, to learn a little of their biographies (with the exception of one, so obscure that she had left no trace on the internet) and order their books from secondhand dealers before I had even left the cemetery. Before the advent of such technology, a book such as this would have taken many years to write, and I, certainly, would not have written it.

My aim has been to entertain while illustrating the inexhaustible depth of our past. The order of the chapters is that in which I wrote them. The order has no other significance.

Alice-René Brouillhet
(1887–1960)

WALKING IN A PART of the cemetery that I had not yet explored, I came across a tomb with five names inscribed on it, the last of which was that of Alice-René Brouillhet, *Ecrivain*, 1887–1960.

The fact that she was inscribed as *écrivain* rather than as *écrivaine* was interesting. The feminine form of the word has come into common usage relatively recently, certainly after Alice-René Brouillhet's death. In Britain and France, change in usage brought about by feminist pressure has gone in opposite directions: for example, the *Guardian* newspaper has banished the word *actress* from its pages in favor of *actor*.* This difference suggests to me that the demand for change arises more from a desire to exercise power than because of any respect or disrespect inherent in the term formerly employed.

Also interesting is the fact that Alice Brouillhet took not only her husband's surname, but his first name, René, and added it to her own first name. This was common practice until quite recently: my mother-in-law signed her name by including the initial of her husband's name. Times have changed.

The other names on the tomb are as follows:

RENÉ BROUILLHET
MEDECIN AIDE MAJOR 5ME GENIE

---

* Thus, Marilyn Monroe was an actor, not an actress.

DECEDE LE 9 FEVRIER 1916
A L'AGE DE 23 ANS

LUCIENNE DIEUDONNE NEE BAUDOIN
(*LEONE DEVIMEUR*)
DECEDEE LE 25 JANVIER 1920
A L'AGE DE 35 ANS

MME VVE BAUDOIN NEE BLANCHE LERUDE
1861–1928
ELISE TOUFFLET
1851–1929

Alice Brouillhet was a war widow. Her husband died aged twenty-two years, eleven months, and eight days. He was a military doctor, having joined the army in 1913. His tomb, like many tombs of soldiers who died in action, is decorated by an effigy of his military medals, in this case the *Croix de guerre*. As far as I am aware, Alice, his widow, never remarried: she remained his widow for forty-four years, having been married to him for six months, though also engaged to him for at least seven months.

What a wealth of suffering these bare biographical facts conjure! (I am here, of course, giving rein to my imagination: the truth might have been quite otherwise.) I surmise that she did not remarry for at least one of two reasons, possibly for both. The first was the decimation of the generation of men into which she might have remarried, which made eligible men so rare in post-war France and both widows and spinsters so numerous. The second reason was that she might well have felt that to remarry was to betray the memory of her poor husband, whose flame she kept alive within her like the flame at the tomb of an unknown warrior. Memory of past loss decays, especially with the accretion of new and happy experience, and one can easily imagine a state of mind in which the preservation of the memory of a good, decent, and optimistic young man, his life cut cruelly and undeservedly short, would be an inescapable duty and constitute henceforth the main purpose of an existence. Thus happiness is a state that is to be avoided as a betrayal.* Moreover, it is my view that the modern idea emanating from psychiatrists that a period of grief lasting longer than some specified – and rather short – length of time is, *ipso facto*, pathological is, if I may so put it, deeply shallow†.

After the war was over, Alice Brouillhet published five novels, the last in 1930. To judge from the three that I have read‡, and the short travelogue she published in 1931, she

---

* A trivial example of this, no doubt, was the feeling both my wife and I had after the death of our beloved dog, Ramses. We thought that to have another dog soon after his death would constitute a betrayal of his memory and be an indication that we had not loved him as much as we thought that we had or as much as we ought to have done. It would also have been unfair on the new dog, insofar as he would suffer in our affections by the comparison with Ramses.

† My mother, a refugee in England from Nazi Germany, was engaged to be married to an RAF fighter pilot. He was killed in the defense of Malta, and after her death I found the telegram from the War Office informing her that he was missing in action, presumed dead, as well as the letter from his commanding officer describing how valiantly he had died and his last letter to my mother, written on the eve of his death. These documents were tied together by a faded red-satin ribbon. I suspect that my mother never recovered fully from the loss or, as the cant phrase now current has it, gained closure.

‡ These are: *Yamunâ le solitaire* (Paris: Éditions "Athena," 1922); *Belzébuth crucifié* (Paris: André Delpeuch, 1929); *La Dame de jade* (Paris: André Delpeuch, 1930). The second of these was dedicated to her "sainted" mother, presumably the Mme Vve Baudoin of the tombstone who died in 1928. I noticed that *La Dame de jade* was printed under the "direction" of G. Baudoin, presumably her brother.

consoled herself by traveling widely in what was then the French Empire, in Indochina, the Maghreb, Sub-Saharan Africa, and the Levant.

4   The travelogue, *Sous le ciel africain: 52° à l'ombre (reportage)* (Under the African Sky: 52 Degrees in the Shade [Reportage]) is a strange little book of ninety-six pages.[1] It starts with the author on board a boat, the *Haïti*, from Bordeaux to Casablanca. The author offers no explanation anywhere as to the origin or purpose of her journey, though since it consisted almost entirely of visits to clinics and hospitals in Morocco and Algeria, I assume either that she was on some official tour or that, her husband having been a doctor, she felt obliged, as if by apostolic succession, to maintain an interest in medicine.

On the journey out, without meaning to or not, she illustrates the gulf between the colonizers and the colonized. In the first-class saloon, "a native performed an exotic dance, accompanied by the claps of passengers lolling on the bridge":

> His two shirt tails fluttered over his trousers. The soldiers [on the boat] showed their appreciation by bursting out laughing. The Arab suddenly stopped his performance: "Ah, since you're fed up with the dance."[2]

This is surely very painful. The dancer probably didn't think of his performance as just a mild diversion of bored passengers to while away their time, but as a genuinely artistic expression. One is reminded of *The Seagull*, in which Arkady's play within the play, to which he attaches such importance, is the occasion of his mother's laughter. How easy it is casually and without thought to give offense! Or perhaps – worse still – the soldiers didn't care whether or not they gave offense.

Arriving in Casablanca, Alice Brouillhet is taken in hand

by a soldier – a junior officer, I surmise – who walks with her in the Casbah:

> In the interior of the houses, some natives, kneeling on dirty mats, shout and gesticulate, while grumpy children fight among themselves to gather the *sou* that my soldier has thrown to them.[3]

5

The scene does not appeal to the author, who makes haste to leave this "foul alleyway."

The next day, she visits the hospitals of the city. There she witnesses an Arab arriving who, on embracing a doctor, says "I've heard that you'd performed miracles here, I've come eighty kilometers on horseback to see you, take care of me."[4]

This short passage took me back to the time, between forty and fifty years ago, when I worked for a time in Mpilo Hospital in Bulawayo, in what was still Rhodesia. This was towards the very end of colonial regimes in Africa. I remember an old patient in heart failure who had walked (not ridden) fifty miles through the bush – that is to say, eighty kilometers – to the hospital to receive treatment there, because it was known to perform miracles. Having received his treatment, he walked back.

When it came to the colonial regime, Alice Brouillhet was no André Gide or Albert Londres, who denounced the abuses that they saw on their travels in the French colonies.[5] On the contrary: her belief was that the French had brought many improvements. For example:

> Syphilis is widespread among the natives [of Algeria], it has been estimated that three quarters of the population are affected. The cost of arsenical and bismuth

medicaments, etc ... furnished free by Algeria and the Ministry of Hygiene is as much as two hundred and fifty thousand francs.[6]

6

Contrary to the detractors, she says:

the Arabs are not treated in North Africa like slaves. They are cared for [medically] at our expense and those who work for us are more than sufficiently paid. Posts as civil servants are even reserved for them, and the generosity of France does not stop there.[7]

The last words of the book are: "France! A small point on the large map of the world, a little star that spreads its light over the whole earth!"[8]

There are judgments in the book that would, at least in France, end the author up in court. Here she speaks of incidences of hereditary syphilis among the Moroccan Arabs (they are much fewer among the Jews, who for other reasons are much easier to assimilate):

Cases of hereditary syphilis are very frequent. This illness evolves in a different way among the Arabs. It manifests itself by mutilating marks of the face or limbs. Nervous lesions are extremely rare, because the natives are very sober and make no intellectual efforts.[9]

No doubt these unfashionable sentiments, which were, however, conventional at the time, at least among citizens of the colonizing countries, would incline a modern reader to abandon Alice Brouillhet forthwith as being beyond the pale, but I think this would be a mistake, as I hope later to prove. Very few people, after all, are able to examine with dispassion the conventionality of their own opinions or question very deeply their own assumptions.

Another story in the book had a peculiar resonance with me. I have long followed (with dismay) the spread of tattoo-ing in the population, which seems to me a peculiar admix-ture of self-mutilation and downward cultural aspiration. The following passage, then, caught my attention. An officer of the French Foreign Legion is speaking to the author:

> I know that there are distinguished men in the Legion, I discovered a sergeant of the *goumiers* [Moroccan troops who served as auxiliaries to the Legion], the son of a great radiologist, a former Legionnaire. Desiring to make money, this young man had trafficked drugs in England. He was arrested in London and imprisoned. Some pris-oners who were sailors tattooed him by force. The poor fellow, afflicted with shameful tattoos, didn't dare return to his family who anyway wouldn't have wanted to know him. He joined the Legion ... and under his broken appear-ance, I recognized a man of the world.[10]

Was it his tattoos or his criminal record that would have caused his family to reject him if he had returned to it? And note that it was deemed sufficient by the officer that the young man should have been the son of a famous radiolo-gist for him to be "distinguished." He was of good family, when being of good family was far more important than it is now, or at least is admitted to being.

There is one curious irony in the book. Speaking of the Jews, the author says:

> The Israelites of Morocco have always been pillaged, maltreated by the Arabs and confined to the Mellah [the

city within a city whose walls supposedly protected them from riots by the Muslim majority]. Looting and murders were frequent in the ghetto. Our protectorate [of Morocco] has brought liberation ..."[11]

8

The irony was that, ten years after of its publication, a regime came into power in France that reversed the liberation of the Jews in the Maghreb and, in its own territory, committed an atrocity with a thoroughness that the pre-modern polities of the region could never manage. Despite the Vichy regime's recent record, however, the Jews, when the lands of the Maghreb achieved or recovered their independence, chose, practically with unanimity, France as offering them greater safety and a better life. I do not think anyone would deny that it was a wise choice.

This slim volume is furnished with fourteen black-and-white photographs, all but one of them of medical establishments. They are all of impressive or even elegant construction, consistent with the artistic style of the country, and there is no pullulation around them, no air of desperate overcrowding such as has overtaken hospitals even in rich countries. On the contrary, they are redolent of calm and quiet instead of chaos and clatter. Appearances can be deceptive, of course: Victorian asylums were frequently magnificent in their exteriors, Versailles of madness as it were, but desolate and uncomfortable within. Still, a splendid exterior is a splendid exterior, and adds something of value to the world, even if what goes on within is of doubtful value (not that the doctors of the time would have known it).

Alice Brouillhet's novels have a strange atmosphere, a mixture of decadence and spirituality. Their plots are rudimentary. In *Yamunâ le solitaire*, for example, published in 1922, two young Parisians, a painter, Maurice Hubert, and his friend, Daniel Jérôme, journey together to Damascus (whether before or after the war, that is to say before or after Syria became a French mandated territory, is not clear). Daniel is fleeing a broken love affair with Geneviève Varly, whom he mistakenly accuses of having slept with a cynical acquaintance of his called Emile Lambert. In Syria, the two young men meet a half-French Hindu called Yamunâ, a semi-mad dilettante and aesthete of otherworldly virtue and mystical inclinations. While on a visit to Yamunâ's beautiful and isolated retreat outside Damascus, Daniel falls desperately ill with fever of an unspecified nature and Geneviève, who has always loved him, make the difficult journey from Paris to his bedside on learning of his illness. Alas, too late, and he dies after their reconciliation. Yamunâ, who has eschewed all fleshly contact, catches a glimpse of Geneviève naked and is briefly tempted by her, but in the end returns to his chaste and solitary life, in which he remains perfectly content after recovering from his brief erotic awakening.

9

Even a bad novel can be instructive: at the very least it will tell us something about the time in which it was written. The whole story turns on the reason for Daniel's decision to accompany his friend to Syria. Having learned of Geneviève's supposed easy virtue, Daniel says to his friend:

> So, this failure [Emile Lambert], as you call him, knew how to please Geneviève Varly. This failure has obtained from her what I should never have permitted myself to ask of her outside marriage.[12]

The war, shortly after the end of which this was written, had a loosening effect on the morals and manners of society, but not universally or all at once. Victorianism survived. Alice Brouillhet would hardly have written this had she felt it was as stilted and absurd as it now seems to us. It is difficult to imagine a young man now saying "what I should never have permitted myself to ask of her outside marriage" before breaking up with the woman he loved. But we should not complacently imagine that we have settled relations between men and women satisfactorily once and for all, just because we smile at Daniel Jérôme's little speech. To this day, even the most promiscuous among us usually wants the exclusive sexual possession of someone else and is outraged to discover that we do not have it.

And the author is not quite as naive as her character, with whose rejection of his lover we are supposed to understand and sympathize, might suggest. En route to Syria, the two young men pass through Egypt. On the day of their arrival in Cairo, they witness something that shocks them:

> A little further on, in a little square, two little girls were playing. On seeing the two foreigners, the older of them, who might have been eleven, approached them and whispered some words with a mysterious air into the ear of Maurice Hubert; realizing that he didn't understand Arabic, she opened her gandoura [gown] with a majestic gesture and showed him her thin nudity.
>
> "Baksheesh! Baksheesh!" she said.
>
> In her turn, her companion approached Daniel Jérôme, and after having revealed her skinny chest, held out her hand in murmuring:
>
> "Signore! Baksheesh!"
>
> Daniel Jérôme and Maurice Hubert withdrew.
>
> "In truth, what a nice country," remarked Daniel, "a country in which they offer foreigners the nudity of girls of ten years old in return for some baksheesh."[13]

Cleary Daniel and Hubert blame the country rather than the people who visit the country. This put me in mind of

some verses of Sor Juana Inés de la Cruz, a seventeenth-
century Mexican nun, poet, and mystic, that a taxi driver in
Mexico City recited to me thirty-five years ago, and that I
committed at once to memory:

> Oh, who is more to blame?
> She who sins for pay,
> Or he who pays for sin?

I assume that Alice Brouillhet is describing what she has
either seen herself or been told by a witness whom she considers reliable, in which case Western pedophilic tourism to
impoverished countries is no new phenomenon. A far better-
known writer than Brouillhet, André Gide, indulged in and
justified it, at least for himself, and, were it not for the Coronavirus epidemic in which I write this, the affair of Gabriel
Matzneff would still be making headlines. Matzneff, a cultivated and by all accounts witty and charming man with
strong connections in the Parisian intelligentsia, for many
years not only patronized pedophilic prostitution in an
impoverished country, the Philippines, but made no efforts
to disguise the fact that he had done so, certain of his protection as a member of a charmed circle, and that his refined
prose style would cover a multitude of sins.

There is no new thing under the sun; and I suppose that
Yamunâ le solitaire might be used as evidence that a strict
sexual code, by promoting sexual frustration, also conduces
to sexual depravity: except, of course, that a loose sexual
code conduces to exactly the same thing. Thus there is no
escape from human depravity.

The character of Yamunâ, aesthete and mystic, put me in
mind of that Lebanese purveyor of spiritual kitsch, Kahlil
Gibran, whose major – most popular – work, *The Prophet*,

was published in the year following the publication of *Yamunâ le solitaire.*

The last novel that Alice Brouillhet published (in 1930) was *La Dame de jade.** It is very unexpected, a work of science-fiction, or at least of futurism. The date of the action is not specified, but is at the very least in the next century (ours); in the meantime, the climate has changed drastically:

> In those time, the Europeans, fleeing the glaciers that progressively covered their continent, took refuge in Africa to find a more moderate temperature; then, little by little, the air cooled, and the snows hardened into glaciers.[14]

Chad, because of its distance from "the great frozen rivers" of Europe, had become the capital of France, and the father of the heroine of the book, Fabienne Savignan, a scientist, has led an expedition to the equatorial regions of Africa in order to survey them and find a more suitable place for human habitation:

> The scientist, Claude Savignan, had decided to go towards the Equator in order to take a survey. None of the audacious people who, impelled by the hope of taking advantage of its heat, had left Chad, Ouadaï, Borno, Sokoto, Adamaouna, had returned. The principal towns of these states were still flourishing markets, but the relentlessly progressive cold risked paralyzing their activity.† [15]

---

* Her last book, as far as I am aware, was published in 1953, and was titled *L'Étoile des catacombs: La Passion de Sainte Cécile*, whose nature I have not been able to discover. She published nothing between *Sous le ciel* and *La Passion.*

† I write this as COVID-19 (or the official reaction to it) has relentlessly paralyzed the activity of the flourishing markets of Europe.

As I was growing up, fear of freezing was indeed the principal anxiety evoked by the prospect of climate change, before it was far surpassed by the fear of overheating.* There is a fashion in fears, as in everything else.

Things are pretty bad in the future depicted in *La Dame de jade*:

> Timbuktu, which owed its prosperity in the XXth century to its proximity to the ocean and to the Niger, no longer attracted merchants; the sea sown with icebergs frightened off the sailors, the ocean currents were no longer practicable, and the snowstorms rendered communication by air or rail impossible.[16]

Once again, Alice Brouillhet praises French colonialism, at least by comparison with others:

> Knowing by long experience that the French people were the most conciliatory, the Africans by preference lived in the center of Africa.[17]

Every nation, I suppose, maintains illusions about itself, and I suppose also that, within limits, it is just as well that it does, for otherwise collective achievement would be impossible.†

Chad has become a cosmopolitan place, with an Indochinese quarter, but the races, though they associate together, rarely mix. Claude Savignan, however, before his departure for the equatorial regions of the continent, lived in the Pagoda of the *Dame de jade*, having been invited there by the

---

* Of course, the fact that we were mistaken before does not by itself prove that we are mistaken now.

† Whether this was the case in 1930 is an empirical question. Was there net voluntary movement into or out of the French colonial empire in Africa? It seems to me unlikely that Alice Brouillhet considered this question.

venerable Mat-Giang, whose life in some unspecified way he had saved.

To place the action of a book in the distant future is to give the author the chance to comment acerbically on the present, which Alice Brouillhet duly takes. At a banquet, a historian looks back at the French of the twentieth century. He says that the literature and art of an epoch are the best reflection of its reality, and hence (from them) draws the following conclusions:

> This people consisted of the jealous and the blood-thirsty.... The majority of legitimate unions [marriages] ended in murder or suicide, all methods being employed, poison, sharp instruments, firearms. Irregular unions were hardly happier.[18]

Brouillhet, through the mouth of her historian, satirizes modern criminology and jurisprudence, as she sees them:

> Under the happy rule of this sentimental people, men risked committing a murder only if they had relatives, for they knew that was enough for their lawyer to secure an acquittal, for him to evoke in a trembling voice the honorable and proud old man with white hair or an admirable mother who so anxiously awaited the verdict, or the children, innocent victims. The heart of men was easier to touch than their mind.* [19]

---

* Fifty years ago, I had a cousin accused of a very serious crime. His advocate evoked the distress that imprisonment would cause his respectable mother (my aunt). This appeal was successful: the judge sentenced him to two years' imprisonment, suspended for two years. My cousin never committed another crime, and indeed became extremely successful.

If this did not work, the accused's advocate had a last resort: the doctor.

> To justify crime, they had created the medical expert who, in front of the judges, exposed with delicacy and brio the range of hereditary and acquired cases of absence of responsibility.* [20]

15

The lot of writers in France was not a happy one – at least until 1930, when *La Dame de jade* was published:

> The writers of the XXth century – who were too numerous – did not earn a living; happily, certain well-off women gave literary teas in their salons where hungry men of letters came to be comforted and to listen to their literary brothers declaiming their poems, and sometimes their own. [21]

The plastic arts were exercised in a peculiar manner:

> The great painters painted thin and tall women; beings ill-favored by nature; men with twisted calves and flattened skulls; women with red faces and livid flesh. The unimportant artists confined themselves to normal women in whom no one was interested. Others devoted themselves to geometrical lines, or in sticking on the same canvas the things they happened to have seen during the day. A bus next to a musical instrument, a ballerina next to a plunger. As for the sculptors, they claimed that only (!) the "idea" counted ...[22]

---

* I was myself an expert in murder trials, sometimes presenting evidence for the defense, sometimes for the prosecution.

Thus Alice Brouillhet relayed the prejudices of the common man faced with what was then modern art, a prejudice that I veer between holding myself and despising in others. Only five years before the publication of her book, the great Spanish critic José Ortega y Gasset, wrote an eloquent essay, *The Dehumanization of Art*, on the subject of the difficulty of modern art – that is, of the art that was modern at the time that Alice Brouillhet was writing. Here is Ortega y Gasset:

> It [the new art] divides people into two parties, the one, tiny, composed of the very few who are favorable to it; the other, the great majority, who are hostile to it.... When the dislike of a work of art arises from an inability to understand it, a man feels humiliated, there is an obscure awareness of his own inferiority in the face of it for which he must compensate by an indignant self-affirmation ...[23]

Although intelligent and cultivated, Alice Brouillhet belonged to the part of the humiliated.

Her short dystopic novel lacks the prophetic quality of, say, *Brave New World* or *Nineteen Eighty-Four*. It is muddled and without an overall point of view or target. This is sufficient to account for its failure to survive, for the fact that it has never been reprinted. But that does not mean that it entirely lacks perspicacity. There is, for example, a suggestion or hint that political Islam will provoke a revolt against European domination. An African leader of the future in which the action of the book takes place, a Muslim, expresses with concision the thought of many an Islamist of today:

> The ambition of certain of their chiefs [those of the Muslims], the softening of their soldiers, the loss of faith, precipitated decadence. It is vital that we give to

our people the preponderance to which it has a right, and woe to those who stand in their way.[24]

Alice Brouillhet's older sister, Léone Devimeur-Dieudonné, buried in the same tomb, was also a novelist, if someone who wrote only one book can be so called. *La Colombe blessée* (The Wounded Dove) was published in January 1920, the month in which the author died, aged thirty-five. As the protagonist of *The Wounded Dove*, a narrative in the first person, dies by suicide at the end of the book, one cannot by help but wonder whether the life (or in this case death) followed art. After all, the great majority of first books are strongly autobiographical.

Léone Devimeur-Dieudonné, née Baudoin, left few traces – as, of course, most of us did before the coming of the internet and social media.* I have found a Léone Devimeur of at least approximately her age who was an actress, and who appears in pre-war photographs in what for the time must have been suggestive poses. To put it no higher, or lower, she is very coquettish. If this indeed was she, the war must have come as a reformative experience, for she became a nurse and must therefore have revised her conception of what life was about.

In fact, her one novel is, in my opinion, the superior of any of her sister's. It is almost an extended version of Chekhov's story "Lady with Lapdog", but set in France rather than in the Crimea. The two sisters, Alice and Léone, must have had some contact with the literary world of their time, for both *La Colombe blessé* and *Yamunâ le solitaire* have laudatory prefaces from Henry Bidou, a remarkable and well-known

---

* There will no doubt be a tendency in the future for historians to judge a person's importance by the size of his electronic trace. If the important leave a trace, those who leave a trace will be important.

figure, a venturesome war correspondent despite having had a leg amputated, and a prominent literary critic for many well-known publications, dying in 1943 in that town of ill fame (at the time), Vichy. In the preface, Bidou says, "Hardly had the page on which the death of Jacqueline been described than the hand which wrote it became motionless in its turn. The graceful genius that had recounted it was silenced, and like those who are depicted on tombs, she put a finger to her lips."[25] Does this imply some secret that should remain as such?

Jacqueline is a naive young girl who is brought up in the countryside of Burgundy by her beloved grandparents. She has been entrusted to them for her upbringing by her worldly and frivolous parents (money never presents a problem in the book, nor is the source of its plentiful supply mentioned or even hinted at), who have taken medical advice that Jacqueline is of too delicate a constitution to survive a childhood in Paris. In those days, when doctors were in fact able to do very little for their patients, their instructions were received with superstitious awe and obeyed to the letter.

Jacqueline grows up surrounded by natural beauty and sees nothing of the world except to go on holiday to another beautiful house owned by her grandparents in Brittany. But suddenly her parents, who have entirely neglected her for years, reappear in her life and take her on holiday to Switzerland. Their object in doing so is to marry her off, and they introduce her the handsome, charming, worldly, sensual but shallow, and ultimately cruel man who is to become her husband, Pierre Fresnois. He is, in fact, the first man she has ever met.

The marriage, of course, turns out badly. Pierre drinks, gambles, and has affairs. Eventually Jacqueline meets a better man, Claude Vernier, who is all that Pierre is not: kind, intellectual, refined, mannerly. He is also a playwright of some distinction. They fall in love, Jacqueline finding in him all that is missing in Pierre.

Claude wants to marry Jacqueline, but of course cannot do so unless she divorces Pierre. This she would be willing to do, except that divorce would profoundly shock and upset her grandparents, who hold to the old-fashioned view of marriage as an unbreakable sacrament, and she cannot bear to cause pain to those to whom she owes so much and whom she loves so tenderly. But Claude becomes impatient: he takes her reluctance to divorce Pierre as a sign of ambivalence towards him, that in part she loves her desultory husband. Claude therefore demands divorce and marriage as signs that she loves him alone, failing which he will leave her; he does not understand the strength of her unwillingness to upset her grandparents. In the end, he does leave her, undertaking a long voyage without any way of being contacted. Jacqueline, desperate, throws herself from a cross-Channel ferry (there are, incidentally, several disobliging portrayals of the English, stolid, lumpen, and unimaginative, in this book, though at one point Jacqueline quotes lines from *Othello* in the original) and drowns.

The whole story turns on the horror of divorce which now seems to us rather peculiar, even primitive, though it persisted to a high degree into my childhood, when the divorced were still spoken of *sotto voce* as if they had committed some nearly unpardonable sin.* It is hard for us now to imagine this attitude, though it existed within living memory. But it cannot really be said that, since the relaxation of the divorce laws, relations between men and women

19

---

* In those days, divorce was possible only on proof of cause: desertion, cruelty, or adultery. After my mother died, I found among her papers the reports of the private detective she set upon my father to prove his adultery as a preliminary to divorce proceedings. In the end, my parents separated but did not divorce. These papers now seem as dated as patchouli or antimacassars.

have become easier, unproblematic, or even improved. They're a little different, that's all.

How far this little book, which is written in an unaffected but (or is it therefore?) affecting way, is autobiographical I cannot say. There is the fact that most first fictions are autobiographical; that the author might have been an actress and therefore knew playwrights (Henry Bidou, who wrote the preface, wrote a play); and that the protagonist died by her own hand just days before the author. The protagonist, however, was twenty-three when she died, the author thirty-five. Without more research, I cannot know for certain, and sometimes one prefers to speculate, not to know.

To return now to Alice Brouillhet: she wrote one book that was truly remarkable and that deserves to live, *Les Héros sans gloire*, "Heroes without Glory," published in 1927. It is a book dedicated to the memory of her sister, and there is a tribute to her by a military doctor called Dr. Lafond:

> Doctor Lafond ... certifies that Mme Léone DEVIMEUR-DIEUDONNÉ, née Baudoin, was a nurse in the Gallia Hospital, Cannes.... Gifted with a superior intelligence and a burning patriotism, this nurse placed her limitless devotion at the service of the wounded, loving above all to care for the most gravely ill, allowing herself to be put off neither by tetanus nor gas gangrene. During the time that she stayed in my service, she was a precious help to me because of her high intellectual culture, her knowledge of anatomy and her devotion to antisepsis. I am happy to render homage to her great heart as a Frenchwoman.[26]

Heroes without Glory is a collection of notes about the more than 1,500 French doctors who gave their lives during the Great War. Some consist of a very few details only, but oth-

ers contain extracts from their letters or diaries, furnished
by relatives. It is a work of astonishing dedication to what
must have been for the author a difficult and painful task,
published eleven years after her husband's own death, and
surely it is to be construed as a monument to his memory, a
prolonged posthumous act of love.

21

Not surprisingly, perhaps, one of the longest entries is
her husband's, for she had his letters easily to hand. But she
gives him no pride of place, his entry appearing in strict
alphabetical order like all the others – as he would undoubtedly have wanted, for if there is one thing that unites all
these records it is the complete lack of self-importance of
the subjects, a lack, which, for good or ill, I doubt that would
find among such a body of men today.

She extracts entry from his diary, which is addressed
to her:

> *November, 1914.* If something happens to me, a letter
> will be found in my wallet, a letter for you. Know from
> now on that my last thoughts will be for you, my only
> memory of happiness ...[27]

And indeed, that last words of many a dying doctor recorded
in this book were along the lines of "Tell my wife that my
last thoughts were of her." Witnesses of their husbands'
deaths in the field often wrote this, or something similar, to
the widows. Was this simply an attempt to comfort them in
their loss, or was it the literal truth? I suppose that there is
no rational way of deciding, but I prefer to think of it as the
latter.

Dr. Brouillhet describes of the life on the front to his
fiancée:

December, 1914. My darling, it is midnight, I have just returned from Mass with the officers of the battalion; this Mass takes place every Sunday.... The Germans must know the exact time of this Mass because every time we leave they sprinkle us with shells.[28]

22

After six months of war, his patriotic exaltation has not waned:

5 January, 1915: I don't want anyone to complain of me, I do my duty like the others, and I have only one dream: to advance with our victorious armies and then quickly come back to you after the final success.

5 April, 1915: Yesterday, relieved [by another regiment, after more than six months continually in the trenches without a day off], departure in the middle of the night. I was with the commandant, it poured with rain, we spent two hours under a tree. The commandant gave some orders, the men filed off in silence one by one, many slid or fell on the wet ground. The relief accomplished, we went quietly so as not to attract the attention of the Germans, and then we stopped at the cemetery. A few words by the commandant about the glorious dead. We rendered honors. As soon as we had crossed the the first few kilometers of the dangerous zone, the band played the *Marseillaise*. I assure you that it was moving.[29]

1 May, 1915: Why do you think the war will soon be over? There are fortresses [on French territory] which we which we can liberate only very slowly and with enormous losses. Or we could sing a peace with the Germans still on our territory, which would be shameful, unthinkable.

26 June, 1915: To achieve victory, it is necessary for every one of us to believe completely in it at the cost of the greatest efforts, the highest sacrifices.[30]

23

Dr. Brouillhet was certainly not spared from seeing the worst, so his patriotic exaltation was certainly not that of civilians who lived in safety:

19 December, 1915: We went to bed at 3 in the morning, and, by 8 o'clock, two thousand had been killed between the French and German lines.[31]

Surely a sentient being from another planet would find it extraordinary that, amid this hecatomb, doctors such Dr. Brouillhet (and many others mentioned in the book) provided medical care for the wounded enemy, even when it was dangerous to do so, whom only moments before they had been doing their best to kill and who had been doing their best as well to kill them. What a peculiar morality, what a strange sensibility or conception of civilized behaviour! Was it not straining at a gnat having swallowed a camel?

In caring for a German officer, I was violently felled by a shell, which gave me a large contusion in the lumbar region; I continued [to work] the following day until midnight. Today, I have two large bandages and cannot move.[32]

Many of the doctors recorded in the book who were injured in action, even fatally, refused to be evacuated until they had treated all the soldiers who were injured with them as best they could. Of course, Alice Brouillhet may have edited out any instances of cowardice in order to leave an impression of universal bravery, but I suspect that in the great majority of cases the social pressure to be brave overcame the instinct to survive.

Dr. Brouillhet knew – as how could he not? – that he was likely to die or be killed. Three months before his death, he was transferred to a town called Revigny, on the Meuse, "which must have been a nice place before the war," but which "the Germans bombarded and burnt" so that "the majority of the houses no longer exist."[33] On January 29, 1916, he wrote to his wife:

> Know that whatever happens to me you will have the right to be proud of your husband. If I do not return from this hell, I beg you to be very strong, very brave.... In asking you to survive me, I know that I am imposing a greater sacrifice on you than if I asked you to follow me in death. Yes! Yes! If I go, you, you, you will live to keep my memory alive. What is more, your life belongs also to God, I repeat, you must be brave.... I know that for my part, I could not envisage life without you! But God preserve me from that frightful pain! I have already suffered so much. Remember that for me you are impossible perfection made possible.[34]

Alice Brouillhet made a magnificent effort to raise a memorial to her husband of only a few months.

Dr. Brouillhet must have sensed his own impending death, that he had not long to live, for he continued:

> As for me, always remember that my supreme thought will be for you, that last image that will pass before me will be yours! But it will be very hard to tear myself from you.... However, how many unfortunates have died without having known, unlike me, the joy of an ardent and pure love. The love that you inspire in me is so elevated, so unique. Ah! what would I not give not to die far from

you, to have the certainty of being able to hold you against my heart at the last moment! It would be so consoling to me to be able to say that "after" your dear little hands caressed me and your lips kissed my forehead.[35]

25

The writer was twenty-three at the time he wrote this. Here is proof, if proof were needed, that what a man has lived and experienced is not be measured linearly, as straightforwardly the length of time he has survived.

Six days after writing the above, he wrote his last letter:

I am worried, I was injured while mounting my Arabian horse…. I have been looking after so many gravely ill Kabyle soldiers that I wonder if I wasn't infected while bandaging. I don't always have the time to practice asepsis of the hands and to clean my nails.

With the doctor unable to continue his work fully, his commanding officer asked for a replacement, after whose arrival he would take leave to be treated in Paris or Bordeaux.

But don't worry, it can't be serious. And even if it were, you must understand how nice it would be for me to be you, but I repeat, don't be worried, and wait for me soon. I don't want to leave my post before my replacement arrives. It will be time, because my heart attacks* keep repeating since I mounted the horse.[36]

He was indeed transferred to Bordeaux (where he had studied medicine), but died the day after his arrival, on the 8th or 9th of February 1916.

---

* I would here imagine that he means the tachycardia and arrhythmias that he experienced as a result of the infection.

The nurse who had worked with him, of the name of Janin, wrote to his widow, Alice Brouillhet:

26

> I understand the suffering of him whom you mourn. To feel that you will die at the age of twenty-three when life is smiling on you, when you love and are loved, what an agony for a doctor who watches and analyzes the different phases of his illness and knows that death is ineluctable. And you, Madam, what must have been your sufferings to observe the struggles of him whom you loved so well.[37]

I do not think that anyone would write today in such a florid (but nevertheless sincere) way. Whether life could truly be said to have smiled on Dr. Brouillhet when he spent practically the whole of his short professional life in the throes of this terrible war may be doubted, but M. Janin was presumably thinking of the post-war period to come, when the young doctor would have enjoyed the calm and contented life of a happily married bourgeois. M. Janin continued:

> in spite of his physical suffering, he examined his illness as a doctor and feared a fatal outcome. With a sang-froid that gave me pain, he confided his last wishes to me, and it was you who were his sole concern. He gave me two letters, one to keep that I was not to deliver unless his sad prognosis was fulfilled, and although I wanted to stay with him to look after him, he sent me to Paris to take the other to reassure you.
>
> I thought it would be a comfort for you to know that there was someone devoted to him whom you loved and who had shared your anxieties, because I liked our poor doctor, who was so good to me, very much.[38]

Heartrending as this story is, it is not the worst relayed in this amazing book – though, of course, it is not possible or desirable to construct a linear scale of human suffering that, apart from being nonsensical in itself and a diversion from the effort to enter into the reality of other people's suffering, would set up a peculiar and unhealthy race of competitive suffering victimhood.

In a sense, then, it is invidious to choose a story for specially dramatic qualities, but that of Dr. Etienne-Joseph Jaubert, head of the French medical mission to Serbia during the terrible epidemic there of typhus in 1915, has a particular resonance as I write this, confined to my home during the coronavirus epidemic of 2020.

Dr. Jaubert was a veteran of the typhus epidemic in Tunis of 1909 and by the standards of the time was no longer young in 1915, being then fifty-two. There was a call for French medical volunteers to go to Serbia, though to do so was advertised as "certain death"; a hundred were needed, and three thousand five hundred volunteered. When Jaubert arrived at the typhus hospital, known locally as the Death Hospital, all fifteen of the doctors had been infected, there were three or four patients to a bed and there were a hundred and twenty deaths a day. The mission immunized a million and a half people in four months, including the entire Serbian army, and the epidemic was halted.[39]

He described the situation in Serbia when he arrived:

On our arrival in Serbia, we found ourselves in the middle of a frightful situation. 50,000 Serbs had been slain by the typhus, that is to say many more victims than the war up till then had caused. The hospitals were full. At Belgrade, 150 a day were dying; 125 of the 350 doctors who practiced in Serbia were dead, a terror reigned.[40]

His mission accomplished, Dr. Jaubert was only at the beginning of his sufferings. The Austrians invaded Serbia, and the medical mission had to retreat before the onslaught through Albania and Montenegro:

> After retreating through the whole of old and new Serbia, after having crossed part of Albania, we went through Montenegro with the remnants of the [Serbian] army; for two months we marched through terrible terrain; we crossed the lost mountains of Montenegro, at more than 6,500 feet, at 24 degrees below freezing; we did 600 kilometers on foot, hungry ... by icy paths along precipices, down which we just avoided falling a hundred times, crossing rivers on foot and passes at 5,000 feet where we were almost buried in snow and almost died of cold; all we had to eat was a little inedible black or maize bread, and a little stony cheese bought at an enormous price. We didn't undress for two months, we slept on the ground, usually without straw, shivering, sometimes without being able to stretch out, squatting in Albanian cottages, often a hundred where there was room for ten. The Albanians (many of them were Christians) did not attack us, the French, but they killed a great number of Serbs, whom they don't like; we had to abandon everything, except a canteen carried by horses, most of which died en route; many rolled down the precipices and were killed ...[41]

When finally they arrived at their destination, the Albanian city of Scutari, from whose nearby coast they hoped to be evacuated by the French Navy (dangerous because Austrian, or what Dr. Jaubert calls *austro-boche*, submarines were blockading the coast), conditions were terrible:

We are bombed every day by Austrian and German
planes.... Numerous soldiers are dying of hunger ... in
the streets ... everywhere there are cadavers of horses,
dismembered by the Albanians.[42]

Perhaps the most astonishing words of Dr. Jaubert's account
are the following: "Certainly the retreat was terrible, but our
confidence and our energy are intact."[43]

There was a special medal for those who worked to contain epidemics, the *Médaille des épidémies.*

Dr. Jaubert was evacuated back to France, where he filled
various posts, the last being consultant in Calais in 1918:

It was in the night of 11th to 12th August ... that Dr Jaubert was mortally wounded. When the alert sounded, he
was at his post, a huge shell fell on his unit, and by a kind
of impious irony exploded on the sacred emblem of the
Red Cross which he had had drawn on the ground for
better protection. He alone amongst all his patients and
his staff whom he looked after and who were still under
his care, he alone was struck, standing as a soldier, as
medical consultant. His last thought was for his son at
the front. "I am hit!" Then he fell into a coma; he expired
half an hour later, despite the care he was given. He had
five penetrating wounds; shrapnel from a shell in the
head, one in the chest, one in the left clavicle, one in the
region of the liver and one in the knee joint. The following day, a letter arrived promoting him to the rank of
colonel. Dr. Jaubert did not have the joy of knowing it.[44]

On almost every page of Alice Brouillhet's book (439 pages
long) one finds stories almost equally tragic and affecting.
There is almost none without its story of heroism, explicit or

implicit. Some of the doctors were killed soon after arrival on the front; others survived until the last days of the war, or even after the armistice. Many died of illnesses contracted in the trenches, or of exhaustion. Some died in captivity, probably of malnutrition, while doing their best to care for their fellow prisoners.

Most of us think of this war (if we think of it at all) as the catastrophe of catastrophes in modern European history, not only as an evil in itself but as the bringer of all the subsequent evils of unparalleled dimension. We think of it as having been meaningless, in the sense that it was fought over no matter of principle, the two sides, the Allies and the Central Powers, being morally indistinguishable. Millions were killed, or died, for nothing.

As this book makes clear, it did not seem so at the time to those who participated in it. The phrase *Mort pour la France* (Died for France), which one finds in every cemetery in the country, was not an empty one: dying for France is what they thought that they were doing. There is no single instance in this book of cynicism towards the war effort, or any semblance of doubt as to the justice of the cause for which it was supposedly being fought. Of course, the author may carefully have edited out any contrary sentiment, any evidence of cowardice, disillusionment, opposition, or despair among the doctors. It seems to me unlikely, however, that she has given an entirely misleading impression of their sentiments of the time. When people are caught up in a terrible situation, either by choice or by force of circumstance, they are reluctant to see it as meaningless or arbitrary, for to do so would make it all the more insupportable. She has raised a monument to mass heroism, of which her ever-to-be-lamented and never-to-be-forgotten husband was an example.

The question naturally arises as to whether such mass

30

heroism or conformity to the ideal of patriotic duty was a good thing, or whether a more critical attitude towards the war might have been better and brought it to an end sooner. I myself can give no unequivocal answer to this. Conscientious objectors and people such as Bertrand Russell, who went to prison for objecting to the war, showed great moral courage in the face of popular patriotic belligerence. To sacrifice your life for what is essentially an accident of birth – the country you happened to have been born in – seems absurd. Vanishingly few, if any, people fought for a side other than their own because they came to the conclusion that the other side had right on its side. My grandfather, a doctor, won two Iron Crosses during the war, and no doubt thought that he was fighting for justice, which was on the German side.* But had I been a young man in England at the time of the outbreak of the war, I think I should have answered the call to the colors, and quite possibly been killed by my choice. This all appears ludicrous.

And yet reading *Les Héros sans gloire* one cannot but be moved by the nobility described in it, not just in one or two cases but as a characteristic of the population as a whole. The relation between the wisdom of any collective action and the moral quality of the individuals involved is clearly a complex one. But Alice-René Brouillhet's book, difficult to find and expensive to obtain, deserves to live.

---

* His military service and decorations no doubt were to his advantage during the first years of the Nazi regime. Jewish, he was eventually deprived of his property, his citizenship, and his name. He saved his life by going to China, where he died in 1944.

A Note on the Texts

One of the things that has stuck me about French books of
the interwar period is their low quality as physical objects,
by comparison with those published before the war and
those published, say, now. The paper on which they are
printed is of very low quality, rough and yellowing, and the
bindings fragile. Books of the Victorian era were incompara-
bly better-produced. This is one small and insignificant testimony to the effect of the war on the French economy.

My copy of *Les Héros sans gloire* once belonged to the
Cercle Militaire of Rennes. Assuming that it was not stolen,
it was deaccessioned, presumably as being of no interest to
present-day soldiers. It was published by Charles-Lavazaulle
and Company, military publishers, who went into liquida-
tion in 2018. The only other of its publications that I have
in my library is *Principes généraux de la philosophie sociale et
politique du maréchal Pétain* (The General Principles of the
Social and Political Philosophy of Marshal Pétain), by
Franck Allengry, published – on glossy, good-quality paper –
in 1943. Alengry (1865–1946) was the rector of Besançon
University and author of academic studies on Turgot, Con-
dorcet, and Compte, and of a three-volume work on the psychology of education.

Eugène-Melchior de Vogüé
(1848–1910)

EUGÈNE-MELCHIOR DE VOGÜÉ was one of the Immortals, that is to say a member of the *Académie française*, to which he was elected at the early age of forty.* But literary immortality, if such exists, is not to be conferred by mere membership of an academy, however august, or even by the Nobel Prize. I think it safe to say that very few people have heard of Vogüé today, and even fewer have read him. True, I once fell talking to a man during a promenade in the cemetery and mentioned my project of writing a book about the forgotten writers interred there, and he asked me for some of the names of those I proposed to write about.† I mentioned Vogüé first.

"The generation before mine would have read him," said the man, "but no one reads him now." As my interlocutor was aged eighty-six, I felt reassured that Vogüé could be safely included among the forgotten. Even in the days of his literary fame, he must have been a minority interest. The first edition of his most famous book, *Le Roman russe* (The Russian Novel), published in 1886, and which led to his election to the Academy, was of 1,650 copies, total sales eleven years later having risen to 3,850 copies.[1] As Vogüé was considered an important writer at the time, these figures

---

* I am grateful to M. Michel Fleury for drawing my attention to this author.

† He asked me where I was from. When I told him that I was English, he replied, "Nobody's perfect."

give some idea of the size of the French literary public of the time – probably the most literary of all publics.

Eugène-Melchior de Vogüé was born into the cadet branch of one of the oldest aristocratic families of his part of France, as it happens in the *département* in which I have a house, the Ardèche. The family having been relatively impoverished by the French Revolution and deprived of its automatic right of social distinction, Vogüé's father was sunk in a kind of melancholic reverie, "the age-old and lamentable ... inner emigration" of the surviving aristocrats.*[2] Vogüé's mother was of Scottish aristocratic origin, but as far as I can tell he never evinced any interest in that part of his heritage, nor was English literature of any importance to him: unlike classical, French, German, Italian, and, later, Russian. Britain was thus a very marginal cultural presence to him, if it existed for him at all.

He grew up in a somewhat gloomy château, made all the gloomier by the absence of guests and his father's inability to express any of the affection that he felt for his older son. Vogüé was also sent to two religious boarding schools, gloomy in a different way, where he largely followed his own inclinations as far as reading was concerned, his favorite author being Chateaubriand.† Thoroughly imbued with romanticism, aged sixteen he wrote of himself in a letter to a friend:

> Ah! My dear friend, how happy and unhappy one is to have one of those fragile poetic natures in which the

---

* The concept of inner emigration was to become important for intellectuals who did not leave Germany during Nazi rule. To a lesser extent, intellectuals who dislike contemporary culture experience something similar.

† He was later called "the Chateaubriand of the Third Republic" by Jules Lemaître, in his wonderfully succinct portrait of Vogüé, in his *Les Contemporains, sixième serie* (Paris: Lecène, Oudin et cie, 1896), 328.

least fiber, touched too brusquely, breaks, in which the tears of the heart, if not those of the eyes, constantly murmur in the breast! When I cast a long look on this invisible part of my being, my first thought is to feel very unhappy, but my second is even more to think myself to be happy, such that I would not change with anyone this soul full of sad dreams, unsatisfied loves, but also of ineffable consolations.[3]

His family had a long military condition, and Vogüé's father wanted him to attend the military academy, St. Cyr, with a view to a military career. Vogüé, however, very early decided that the military life was not for him. On the contrary, he wanted to travel and write, modeling himself on Chateaubriand. When he was twenty-five, he wrote:

> From the age of sixteen, all my studies, thoughts and hopes have been directed to a single end, a single instrument of human activity: the pen. To be someone in the pure world of letters, beyond political preoccupation, such is the only ambition that I have ever loved, the only way to fame and fortune that seemed to me seductive.[4]

The Franco-Prussian war broke out, however, and profoundly changed his trajectory in life as well as marking his character. His younger brother, Henri, followed the family tradition and was a cadet at St. Cyr. Henri was named as a sub-lieutenant to a regiment that Eugène-Melchior then also joined, feeling it to be his patriotic duty to do so. At the Battle of Sedan, Henri was badly injured (Eugène-Melchior having been more mildly injured). The older brother dressed the younger's wound and put him in an ambulance, being then captured by the Prussians and held prisoner in Magdeburg. Terrible as the war was, with over 180,000 deaths, the laws of war were in some respects more civilized in 1870 than they were soon to become. Vogüé was allowed out of prison camp by day, on his promise to return at night, and he was even allowed to attend the Magdeburg opera, where he attended an impressive performance of Weber's *Der Freischütz*. He was also allowed a trip to Berlin, a city that did not please him.[5]

He was a prisoner of war for six months, expecting a joyful reunion with his brother, but returned to Paris to discover that Henri had in the meantime died of his wounds.[6] He arrived in time for the terrible events of the Paris Commune, a witness to the slaughter. He wrote eloquently in his letters:

> The desperate population of Belleville and Montmartre seems ready to resist to the last extremity. These unfortunates would rather be hacked to death than accept the king that they accuse the Assembly of wanting to bring back. How will this horrible crisis end?... Good God, are we in the Nineteenth Century, or will we fall back into barbarism? Did the Wars of Religion ever present such refinements of atrocity?*[7]

In another letter he wrote:

> Ah! You must see how these strange *illumines* [visionaries] die. All day they shot them around me: stoical and scornful ... dying upright, leaving to their children the continuation of the unfinished work. Their women threw lighted cotton and petrol under the feet of the sol-

---

* The French Wars of Religion lasted between 1562 and 1598. Some two to four million people died in them, of the violence and the disruption it caused. This would be the equivalent of six to twelve million today.

diers; captured, they die without complaint, like she-wolves in the teeth of dogs.[8]

All this he lived through and experienced by the age of twenty-three! A man would have to be shallow indeed not to develop a serious outlook on life afterwards! It was perhaps fortunate for him that he died in 1910, for two of his four sons died in the First World War. His first son, named Henri, presumably in honor of his deceased brother, was born on September 1, 1879, nine years to the day after Vogüé's brother was fatally wounded at Sedan. (The Empress of Russia wanted to be the younger Henri's godmother, Vogüé having married a Russian aristocrat, but she died before she could act on her wish.)[9] The younger Henri was killed on October 10, 1915.[10] At least Vogüé's comparatively early death preserved him from a grief that would surely have been unassuageable.

The civil war over, Vogüé was invited by his older cousin the Marquis de Vogüé (whom he called Uncle, as I did my cousins of an older generation when I was young) to be an attaché at the French embassy in Constantinople, the marquis having been appointed ambassador by Adolphe Thiers, the first President of the Third Republic.*

This might seem to modern sensibilities like nepotism, but better, perhaps, an honest nepotism than a dishonest meritocracy. By an honest nepotism I mean the appointment of people to positions by personal connection, but not by such connection alone: the person appointing must know that the appointee has the necessary abilities for the

---

* Adolphe Thiers was an historian and politician (1797–1877). He was prime minister under Louis-Philippe (1840) and later president (1871–1873). He is also interred in Père Lachaise, in a far grander tomb than Vogüé's, though he was of far humbler birth. Thus the whirligig of time brings in his revenges, or at least expresses his scale of values.

position, which, because of his intimate knowledge of him, he has been able to assess close-up. By contrast, a dishonest meritocracy is an impersonal selection process that allows little or nothing to personal knowledge of the appointee, being purely "objective," though what is tested may have little or no bearing on the job to be performed. Be that as it may, Eugène-Melchior's subsequent career proved that the judgment of the marquis, scion of the senior branch of the family and himself a distinguished writer, historian, and archaeologist, was sound enough.

Vogüé remained five years in Constantinople and early in his posting traveled extensively in what is now Syria, Lebanon, Israel, and Palestine, all then part of the Ottoman Empire to which he was accredited, and also to Mount Athos in Greece. His travels furnished the material for his first book, *Syrie, Palestine, et Mont-Athos: Voyages aux pays du passé* (Syria, Palestine, Mount Athos: Journey to the Countries of the Past), published in 1876, two or three years after he compiled it from his travel notes in Syria and Palestine and a year after his journey to Mount Athos.

The book is inscribed to his lifelong friend Henri de Pontmartin, and in the dedicatory epistle Vogüé voices some of the anxieties that persist in France, with what justification I leave to others to decide. Speaking of his own book, he says:

> What audacity at the present moment to throw into this troubled land, so unwelcoming to letters, so deeply unsettled by regrets, fears and hopes, these calm studies! Our Republic, more severe than Plato's, sends those who come to speak of art and of poetry, without so much as crowning them with flowers.[11]

People who do not share the interests or tastes of multitudes, but prefer arts and letters, have perhaps felt something similar at all times and in all places, but there is a special national anxiety, understandable after the recent defeat in the war, about the loss of French influence, and particularly about the international importance of the French language, the latter anxiety persisting to this day. According to Vogüé:

> The Frenchman no longer leaves his boulevard, where he sees everything in his own image: we can see this in distant lands ... where our language, our manners, our ideas, lose ground every day to the advantage of those people who travel ...[12]

Obviously, the author must have seen himself as exempt from his own strictures about his countrymen, and indeed his book is full of curiosity about life in distant places. He strikes the reader as intelligent, observant, and open-minded; his reflections, even when we should now regard them as mistaken, are of an astonishing maturity, certainly by comparison with any that I would or could have made in similar circumstances at his age.

The book would be worth republishing today, so rich is it in material for reflection on change and continuity, the yin and yang of history, always present, always in contention. Furthermore, there are sometimes in it facts or opinions that would challenge our prejudices or preconceptions about the past. I will mention one or two later.

As you would expect from the title, the book starts in Asia Minor and continues on to Syria (a geographic expression that in those days included Lebanon). On the train to Ephesus, the author's first experience of life in the East is not favorable. He sees some camels being led by an Abyssinian:

Man and beast regard us with that great look of aston-
ishment and resignation that is common to the human
and animal races of the Orient.... Fever, pale sovereign of
all Asia Minor, inhabits these humid valleys almost
alone: one could represent this poor Asia as a spectral
fever sitting on ruins.[13]

From Ephesus, he takes a ship to Rhodes, which (at the
time) was part of the quickest route to Jerusalem. On the
bridge of the ship, he observes some of his fellow passengers, some of them pilgrims:

This pious traveler [an American pastor] is on mission
to Jerusalem: standing in a long embroidered dressing
gown with white cravat, his sad face with a mystic gaze,
he leaves through his Bible by the light of a candle, posing for Rembrandt or Holbein as do the Greeks for Dela-
croix. A little further on, the Patriarch of Antioch,
returning from the synod of Constantinople, is sitting in
a large armchair. This old man, dressed and coiffed in
black, with a long white beard, emaciated features and a
listless look, stiff and solemn like Byzantine mosaic, is
really imposing in his pontifical immobility; by contrast,
his two acolytes are very agitated, talkative and dirty.
They recite the Orthodox liturgy all day in a nasal tone
with the same patience with which the American reads
his Bible. Beside them, some Arabs from Damascus pray
gravely on the bridge at the hours prescribed: a servant
brings them a rug which he spreads for them, and the
believers prostrate themselves three times in turning
towards Mecca, without much success, I must say, for
the compass flagrantly deceives them; but it is the faith
which saves.[14]

40

From this, Vogüé draws a conclusion (he was only twenty-three or twenty-four when he drew it):

> It is only in the East that can gather in so narrow a space the most striking specimens of races and religions so different. One feels very quickly, on seeing the gulfs which separate them, how chimerical are the dreams of social and religious unification of the world ...[15]

41

He goes on to say that each religion, in each race, must obey its own laws of development: a thought that the makers of foreign policy might do well to consider.

Vogüé was a believing, or at least a practicing, Catholic (the two are not the same at all). Over and over again in the book, he expresses tolerance for religious conceptions not his own, which suggests a relativistic turn of mind. Speaking of ancient Greece, he says:

> Before condemning paganism *in toto*, it is necessary to have passed under the clement skies of which it seems to be the natural emanation. Insensibly the genius of the place invades and penetrates you; you feel yourself becoming pagan, fatalistic, happy; you wonder with regret why you don't live this secure life under the consolatory tolerance of those gracious gods.[16]

Vogüé, in fact, seems to me to have been a Catholic because it was the religion of France, rather than because Catholicism required belief in undoubted theological truths. In other words, his love of country was primary, preceding any genuine religious feeling he may have had. I am not alone in this thought, for Léon Le Meur concludes the penultimate paragraph of his work on Vogüé with the following words:

> . . . we do not have the right to suspect the sincerity [of his profession of faith] and to suppose that the external attitude of Vogüé, his official Catholicism, did not correspond to a profound feeling.[17]

42

The author would surely have asserted this only if others had suspected what I suspect, namely that Vogüé's religion was cultural rather than theological. I have known many other people who held to religious observance for cultural reasons; whether such observance can long survive absence of true belief, or exert a preservative cultural effect, is an open question, but I am rather inclined to doubt it.

Vogüé's observations of Beirut and Damascus almost induce a state of *déjà vu*:

> It is difficult for us to realize, in our old Europe where religious feeling plays a more and more restricted role, the way in which it seizes and penetrates you in this other moral world. It is the ambient atmosphere; in its various forms, it is mixed in all aspects of social life, it contains all the national aspirations of the numerous and divided groups of which eastern society is composed.... The European traveler who brings his *moderatée* ideas here believes himself at first to be in a madhouse.[18]

Vogüé goes on to say that he supposes that the atmosphere was similar to those during the French Wars of Religion in the sixteenth century, whose atmosphere he now understands, or thinks he understands, the better, the underlying assumption being that all societies go through the same stages.

He makes mention of the events of 1860 in Damascus, in the course of a war between the Druzes on the one hand and the Maronite Christians on the other, in the course of which several thousand Christians were massacred in Damascus and their entire quarter of the city destroyed (the photographs of Damascus then resembling those of Aleppo or Mosul a century and a half later).

43

Ever since then, says Vogüé, a feeling of terror hangs over Damacus like a cloud. "On certain days, for no apparent reason, a shiver passes through the town and everyone quickly locks up his clothes and precious objects and gets ready to flee to Beirut."[19]

In Syria, Vogüé comes across an Italian anchorite, who has lived in the desert for seven years, but immediately asked Vogüé for news of the Franco-Prussian war and Italy's attitude thereto. (This suggests that he could not have been altogether isolated in the intervening period.) Vogüé comments:

> Ah, padre Antonio, is it worth going to the trouble to making oneself a hermit and burying oneself in the Gorge of Kadischa only to talk politics to travelers? Will then man never leave his miserable worries over such fleeting things?[20]

I was reminded of the chapter of in Doctor Johnson's *Rasselas* in which a hermit confesses to Rasselas and Imlac that "the life of a solitary man will be certainly miserable, but not certainly devout."[21]

At Baalbek, the ruins are so magnificent that they make Vogüé wonder whether there has been any real progress at all:

> What are we... by comparison with these ancestors, what is our vaunted progress? Have we ever put steam, electricity, all the mechanical contrivances ... of which we are so proud, at the service of art and religious thought?[22]

These questions continue to haunt us. Yes, we can now communicate instantaneously, but do we have anything to communicate?

44

To quote every interesting description or reflection in Vogüé's book would be virtually to reproduce the book whole. He notices at Beirut, for example, that during the month of Ramadan the men who fast go straight to tobacco rather than to food once the cannon shot announces the definitive end of daylight. He mentions that in Egypt he has seen the leader of the caravan of pilgrims on the annual *Hajj* ride on his horse over the prostrated bodies of the faithful who, thus ridden over, stand up afterwards unharmed and rejoicing.[23] He recounts the curious effect of the monotony of riding through the desert:

> Here, as in life at sea, the bored mind endows the slightest incident with enormous proportions and a relative interest that those who have not had this harsh experience will find difficult to understand. Meeting a jackal or a herd of gazelle are the great events of the day's journey.[24]

In other words, importance is not a natural quality, like size or weight: it is the mind that imposes significance on events.

Vogüé met Abd-el-Kader, the leader of the revolt against French rule in Algeria, whom the French forced to surrender and eventually exiled to Syria, in his house in a village just outside Damascus:

> He [received us] in the very simple and very modest house in which we found him. Abd-el-Kader has a fine head, grave and mild, but susceptible to light up when speaking of religion or war. Thanks to his hair, which he care-

fully dyes, he appears much younger than he is…. [He] has an uncontested authority over his Algerian compatriots, who are very numerous in Syria. This authority allowed him to render tardy but important services during the massacres of 1860. Immediately after those bloody days, the Emir [Abd-el-Kadr] confined himself for two months in the great mosque to purify himself of the stain in the eyes of the faithful of having saved the lives of infidels.[25]

Vogüé's account of Jerusalem in 1872 is immensely interesting. One feels by the end of it that he knows it intimately, though in fact he spent only ten days there. (The journalistic rule is that a journalist should spend three days or three years in a place: three days for strength of impression, three years for depth of understanding.) Religion – Christian, Jewish, and Muslim – was the *raison d'être*, or at least the obsession, of the Jerusalem of Vogüé's day, as perhaps it still is: religion in its worst, most sectarian and divisive form:

These are the principal actors who argue over this narrow scene. I cannot enter into the tedious details of the intrigues, conflicts, conspiracies, which every day entangle these hostile groups in this field of discord; religious proselytism and earthly covetousness maintain them in that state of permanent fever which so greatly surprises the stranger and will grip him if he is not careful. Need I repeat that sadly the Christian takes part in these petty quarrels, in the very place which ought, *par excellence*, to be the temple of peace and charity?[26]

The Greek Orthodox appall him by their ridiculous annual ceremonies. A huge crowd of the faithful waits impatiently for the Patriarch to deliver the flame that an angel is supposed to have brought him, horsemen waiting outside the church to take a torch of that holy fire to distant villages:

46
> A furious frenzy takes hold of this turbulent Greek crowd, a savage clamour shakes the sky; it is rarely that this ceremony, evidently a pagan legacy, ends without serious accidents; we recall the famous catastrophe of 1833, when more than three hundred people died of suffocation ...[27]

As for the Armenian Patriarch, he

> is a man still young, of giant stature, with a noble and intelligent face. He was, would one believe it, a student of law in Paris, where he learnt photography, which he practices with success.... As a result of a cabal that formed against him, they have tried to poison him twice; saved by his strong constitution, he had the guilty thrown into monasterial prison, but he no longer dares to eat any but dishes prepared by his sister.[28]

The Protestants are not attractive, though they have the virtues of their vices:

> The Anglican and American missionaries arrived the first, preceded by their obligatory load of Bibles: as full of money and zeal as they could wish, they have raised comfortable buildings, a bishop's palace, a chapel, and have sown the city with stores of Bibles. . . Protestant activity among the natives is practically nil: this northern form of Christianity finds the Eastern mind absolutely stubborn.[29]

Vogüé doesn't have much time for the Jews either, who were 14,000 of Jerusalem's population at the time of 26,000 (the

Muslims were 5,000). He particularly dislikes those from Eastern Europe who, like precursors of Zionism, arrived in Palestine to stay:

Imagine, the two sides of an alley, with fetid drains and a thousand tiny shops, in each of which presides an old man worthy to pose for Rembrandt, or a witch, without counting the children with long hanging curls; for these are the Jews of the north of Europe, a few from all parts, but especially from Poland, Russia and Wallachia, and who have kept the strange and sordid costume that everyone knows: long black coat, patched and greasy, conical hat, peasant's cap or, strange headwear under this leaden sky, the immense fur hat much wider than the head. A few old men with a white beard still have a certain majesty; the others offer types that realist paint-ers might dream of to personify rapacity and usury: the hooked nose, the two ringlets like corkscrews hitting the temples, the distinctive sign of the *Caraite* sect, red-eyed, scratched and blinking, weak from Mosaic maladies.... Nothing could overcome contempt for this resigned and repellent dirtiness.[30]

The only groups for whom Vogüé had any real regard were the Ottoman Turks, who not only hold the territory with a handful of men, thereby proving that they did so with the consent, or at least the absence of opposition, of the popula-tion, but both exhibit and guarantee a certain tolerance,* and also the Orthodox Russians, so different (in Vogüé's opinion) from the weak, effete, and degenerate Greeks. For

---

* Vogüé mentions, for example, that Turkish troops keep order at Christ-mas celebrations in Bethlehem and behave respectfully at Christian reli-gious processions.

the monks of Mount Athos he had nothing but contempt. The final sentence of his book, which recounts his departure from Athos, reads:

48

> The dark mass of Athos descended into the depths of the sea, as its outdated inhabitants descend into the past.[31]

Very different, in his opinion, were the Russian Orthodox. It is interesting that his admiration for Russia preceded his subsequent posting at the French embassy in St. Petersburg. At Jerusalem:

> The [Russian] consul, housed in an elegant villa ... received us affably, and showed us in detail, with an understandable pride, the works due to the charity and wisdom of his compatriots. A hospital of sixty beds, spacious and comfortable, a pharmacy, a hospice in the old sense of the word, a house set up for poor pilgrims with neat rooms for those better-off and a chapel, a large and beautiful church, numerous dependencies, nothing was missing from this little Muscovite quarter. Doctors, pharmacists, nurses, lady almoners,* looking after the ill and the indigent. I cannot dwell on the thousand little details that reveal a hand as generous as it is far-sighted; to give to the smallest things their true value and supreme interest it is necessary to understand the irresistible impression of the power, wealth, perseverance and vitality that they create.[32]

It may be anachronistic to do so, but it is difficult not to read into this passage, and several others, a foretaste of the

---

* As hospital social workers, all women, often voluntary, still were called in some hospitals in England at the beginning of my career.

praises of the Bolshevik regime that foreigners were to sing
after the revolution. Vogüé compares the millions spent by
the Tsarist government on their coreligionists in the Holy
Land with the "few miserable thousands of francs that other   49
powers send to their coreligionists," and the genuine Russian faith with the "mechanical formalities of the Greek
believer."[33] Soviet faith was often compared favorably by
intellectuals to Western nihilism and despair during the
1930s, precisely when oppression was at its worst.

Although ten years later, in *Le Roman russe*, Vogüé was
roundly to condemn the effect on the Western mind of what
he calls *the poison* of Rousseau's noble, pre-political savage,
he paints a picture of the Russian peasant pilgrims that is
similarly overoptimistic. He is like those Slavophiles of the
nineteenth century who believed that the Russians, though
materially backward, were spiritually superior to Western
Europeans:

> In saying that the future belongs to these men, I am
> obliged to recognize it as their due, since they are simple,
> pious and good. They do not know as well as we how to
> harness the forces of nature or to play with the subtle
> wheels of the political machine; but they do not know
> our revolts, our doubts. They do not yet know all our sci-
> ences, our arts and our letters; buy they possess the three
> great sciences that we have lost, namely faith, sacrifice
> and respect.[34]

In the light of subsequent history, this could hardly have
been a worse or less accurate prognostication. The simple,
good, and pious people were destined for civil war, repeated
famine, and mass murder. Yet this kind of hope for people
who are deemed simple, good, and pious by the overedu-
cated intellectuals (in contrast to themselves) is a repeated

error or illusion. I met it in Central America during the civil wars there; if the present situation was dreadful, it could only mean that there was glorious future waiting to be born.

50   Vogüé soon changed his mind, at least about the Russian literature of his time, which he believed to be superior to any in Europe. After a brief time in Vienna, he was posted to St. Petersburg, where he set about mastering Russian and making a study of Russian history and literature. This resulted in the book regarded as his masterpiece, the work that secured his election to the Académie française, *Le Roman russe*, "The Russian Novel."

His first writings on Russia were historical essays that can still be read with great pleasure and instruction of the non-specialist. The first to be published in book form was *Le Fils de Pierre le Grand* (The Son of Peter the Great). It is not a work of original research but no less valuable for that, and in my view rises to the level of literature. It reminded me strongly of De Quincey's beautiful and moving essay, also not a work of original research, "The Last Days of Immanuel Kant," for we know in advance that the life of Alexis, son of Peter the Great, is moving inexorably to a tragic and horrible end:

> the son of Peter the Great belonged to the fatal lineage which haunted the tragic Greeks; before this tortured prince, Clytemnestra would have cried out once more: "It is Destiny that has committed this crime!"[35]

Vogüé does something in this essay that is not easy to do, at least not for writers of present-day sensibility, namely create sympathy for a victim of cruelty, oppression, and injustice who is himself a deeply flawed man, as was the Tsarevich Alexis (quite apart from the imperfections consequent upon being a human being, it is difficult to see how having Peter the Great for a father could have resulted in anything other than disaster for a son). Alexis was by turns weak, foolish, obsequious, imprudent, cowardly, and vacillating, though there was also nobility in his undying and never-renounced love for his wife of lowly origin, Euphrosine, not entirely reciprocated.

51

The story is told with delicacy and evident but not obtrusive sympathy. There are passages on historiography that we might do well to ponder today. Writing of the almost automatic resort to torture of Peter the Great, Vogüé says:

> But however revolted by this spectacle our souls may be, let us remember that we are not worthy to read history if we judge the men of the past by the lights they did not have, if we condemn them by our laws, not theirs, if we separate them from their times, their milieu, the air they breathed ...[36]

No one could possibly imagine that Vogüé was therefore a complete relativist about torture. On the contrary (having no knowledge of the horrors of the twentieth century to come), he regarded himself, and us, as fortunate to live in an age when such methods had passed into desuetude, moral and practical.[37] He was a man who could keep the arguments in favor of relative and absolute moral standards in mind at the same time, in a kind of perpetually unstable equilibrium. This was important to him, for very near the end of this essay of two hundred pages, he writes:

> Ah! let us not write history from the childish point of view that the human mind is an unchanging terrain of eternally uniform character; it has not escaped the incessant work of centuries any more than has anything else; in failing to understand this truth, everything in the

annals of the past will be mystery and scandal to us, and we will not perceive that radiant law of progress which raises the refined consciousness of humanity towards ever greater justice.[38]

The law of progress may have seemed more radiant in the 1880s than it seems now, but there is no doubt that it is as important for our mental equilibrium to understand the achievements as well as the disasters of the past, and to appreciate them thankfully.

Vogüé begins his essay on another tragic episode in the history of Russia, the ascent of the Emperor Paul to the throne after the death of his mother, Catherine the Great, as follows:

> You don't have a seat at the theatre tonight? Or perhaps the play being given is mediocre, badly plotted? Console yourself if you have history books on your shelves. History is the inexhaustible repertoire of the great human farce, the masterpiece of irony and pathos which has never ceased for a single day ever since the curtain went up on this ancient scene.[39]

There soon follows a passage about the lives of potentates that put me in mind of *Richard II*:

> Insinuate yourself into their lives, pull off their masks, look beneath the majesty of phrases and the ceremonial robes; you will see that these great companions are made of the same poor and rotten flesh as you, that they laugh and cry like you.[40]

Here is Richard II:

For you have but mistook me all this while:
I live with bread like you, feel want,
Taste grief, need friends: subjected thus,
How can you say to me, I am a king?*

In the diary that he kept in Russia during his diplomatic
posting, not intended for publication, Vogüé compassion-
ates the Emperor Alexander II, whose assassination by
young revolutionaries was one of the two most disastrous
political assassinations of the era (the other being that of
Franz Ferdinand, of course). Vogüé depicts the Tsar before
the assassination as almost a prisoner of the Winter Palace:
the allegedly absolute ruler of one-sixth of the world's land
surface is confined to a few rooms, admittedly of the greatest splendor (which, perhaps, made his confinement all the
more ironic), by fear of assassination. Vogüé writes with real
feeling of the death of the Tsar, who was on his way back
from the military parade that he had been advised not to
attend because the secret police knew that there was a conspiracy afoot to kill him. A bomb was thrown at his proces-
sion, which the Tsar survived but which killed several
Cossacks. His coachman wanted to continue, but Alexander
insisted on inquiring as to what had happened, and a second bomb was thrown. When Vogüé hears of the assassination attempt:

> I return to the [French] embassy. Chanzy [the ambassa-
> dor] arrives after a few moments. He was able to pene-
> trate the palace to the Emperor's bedroom. He saw the
> dead man, on a divan next to his desk. His two legs were
> literally detached, his face covered in blood, horribly
> contracted.[41]

---

* *Richard II*, Act 3, scene ii.

According to Vogüé, Loris-Melikov, the minister of the interior, was in the next room. He said that he had been on the tail of the plot to kill the Tsar, two of the conspirators having been arrested and admitted their part in the plot. They said, "We are fifteen who have sworn his death, the blow is too well prepared, you will not stop it." Loris-Melikov begged the Tsar not to leave the palace until he had all the plotters in jail, but the Tsar insisted. Here was a real Cleopatra's nose moment in history: had Alexander not been killed, the history of Russia and the world might have been very different.

Vogüé was clearly very upset:

> I think of this poor man, weak and good, who married me three years ago, who has just died so tragically in blood, in the shame of this crime. Having emancipated fifty million men at a stroke, and to die like this, tracked down like a wild animal in his own capital![42]

It is not fashionable to express sympathy for those deemed highly privileged, but Vogüé recalls us to the understanding that just as the humblest person is worthy of our sympathy and is created equal, so is the most privileged. To forget this is to reduce our humanity a little.

Vogüé's most famous book, *Le Roman russe* (The Russian Novel), is credited with introducing Russian literature to the French reading public and thereby possibly to other reading publics at the time since the influence and prestige of French culture remained great in Europe. The book is still an admirable introduction to Russian literature, and in choosing to write mainly about Gogol, Turgenev, Dostoevsky, and Tolstoy, Vogüé showed remarkable literary judgment. It is easy enough for us now to see that these were great writers, but Vogüé was the younger contemporary of three of them (all of whom he met), and four years old when

Gogol died; to have spotted so unfailingly their enduring worth is therefore no mean feat. If asked to name four writers today who will still be read in 150 years or more, how confident would we be that we could do it? Perhaps this might be because there are no writers of such stature today or because literature does not have the vital importance that it once had, or simply because too many books are published; or it might be because we are lacking in the acute judgment that Vogüé had.

Vogüé tells us things that may be commonplaces today but that would have surprised his contemporaries. Until the emergence of the Russian novel in the 1840s, Russia had made no great contribution to European civilization, despite its status as a great power, but suddenly its literature (in Vogüé's opinion) surpassed all others in depth. One of the reasons for this was the effect of censorship. Anything remotely political or connected to political philosophy was heavily censored, which meant that such matters had to be approached indirectly. Whereas in other countries the novel was only one form of expression about the most important questions of life, in Russia it was *the* form of such expression, so that it tackled both the problems of everyday existence and the deepest philosophical questions at the same time, in a manner in which they were indissolubly linked. The necessity to avoid the censorship but at the same time expatiate on the problems confronting Russia and, indeed, the whole of humanity, led to a wonderful subtlety:

Tell all the truth but tell it slant —
Success in Circuit lies
Too bright for our infirm Delight
The Truth's superb surprise
As Lightning to the Children eased
With explanation kind

> The Truth must dazzle gradually
> Or every man be blind —.[43]

56   Of course, this situation was not enough by itself to call
forth literary genius, whose existence must be to a large
extent a matter of chance. If John Stuart Mill had lived in
Russia, he would have been forced to write novels rather
than tracts, and one fears to imagine what they might have
been like: the work of Chernyshevsky, perhaps, whose
dreadful didactic novel, *What Is to Be Done?*, was a favorite
of Lenin's.

This raises the question of art and censorship. When the
matter is discussed today, it is usually in the simplified form
of Art *or* Censorship, as if censorship were utterly inimical
to art. This is completely ahistorical. In fact it would be
more true to say that history would suggest that some form
of censorship is a precondition of art, at least of great art,
the vast majority of which in human history was produced
in conditions of censorship. Shakespeare wrote in such conditions that we should now find worse than those of a Latin
American military dictatorship. It is the prohibition against
saying certain things that stimulates the author's
imagination.

This is not to say that any and all censorship has this
salutary effect. It can be so drastic that practically nothing
at all of any interest can be written. Even worse, it can not
only forbid but it can decree what must be written. There is
probably no more effective way of killing literature than
this, which helps to explain why literature written under the
tsars in the nineteenth century was so infinitely superior to
that written under the Soviets in the twentieth. Without
intending to, the tsarist government found the perfect recipe for a stimulating form of censorship, a recipe which perhaps can only be filled unintentionally, prohibitive but not

too prohibitive, with a strong element of incompetence. Nor, I hasten to add, is this an argument in favor of censorship in general: for the whole purpose of life and society is not to produce great literature or art. Societies productive of such literature or art are not necessarily societies in which we should care to live, and Turgenev's great work, *Sketches from a Hunter's Album*, which played an important but unquantifiable role in the abolition of serfdom, no more justifies centuries of that institution than does Dostoevsky's *From the House of the Dead* justify the Siberian exile system.

Vogüé is still very illuminating about the works he discusses. His is literary criticism of the kind that existed before the contemporary university killed it: namely that which can be understood by any reasonably literate person. Here he explains why Chichikov, the protagonist of *Dead Souls*, has so little personality, considering the scale and magnificence, if I may so put it, of his attempted fraud:

> Chichikov has to have as little personality as possible, for it is not such-and-such a man that he wants us to see in him; it is a collective image, that of the Russian who not responsible for his own degradation.[44]

I think Vogüé's favourite among the writers is Turgenev, perhaps because his sensibility most resembles Vogüé's own, that is to say aristocratic but not reactionary. Vogüé was called the Chateaubriand of the Second Empire;[45] not by nature, background, or upbringing a republican, he nevertheless saw the futility of trying to put an egg together again once it was broken and served the republic faithfully. After all, France for him was something larger, grander, and more important than the political regime under which it was presently living.

For Vogüé, the life and work of authors forms a whole

and cannot be understood apart.[46] This is particularly so in the case of his Russian authors, partly because the Russian word for truth, *pravda*, is the same as for justice. The Russians therefore did not divide intellectual tasks in the same way as other Europeans: they were intellectual conglomerators rather than dissectors.

Vogüé explains very well how Dostoevsky's experiences first as a man to be executed, then as an exiled prisoner for ten years, affected him for the rest of his life (as well they might). Vogüé calls his chapter on Dostoevsky "The Religion of Suffering," a very good title. Dostoevsky claims that the Russian people have a special or redemptive role in the world's history because they suffer more deeply than any other people and sympathize more deeply with other people. They are, if I can so put it, Christ made population. That the Russian people did have a tendency to sympathize with suffering more than most is testified by an episode that Vogüé witnessed for himself: he saw a group of prisoners waiting to be transported to Siberia who were succored by poor peasants who gave them food and drink without so much as enquiring what the prisoners had done. It was their suffering that counted for the peasants, not their guilt (assuming them to have been guilty). Other peoples might simply have execrated them.

Vogüé met Dostoyevsky and portrays him half-admiringly and half-mockingly:

> Habitually taciturn, when he began to speak it was in a low tone, slow and deliberate, warming by degrees, defending his opinions without any consideration for anyone. In asserting his favorite thesis on the preeminence of the Russian people, he sometimes reached the point of saying to the fashionable women in the circles attracted to him, "You are not worth the least of the

mujiks [peasants]!" Literary discussions finished quickly with Dostoevsky; he stopped me by a magnificent phrase: "We have the genius of all peoples, but in addition the genius of the Russian people; therefore, we can understand you and you cannot understand us."[47]

There might be something in this: it is possible that Mr. Putin understands Western Europe better than Western Europe understands him. But Vogüé was not impressed by Dostoevsky's understanding of the West, and finds his eschatology absurd:

> I always remember a sally of his on Paris, one evening when inspiration seized him; he spoke of it as Jonah must have spoken of Nineveh, with a biblical fire of indignation; I took down his words: "A prophet will appear one night at the Café Anglais, he will write three words of flame on the wall, and Paris will crumble to the ground in blood and fire, with all that makes it proud, its theatres and its Café Anglais ..." – in the imagination of the Seer, this inoffensive establishment represented the very navel of Sodom, a cavern of infernal and attractive orgies that had to be cursed in order not to be too much dreamed of. He expatiated long and eloquently on this theme.[48]

One is rather reminded of Sayyid Qutb, who managed to espy Sodom and Gomorrah in small-town middle America in the early 1950s.

But Vogüé does not deny Dostoevsky his prophetic qualities, at least with regard to Russia. The value of his novel *The Possessed*, which Vogüé says is very flawed, is in its depiction of the handful of revolutionaries, these "souls of icy steel," which he contrasts with "the timidity and irresolution of the legal authorities."[49] Soul of icy steel: could anything better describe Lenin, if one added the word "satanic"?

Vogüé recognized that Tolstoy was one of the greatest writers who ever lived, no mean achievement considering Tolstoy had still a quarter of a century to live when Vogüé wrote his book (in fact he died in the same year as Tolstoy). Vogüé quotes the anecdote of Flaubert, who exclaimed, "But this is Shakespeare! This is Shakespeare!" when Turgenev read him an extract, translating as he went.[50] This anecdote helps to explain why Tolstoy was derogatory about Shakespeare: he knew that Shakespeare was the one writer whom he could not surpass, and Tolstoy was nothing if not egoistic. As my friend Alexander Boot pointed out in his brilliant book on Tolstoy's religion, Tolstoy did not so much worship God as he worshipped himself.[51]

Vogüé has the highest praise for Tolstoy as an imaginative writer, but is not impressed with him as a thinker or philosopher, rather the reverse. He spots, in my view quite correctly, the incipiently totalitarian nature of his doctrines (not coincidentally, the Bolsheviks appropriated him as a kind of ur-Bolshevik). That is why he quotes Turgenev's moving and magnificent deathbed letter to Tolstoy not once but twice:

> My very dear Lev Nicolaevich, I have not written to you for a long time; I was and am on my deathbed. I cannot recover, it is useless to think it. I am writing to you to say how happy I was to be your contemporary, and to express my last, profound prayer. My friend, return to literature! Your gift comes from the source from which everything comes. Ah! how happy I should be if I could think that you had heard my prayer! My friend, great writer of the Russian land, grant my prayer![52]

There may be a nobler letter, but I know of none.

There is something rather curious about this use of the letter, however. Turgenev died in 1883, and Vogüé's book was published in 1885. How had Turgenev's deathbed letter, which was private, and which Tolstoy did not even hasten to read, enter the public sphere so quickly? I have no answer.

After Vogüé left the diplomatic service, he became for a few years (1893–1898) a deputy to the National Assembly for the Ardèche. He did not enjoy his time there, for he was far too upright, straightforward, and intellectually honest a man to flourish in the atmosphere of parliamentary compromise, cynicism, moral corruption, and wheeling and dealing that characterized the Third Republic, and perhaps all parliamentary regimes. He lost little time in writing and publishing a novel that, thinly disguised, recounted his unhappy experience as a parliamentarian: *Les Morts qui parlent* (The Dead Who Speak). He appears as one of the main characters in it, Jacques Andarran, who is more observer than participant in the events around him, and whose biography resembles his. A member of the cadet branch of a noble family with a military tradition (his younger brother is a soldier), Andarran agrees to serve as a deputy for his *département* from a sense of *nobles oblige* rather than from political ambition, though once elected he hopes to be able to do some good – hopes that are soon dashed once he enters the chamber.

His childhood friend, Elzéar Bayonne, is already a deputy, a fiery orator who leads the socialist faction. He is the brilliant son of an assimilated and newly enriched Jewish family that has made its fortune from chemical fertilizers, which it realized would replace the natural fertilizers in which it had previously dealt (few origins could be less noble). Another branch of the family, with whom Elzéar's branch has lost contact, owns a powerful bank, the *deus ex machina* of much parliamentary intrigue.

62 The plot of the book defies easy summary, but its main interest in any case not in its story but in the light it sheds on political life that in so many respects seems contemporary, though it was published in 1899. In the first scene, for example, Elzéar makes a speech about a law before the chamber of deputies that originally had given certain advantages to workers, but that had been emptied of content by seven years of amendments, legislative delay, and politicking. Elzéar says in his speech:

> Yes, we do not regret seeing you deny the working class even these minimal palliatives, which would perhaps have given them the lying illusion of an effort to liberate them. We defended the law in trying to improve it, we would have voted for it because we're not intransigent theoreticians, because you will find us always ready to assist the birth of the humblest flower of justice in the decomposed soil of capitalist society. You have just pulled out this pale flower from the ruins with your own hands: go ahead, we rejoice at yet another of your admissions of impotence; each of your retreats marks for us a step towards the advent of the new social order, the just and rational social order. Ah, *messieurs*, you don't even want a little air or light under the enormous pyramid, each day higher, that weighs on the crushed multitudes. So much the better! This eternally abused people will rise up all the sooner to overturn it from top to bottom. It knows, with its admirable patience that the more cruel today's suffering, nearer and more complete will be their reward, their victory of tomorrow. Thank you, you who force open the eyes of those whom we would not yet have succeeded in unsealing.[53]

As Lenin put it, more succinctly, "The worse the better."

An old deputy enters the chamber just as Elzéar is ending.

"What tune is he still playing, that flautist?" he asks.

But the speech has been well-received, and from sly cynicism his expression changes, and "with the docility of a lost sheep rejoining the flock, he began mechanically to applaud [Elzéar's] last sentence, which he had not heard."

At every point in the book, the political process is shown to be superficial and shallow. Jacques Andarran is elected in a rural constituency where his

> first contact with the sovereign people had informed him: the journalists' rhetoric, the arbitrary classifications in which political parties were nominally divided, the alleged currents of opinion, all these inventions of city-dwellers had no real application to the rural masses, apart from a few leaders ... these masses were above all avid for practical satisfactions, and always in search of a defender against their natural enemies, the taxman, the army recruiter, the lawyers, but nevertheless capable of idealism when under the temporary magnetism of a man's voice ... the flock didn't choose between two doctrines, but between two shepherds.[54]

When Andarran arrives for the first time at the National Assembly, Elzéar shows him around. "What the devil are you doing in this ridiculous place?" he asks him. "I've come to try to do a little good," replies Andarran. "A strange place to choose," replies Elzéar. "I'm going to introduce you in the circus where we're going to eat you alive."

> He points out M. Chasset de la Marne, leader of the center-left: "Plenty of talent, speaks very well, to say nothing at

all.* I won't present him to you: an introduction by me will warn him forever against you. He thinks I want to deprive him of the capital he doesn't have and of what he has instead, the eighty thousand pounds of income from which he derives his respectability that rotten industrial companies pay him. Don't you think he's right to defend so nourishing a state of society?"[55]

64

Debates are futile. Andarran adapts the old Latin saw *verba volant, scripta manent*: the spoken flies away, the written remains. "Speeches fly away," he says, "the votes count." And the real business is conducted in corridors. "Everyone changes his positions, his votes, according to the direction of the compass."[56]One is reminded of Ledru-Rollin's famous remark, that he had to follow the people so that he could lead them.

The novel is rich in, almost an encyclopedia of, political pathology and petty intrigue. For example, the Panama Scandal is resuscitated when it suits the opposition to bring the government down – not because of any matter of principle.† Behind the intrigue lies the bank of Elzéar's distant cousin; late in the book there is an interesting depiction of the anti-Semitic populism of the time, with no indication that Vogüé himself was anti-Semitic – for he allows the anti-anti-Semite get the better of the argument. (The book was written at the height of the Dreyfus Affair, upon which Vogüé never pronounced, for he had friends in both camps, and wanted to break with neither.)

Although written eighteen years before the Russian Rev-

---

* A perfect description of Nicolas Sarkozy, former president, when I heard him speak in person.
† The Panama Scandal was one of the great *causes célèbres* of the Third Republic, in which vast sums of money were misappropriated during a failed French attempt to build the Panama Canal.

olution, the book features a character who, in the light of experience, prefigures the horrors of totalitarianism. She is the extremely rich and beautiful, but also extremely dogmatic, Russian aristocrat Princess Daria Véraguine, who sets her sights on Andarran. She is a revolutionary socialist who desires a state of complete equality, of necessity brought about by violence, though in the meantime she enjoys her privileged status. In the end, she is the cause of a duel between Elzéar and Andarran's brother, in which Elzéar is killed. Princess Daria assuages her grief by going off the Bayreuth to listen to Wagner in luxury.

Vogüé contrasts the frivolity of politics, or politicking, with the seriousness of military life, engaged at the time on promoting and extending France's colonies in Africa and Indochina. Andarran (who is really Vogüé in this instance) admires the soldierly, practical, comradely life, so different from the temporizing, hypocritical, obstructive, parasitic, essentially worthless existence of the political class. He evidently believes in the *mission civilisatrice* of French colonialism, thereby proving that he, no doubt like us, cannot entirely escape the orthodoxies of his time. But his dislike of and contempt for the political class seems very contemporary and almost universal.

Eugène-Melchior de Vogüé died on the day before his sixty-second birthday.

François-Vincent Raspail (1796–1878)

EVERYONE IN PARIS knows the Boulevard Raspail, but I have found no one of my acquaintance who knew anything much of Raspail, or of what he had done that was of such importance that a grand thoroughfare should have been named after him.* A history teacher thought that he had had something to do with the Revolution of 1848 – as indeed he had – but what, exactly, she did not know.

Raspail was not, perhaps, primarily a writer, but if a man who wrote and published millions of words was not a writer, it is difficult to know who would count as such. Indeed, he wrote so much that a scholar could easily devote himself to his work and not by the end of his life have read all of it: for Raspail seemed to write faster than most people read.

He was a very significant figure in his day, as testified to the fact that the crowd at his funeral was immense, and even the funerals of his wife and daughter, who died before him, were attended by huge crowds, estimated at between fifteen and thirty thousand for that of his wife and up to three hundred thousand for his daughter.†[1]

---

* The Boulevard was particularly detested by the fascist Franco-Swiss architect Le Corbusier. It was completed during his young adulthood, and he took it as proof of the exhaustion of architecture before he, in his own opinion, rejuvenated it, spreading his concrete ugliness through the world like a terrible fungating skin disease.

† Of the funeral of Raspail's wife in 1853, Georges Duveau wrote: "Moving obsequies, which were like a little flame, like a shimmering hope in the desert of the early Empire. Under the eyes of the police, the workers silently saluted the hearse as it climbed to Père Lachaise." See Georges Duveau, *Raspail* (Paris: Presses Unversitaires de France, 1948), 56.

Considering his accomplishments, prominence, and even importance in his own day, Raspail's fall into obscurity and oblivion is strange and stands in need of some explanation. Writing in 1939, Jules Wogue wrote "All that many Parisians know about him is a boulevard, a liqueur [invented by him] and a statue."[2] Daniel Ligou, who edited a collection of his writings published in 1968, begins his preface by with the words, "He is hardly more than a name."[3] In the same year, the American historian Dora B. Weiner began her book on him as follows: "Who was Raspail? Few Frenchmen seem to know."[4] Theodore Zeldin, in his two-thousand-page long *France 1848–1945*, mentions Rapsail *en passant* three times, the third disparagingly.

Perhaps the reason for the neglect is that Raspail spread himself too thin over too many activities for his name to be associated with any one great achievement. He wrote about embryology, botany, chemistry, parasitology, paleontology, agronomy, veterinary science, geology, meteorology, medicine, toxicology, penology, politics, and economics. Among his other accomplishments, he was a good draughtsman and musician (he once calmed a hostile mob with his violin, which had come to riot and ended by dancing). For him, literary activity was always a means to an end, and literary quality was a secondary consideration for him, other than writing so that he should be understood by the average man. If someone were to ask me "What should I read of Raspail?" I should be hard put to reply. It is not like asking the same question of Dickens, say, or of Flaubert, to which one might reply *Great Expectations* or *Madame Bovary*. There is no single work in his immense bibliography by which he could, or should, be remembered: the sum is greater than the parts, and even the value of that sum might be doubted by those with no interest in the history of Raspail's time, insofar as so much of what he wrote has long since been overtaken.

His trajectory in life was certainly a most extraordinary one. He was born in Carpentras in the Vaucluse only three years after it has ceased to be a papal enclave in France, which it had wished to remain.[5] Raspail's father was a café and restaurant owner and caterer, and his mother a very pious Catholic. Raspail never knew his father, who died when the boy was one, leaving his widow very poor. The young Raspail, however, received a very thorough education at the school of the Abbé Eysséric, a Jansenist priest who ran a school in Carpentras, mainly for the children of the poor. Eysséric was a pro-revolutionary priest with an interest in modern science, which he communicated to his brilliant pupil. Raspail was at first destined for the priesthood, as his mother had always much desired. By the age of twelve he was an able scholar of Latin, Greek and Hebrew, and was then sent to a seminary in Avignon, whose clerical superior, Henri-Anne Sollier, was a much less liberal and open-minded man than Eysséric, and whom Raspail detested. Nevertheless, he continued to do brilliantly there, being made first an assistant teacher and then a lecturer in philosophy. At the age of seventeen he was selected to preach a sermon in Avignon Cathedral on the occasion of the anniversary of the battle of Austerlitz, which was so successful that a transcript was sent to Napoleon who, on reading it, said that the young Raspail was someone to watch, for he would go far.

Raspail, however, had had enough of the seminary, and like many a young man training for the priesthood but not completing it, he became strongly anti-Catholic and anti-clerical, often seeing the Jesuits in particular as the *deus ex machina* behind every political development that he deemed undesirable. Raspail remained a deist, however, and was an active Freemason throughout his life. He regarded atheism as extremely foolish.

He returned to Carpentras, where he found work as a teacher, but had to leave because, during the Hundred Days of Naopleon's return from Elba, Raspail showed himself to have been an ardent supporter of the emperor, remaining   69
an admirer of his throughout his life, though he was also an ardent democrat and opponent of all police states. Consistency is not necessarily the first characteristic of all men.

After Waterloo, there was a strong and vengeful reaction by supporters of the restored Bourbons in the Vaucluse against supporters of the revolution and Napoleon, and Raspail felt it prudent, probably even essential to his safety, to flee to Paris. There he lived in poverty, teaching at the Institution Stadler, later the College Stanislas. Dismissed from this post for his political and religious views, he was taken as a tutor to a rich man's children.[6] He read voraciously and attended lectures at the university, making the acquaintance of prominent people. Two of Raspail's personal characteristics are here worth mentioning: first, his indifference to riches; and second, his good relations with aristocrats despite his radical politics, radicals not being immune from social snobbery, which in Raspail's case existed, though only to a mild degree. He also ended a rich man, almost by inadvertence, with extensive property and a magnificent collection of art that he started while in exile in Belgium. (A man who owned paintings by Rubens and Breughel, as did Raspail, would *ipso facto* be considered rich today.)

In the second half of the 1820s, Raspail conducted investigations into and experiments on a wide range of subjects, including on the germination of plants. In the course of the latter, which consumed him for several years, he invented a technique now known as histochemistry. Knowing that iodine reacted with starch, he demonstrated the location of starch in germinating grasses by examining them under the microscope having placed a tiny drop of iodine on the object of his examination. Although it may not have appeared so at the time, histochemistry became of immense importance in modern medicine.

He invented, or at least modified, a cheap and effective microscope that was soon produced by the thousand; he sold the rights to its manufacture, however, to an optician named Deleuil, and made no money from it, unlike Deleuil, who made a fortune.[7]

He is claimed as a forerunner of the cell theory, according to which all living organisms are composed of cells, and he drew theoretical consequences from this for pathology, maintaining that disordered cells either died as individuals or, if they reproduced themselves, could produce deleterious consequences for the organism as a whole by the secretion of toxins. He didn't have concrete evidence for this, but it was a very clever guess.

Nothing in the natural world failed to excite his interest. He wrote about geology, fossils, chemistry, meteorology, and parasitology. He is credited with important advances in the understanding of the role of the scabies mite in the development of that common and unpleasant skin disease. It was he who named the organism *Sarcoptes scabei*.

He turned his attention to medicine, which he connected very strongly with his radical politics. He guessed, from his studies of scabies and intestinal helminths, that many or most human diseases were caused by parasites infinitely smaller than worms and mites, at least thirty years before the germ theory of disease was established. Again, this was a clever guess, for which he had no concrete evidence. But he did suggest, well before Lister, that cleanliness was of the essence in preventing infection after surgery – this, in the 1840s, being (to us, astonishingly) almost the exact oppo-

site of the professional prevailing view, which still saw pus
as a sign of health. He insisted that surgeons should clean
the skin of the patient before operation and also that they
should clean their instruments between operations with
alcohol. He preached cleanliness to the multitudes as a pro-
phylactic measure.

He excited ridicule by promoting camphor in various
forms almost as a panacea, though this is not quite fair to
him because he said that he promoted camphor as the best
disinfectant (in the widest sense) known to him, and that if
he found a better one – which he never did – he would abandon camphor.[8] In other words, he recognized that it was *not*
a panacea. He was certainly not a quack in the sense that, for
lucre, he promoted a remedy that he knew to be useless, for
he strongly believed in it and took it himself.

There were many different forms of camphor, for example
camphorated alcohol and camphorated cigarettes (which he
advocated for lung disease, including the tuberculosis from
which his daughter died).[9] So associated was he with camphor as a seeming cure-all, that when he appeared at the head
of crowd in revolutionary mood in 1848 and broke into the
City Hall of Paris where the provisional government was sitting, Louis Blanc, a member of the government and reform-
ist socialist, exclaimed, "Here is Monsieur Raspail! What
will he do to us? Camphorate us!"[10]

It is easy, of course, to ridicule Raspail's advocacy of camphor, and to blame him for the lack or real scientific evidence
in its favor, but modern notions of what constitutes valid
evidence in favor of a treatment hardly existed then, and in
any case the evidence in favor of orthodox medicine was certainly no better, and many of its prescriptions were probably
far worse in their effect. Camphor does have, at least potentially, many useful biological properties. It is perfectly possible

that Raspail's medical system was superior, and certainly not inferior, to that of orthodox practitioners – which, perhaps, is not saying very much.

72   Raspail never attained any university degree or professional qualification, not through any lack of opportunity, but as a matter of principle, because he was opposed to all forms of institutionalized hierarchy. He was a man of principle, and, like many such when they are completely uncompromising, he was also an awkward customer. There was a strong paranoid streak to his personality, and it is not easy in his case to distinguish justified fear of persecution from delusory fear. The paranoid often conduct themselves in such a way as to invite the very persecution that they fear. For example, soon after the Revolution of 1830, Louis Philippe offered him the *Légion d'honneur* for his scientific work and the directorship of the Parisian botanical garden, Raspail answered the King's intermediary, "Tell your master that I will accept nothing from those who stole the republic!"[11] He was then somewhat aggrieved when Guizot, the prime minister, intervened to prevent the award of a prize to him, which he took as evidence of the regime's further hostility towards him.

The fact is, however, that he *was* persecuted, not only by the July Monarchy of Louis Philippe, but by the Second and Third Republics, all of which imprisoned him.* In all, he spent eight years of his life in prison and nine in exile; one of his most important works was a two-volume collection of his articles about his imprisonment, published in 1839.

He saw spies and informers everywhere, and the modern

---

* He was also imprisoned under the Second Empire, but that was only as a continuation of the sentence — the very harsh sentence — imposed on him by the Second Republic. The sentence was commuted to exile by Napoleon III after the death of Raspail's wife.

view of Louis Philippe's reign, at least, is that they *were* rather numerous. Nevertheless, there is something distinctly paranoid about some of what Raspail wrote. In 1835, for example, a Corsican called Fieschi tried to assassinate Louis Philippe by mounting what was called an *machine infernale* in a building along the route in Paris due to be taken by the king and his entourage. The infernal machine was a collection of twenty-five gun-barrels designed to go off at once as the king went by. Not all of them did, but enough to kill eighteen people, including one of Napoleon's marshals, Marshal Mortier, and two generals. The king himself escaped with a minor wound. Fieschi was captured soon after and guillotined, his decapitated head being painted the following day by Jacques Raymond Brascassat, known more for his landscapes and paintings of farm animals than for such ghoulish subjects.

There was nothing to connect Raspail with Fieschi: the former was en route to Nantes when the infernal machine went off. Nevertheless, Raspail was arrested as he arrived in Nantes and brought back to Paris, the occasion serving as a pretext to arrest all opponents of the regime. Raspail, however, went further than this:

Before the House of Peers, where the case was tried, another circumstance was revealed to everyone's eyes, despite the care that was taken to hide it, the scrupulous deposition of a reliable witness: for it showed that the *commissaire* of police for the district had been warned the evening before of the existence of an infernal machine, and instead of going to the place to verify the fact, he had sent the informer away with marked indifference or even bad temper. Such a revelation caused indignation in the House of Peers and allowed the public to understand that this abominable mass murder had been nothing but another trick, bloodier than the others, to act upon the fears of the bourgeoisie.[12]

74   No other explanation of the policeman's indifference to the information he received, other than that he was party to a giant plot to raise the fears of the bourgeoisie, seems to have occurred to Raspail, for example that under a regime of spies and informers (as Raspail thought that Louis Philippe's was) more false information than true must have been received, far more than could possibly be acted upon. The presumption against information being true was therefore strong. Besides, no infernal machine had ever been known to exist before (in fact, Fieschi was almost an inventor, a forerunner perhaps of the Stalin Organ), and therefore the policeman might well have received information about it in much the same way that a modern policeman might have received information about the arrival of aliens from outer space on Acacia Avenue. It is also a fact that on occasion, policemen have been found to be lazy or incompetent.

Two of Fieschi's co-conspirators, Morey and Pépin, were executed with him, but Raspail was not impressed by the execution:

> Morey and Pépin were really guillotined; they had been the wretched dupes of Fieschi, agent of the Palace, only an effigy of whose head really fell; for we learned later that a mysterious personage had embarked at Brest with his companion. The newspapers only spoke of this circumstance obliquely; the government did not deign to reply to this unexpected revelation.[13]

This all strikes me as authentically mad, albeit that Raspail had no reason to love the government. Here is the very template of conspiracy theory: a vague political aperçu, that regimes often drum up support by frightening disgruntled electorates or clienteles by posing as the sole defense against something far worse, is inflated into a ludicrous plot, in which a regime kills a large number of its prominent members and injures its very head. Surely Louis Philippe would not have agreed to a plot in which he himself would be injured, even mildly, and the method employed was intrinsically so uncertain that its effects could not have been fully calculated in advance.

75

If it was not Louis Philippe, then, who had arranged or agreed to the plot, who was it who actually did so? Again, it would hardly have been any of his entourage that day, for they would not have agreed to be mown down by the infernal machine just to raise public support or sympathy for the regime. Implicitly, Raspail suggests that there was what in modern conspiratorial parlance would be called a *deep state* intent upon preserving itself irrespective of who its head appeared to be. No doubt his imprisonment under four regimes, often under laws passed by previous regimes, and in one case a sentence continued from a previous regime, would tend throughout his life to encourage such a view.

As to the embarkment of a man and his companion in Brest, this is the kind of evidence beloved of, and necessary to, conspiracy theorists. Fieschi was known to have a companion, actually his stepdaughter with whom he carried on an affair for many years; therefore an unknown man and his companion appearing at Brest immediately after the outrage must have been Fieschi. It follows from this that the supposed execution of Fieschi was actually a sham, the victim being either a dummy or a replacement person. Of course, the painter Brascassat must have been in on the plot, having first been bribed.

It is clear that with reasoning such as this, no evidence could ever refute a belief in the plot, and everything could be incorporated into it. This is the beauty of conspiracy theories.*

There were undoubtedly paranoid traits in Raspail's character. On his own admission, he was always very jealous of his wife, though she gave him no reason to be and by all accounts was of such an ugliness that infidelity would have been difficult for her, excellent in every other way as she was always reported to have been. Unlike many jealous men, however, Raspail was not unfaithful himself, believing that public men such as he should not make themselves the object of derogatory gossip, and he was an excellent father, beloved of his children despite (or because of?) his prolonged absences.

His wife always visited him in whatever prisons he was incarcerated, and she died soon after she visited him in the prison of Doullens. Raspail thought that she had been poisoned by arsenic in the prison food, though there was no evidence of this other than that she suffered from vomiting and diarrhea. As we shall see, in another famous case, Raspail had argued that such symptoms do not by themselves indicate arsenic poisoning.

In his writings, even on seemingly innocuous or neutral subjects, Raspail adopted a combative or rancorous tone. It was said that he sought always to crush rather than to persuade. Those who disagreed with him were opponents, usually ill-intentioned. This was a characteristic from early in his career: for example, the embryologist Victor Coste (later to be one of the founders of some of France's most important oyster beds) reproaches Raspail in 1830 for his combative and insulting tone in a purely scientific controversy over

---

* This is not, of course, to say that there are no conspiracies. Machiavelli, in the *Discourses*, discusses the conditions for their success.

the point in embryogenesis at which the human fetus is attached by umbilical cord to the placenta:

> Science is not an arena in which *antagonists* come to dispute or claim victory, but a field of asylum open to devoted scholars, association of whom increases their power.... Enough men speak today of abnegation and devotion when they practice egoism; of love and tolerance when they are carried away by hatred, so that it is time to translate theory into fact, morality into action, and break with this dark and unhappy polemic which disputes rather than discusses, and which serious men have sometimes pushed to the point of suspecting the good faith of their colleagues.... If, therefore, we do not want to waste precious time on these puerile disputes which, of no use to science, only end most often in sterile satisfaction of *amour propre*, we must begin by limiting the field on which we find ourselves ...[14]

This gives a far from a complete impression of Raspail's character, however, for Raspail had undoubtedly been a devoted scholar, spending eight hours each day for several years poring over his microscope, and later offering free medical advice and treatment to thousands of the poor. Naturally, it is possible to interpret these as manifestations of egoism insofar as they served his ultimate interest, but only at the cost of making egoism a tautologically necessary interpretation of human behavior. If providing free advice and treatment to thousands of people at one's own expense of time, effort, and money (or opportunity cost) is not altruistic, it is difficult to know what could be.

It is hard now to estimate how far Raspail was irrationally paranoid. Among his most important activities was the founding and editing of two newspapers, the *Le Réformateur* and *L'Ami du peuple* (both of which he also wrote for, and sometimes the whole of), the former started with capital from the rich but radical Breton aristocrat René-Théophile Guillard de Kersausie, the latter a provocative reference to Marat's inflammatory publication of the same name during the first revolution (Raspail wrote a long and laudatory study of Jean-Paul Marat, a doctor, scientist, and journalist turned political activist, with obvious resemblances, therefore, to Raspail himself, whom Raspail tried to rescue from his reputation as a bloodthirsty mass-murdering demagogue – which nobody could have accused Raspail of having been).

Having founded his newspaper, Raspail later wrote, "I hardly had two of the editorial staff, two friends, on whom I could count, I mistrusted all the others."[15] Whether his mistrust was justified can probably never now be known. He tells the following story:

> Louis Philippe knew my mistrustful attitude perfectly well; and this gave rise to a new trick to tire me out. On two evenings, he sent me the most annoying personage of his entourage: he was a certain *Ganal*, well known for his system of unctuous flattery. This succeeded one day, but from the next day the trick was neutralized ...
>
> One morning, on rising at about six o'clock, I reread the newspaper [*Le Réformateur*] that had just appeared, and saw with astonishment an article that had not passed under my eye when I gave the order to print, that is to say near midnight. This article contained a shameful accusation of cowardice against one of the sons of Marshal Oudinot, who was in the army in Algeria. One can imagine the father's indignation on finding such an insult. As for me, I only discovered the author at six in

the evening, when all my compositors were together. Towards ten or eleven [in the morning], I saw the Marshal's steward enter my office. "You find me," I said to him, "as anxious about this false accusation as the Marshal himself; I still do not know the author of this infamy, I will know him only this evening, when the newspaper will start work again; do me the honor of giving me a rectification or I will hasten to make one myself. All this," I added, "can only come from the Palace, by one of its agents, and I am not short of these lepers, for those lines were not in the newspaper at midnight, when I gave the order to print."

The steward left it to me to write the rectification myself. Almost as soon as the compositors were assembled, I was apprised of the author of the infamy; and I discovered from the layout designer that after the departure of the compositors, a certain gentleman whom he had seen during the stay in the office came to him and told him that he was acting on my behalf, which he believed. As he depicted this gentleman, I recognized this M. Ganal, a kind of looter from the rue de Lombards [a banker therefore]; he played the mental defective so well that he was a protege of H. M. Louis Philippe.[16]

Is this story true? Raspail was not entirely scrupulous with facts once he had the bit between his teeth, though the story could have been true, for there is no doubt that the regime tired repeatedly by means of legal actions and heavy fines close down *Le Réformateur* (and in the end succeeded). Of course, by twentieth-century standards, such methods of oppression were almost gentlemanly, or at any rate amateurish.

We have seen that Raspail thought that his wife had been poisoned with arsenic, and arsenic poisoning played an important part in his career. In fact, the only reason that I had ever heard of Raspail before I looked further into him was that I had taken an interest in arsenic poisoning, criminal, domestic, and industrial, in the nineteenth century. Raspail involved himself deeply in the case of Madame Lafarge, née Marie Capelle, who was accused and convicted in 1840 of having poisoned her husband to death by arsenic the year before.

The story is well-known and is the subject of at least a hundred books. Even today, there are still *Lafargistes* and *Anti-Lafargistes*, that is to say those who believe in her innocence or guilt. Flowers are still placed on her grave a hundred and seventy years after her death, in memory of a wronged woman (and wronged I believe her to have been, even if only because the prosecution did not prove its case even had she been guilty).

Marie Capelle was born into an upper-middle-class family but was soon orphaned and left comparatively impoverished. She lived as a poor relation with people who wanted to get her off their hands, and they found for her a husband, Charles Pouche-Lafarge, supposedly rich and living in a fine château in the provinces. It turned out that he was a boorish, or at any rate unrefined, ironmaster, and that the fine château was in fact an ancient, dilapidated building barely furnished and without comfort, infested by rats and falling apart. In addition, Marie Capelle's mother-in-law detested her, in a way that the coarse often hate the refined (who, of course, may give themselves airs).

On the night of her arrival at her new home in Glandier, Marie Capelle, now Madame Lafarge, locked herself in her room and refused to come out, writing an extraordinary letter to her new husband, asking him to release her from their marriage but allowing her to keep her dowry of 80,000 francs, after which she would travel alone in the Levant.

Over the next few months, however, she developed an affection for her husband, allegedly because he was so considerate to her. The Anti-Lafargistes, of course, interpreted this as a sign of her cunning in her premediated plot to dispose of her husband by poison: everything in this case is a double- or triple- or quadruple-edged sword.

Be that as it may, Lafarge went on a trip to Paris for two reasons: first to try to patent a new process of iron-smelting that he had invented, and second to raise a loan, for he was always in financial difficulties and involved in shady dealings. His wife sent him affectionate letters, as he did to her, and then she sent him some cakes for him to eat at a given time, at which she said she would do in Glandier at the same time, thus uniting them in some vague spiritual fashion. The four cakes that left Glandier arrived in Paris as one big cake, a mystery that has never been solved.

When Lafarge ate of the cake, he was immediately taken ill with severe nausea, vomiting, and diarrhea. He managed to return home to Glandier, where he continued to be very ill with the same symptoms and died a few days later. Poisoning by arsenic was suspected, and Madame Lafarge arrested.

These were the early days of forensic toxicology, yet another of the matters in which Raspail interested himself. The Marsh test for arsenic had been invented (not surprisingly by someone called Marsh) only three years before, and toxicology was to play a large part in the trial and conviction of Madame Lafarge.

That trial, in a town called Tulle, was unfair on many levels. One might have thought that the first thing to prove was that Lafarge actually died of arsenic poisoning; the second that, if he did so die, the arsenic from which he died could only have been administered criminally; and the third that it was Madame Lafarge who administered it. But in fact, the trial commenced with a hostile examination of Madame

Lafarge, her conduct, and her possible motives. This was deeply prejudicial. She *did* have possible motives for poisoning her husband, but so did others, as there are many possible suspects in any good detective story; moreover, her mother-in-law had a strong motive for spreading false rumors about her, rumors that, in fact, were responsible for persuading Lafarge's doctor, Dr. Lespinasse, that Lafarge was being poisoned with arsenic before he succumbed.*

The first toxicological investigations of the case were very crude. Dr. Lespinasse and the local pharmacist simply threw some of the powders subsequently found in the Lafarge household on the fire and smelt the odor of garlic that is characteristic of arsenic alone in these circumstances.

The second toxicological investigations were carried out in Limoges by competent chemists appointed as experts by the court, both on the preserved vomitus and Lafarge's corpse that had been exhumed several months later. These experts found no arsenic in either, and when they testified as much in court, there was at first general rejoicing that Madame Lafarge must now be acquitted.

The prosecutor, however, refused to accept the findings of the experts from Limoges; he managed to obtain an adjournment while he arranged for the great Parisian expert on poisons, Matthieu Orfila, to repeat the tests. Orfila duly found arsenic where the experts from Limoges had found

---

* Interestingly, his conviction that Lafarge was being poisoned did not cause Dr. Lespinasse to suggest that he be moved from the household in which he was being poisoned, by whomever it was. A similar situation arose eighty years later in England when Mrs. Armstrong's doctor suspected that she was being poisoned with arsenic by her husband, poisoning from which she subsequently died. The doctor had been persuaded of Armstrong's guilt by the father-in-law of Armstrong's rival in business, but he did not remove Mrs. Armstrong from the home. Of course, the doctor faces a serious dilemma. Acting on a false suspicion may have terrible consequences, but so may failing to act on a true one.

none, and it was on Orfila's evidence that Madame Lafarge was convicted. If his evidence was not sufficient for a conviction, it was certainly necessary.

Now Raspail was a ferocious opponent, even enemy, of Orfila, who represented everything that he hated. Orfila had risen from Spanish immigrant (he was born in Minorca) to become doyen of the Parisian medical faculty, without whose approval nobody could be appointed to an official medical position. He had a claim to be considered the founder of forensic toxicology and wrote many textbooks on the subject that went through several editions. He was the first to suggest that ingested poisons were distributed via the blood throughout the body and that therefore it was inadequate to search for poisons in the intestinal tract alone, Many poisons, he said, including arsenic, were concentrated in the liver.

Once Orfila, the great panjandrum, had delivered his evidence, Madame Lafarge wrote desperately to Raspail as the only man who could save her. Raspail had already appeared as an expert for the defense in two trials for murder by arsenic poisoning in which Orfila had appeared for the prosecution, with equivocal effect: the convictions were arrived at without regard to the toxicological evidence. Both men claimed victory.

Raspail arrived too late in Tulle to give any evidence: the verdict had already been reached and Madame Lafarge found guilty. Orfila had also left Tulle before Raspail's arrival, which later gave rise to a witty little jingle suggesting that Orfila was afraid of Raspail:

Quand Raspail arriva,
Orfila fila, fila!*

---

* (When Raspail arrived/ Orfila scarpered, scarpered!)

Raspail was no fatalist, and he quickly wrote a long disquisition for use by Madame Lafarge's lawyer at appeal (which was unsuccessful). A hundred and seventy-two pages long, it has a less than succinct title, *Mémoire à consulter, à l'appui du pourvoi en cassation de Dame Marie Capelle, veuve Laffarge, sur les moyens de nullité que présente l'expertise chimique, dans le cours de la procédure, qui vient de se terminer par l'arrêt de la Cour d'assises de la Corrèze, du 19 septembre 1840 ; rédigé, à la défense.**

Since the date of the publication of Raspail's memorandum is October 1, 1840, the trial having ended only twelve days before, and the memorandum must have taken a day or two at least to set up for the press, it is clear that Raspail was a very fast worker.

This work captures Raspail's character and methods very well. He is like a man who accuses a man of being a mass murderer and animadverts on his bad table manners into the bargain. He is so convinced of his case, that he is sometimes unfair; he does not recognize that in certain circumstances less can be more. Nevertheless, some of his criticisms strike home and should have been sufficient to secure Madame Lafarge's acquittal.†

For example, he points out the utter uselessness as evidence of the first investigation. Not only was the test itself highly dubious, but the provenance of the powders tested for arsenic was unsure and they could easily have been interfered with or contaminated between Lafarge's death

---

* "Memorandum to Consult in Support of the Appeal to the Appeal Court of Madame Marie Capelle, Widow of Lafarge, of the Nullity of the Means Employed in the Chemical Expert Report, During the Trial which Has Just Ended in the Judgment of the Assize Court of the Corrèze on the 19th September 1840."

† For some reason, Raspail always spells Lafarge *Laffarge*. I have about twenty of the books on the affair, and Raspail was the only one to spell the name thus.

and when the test was carried out.

He is complimentary about the tests carried out in Limoges: their negative results should have introduced enough doubt for acquittal. (Raspail clearly believed that Madame Lafarge was innocent, but is careful to point out that his arguments would be valid even if she were guilty.)

It is about Orfila's evidence that he is most scathing:

> If the conviction of Madame Laffarge was obtained only with aid of certain expert reports, and notable the last of them [that of Orfila], the accused fell victim to a deplorable judicial error, and an even more deplorable system of chemical investigation.[17]

Raspail accuses Orfila of having begun his verbal evidence to the court by exclaiming, "*Laffarge est mort empoisonné; je vais le démontrer*" (Laffarge died poisoned; I will demonstrate it.) If Orfila did say that, he was clearly going beyond the evidence, but in fact he denied that he said any such thing. In his *Réponse aux écrits de M. Raspail sur l'affaire de Tulle* (Reply to the Writings of M. Raspail on the Case in Tulle), forty-five pages long and also published in December 1840 (they evidently were able to work quickly in those days and did not require our technology to rush things into print), Orfila said that what he actually said at the beginning of his evidence was "*Il existe de l'arsenic dans le corps de Lafarge*" (There is arsenic in Lafarge's body),[18] which of course is very different. Moreover, Orfila says that these words appear in all the transcripts of the trial: and this is borne out, at least to some extent, in the only transcript of the trial I possess.* [19]

---

* What Orfila is here recorded as having said is, "*Je demontrerai qu'il existe de l'arsenic dans le corps de Lafarge.*" (I will demonstrate that there is arsenic in Lafarge's body.)

Raspail as ever has a reply to this, namely that Orfila was so powerful, influential, and corrupt a personage that he was able to pay to have the transcripts of evidence altered to suit himself. According to Raspail, Orfila had his *valets de plume*, his valets of the pen, who would write whatever he dictated.[20] This sounds mad, but it is not totally impossible (no doubt such things have been known in history).

86

Of course, if Orfila said what he said he said, and not what Raspail said he said, his evidence was a good deal less *parti pris* than Raspail alleged.

Raspail tries to cast doubt on Orfila's claim to chemical expertise by saying that he was laughed at during a session at the Academy of Medicine when he claimed that he had tested the bouillons of two hundred Parisian restaurants and found that they had all contained arsenic, a ridiculous claim that he had since been forced to withdraw, the arsenic having come from the chemical reagents he used to perform the tests. Orfila says that what in fact he told the Academy of Medicine was the following:

> I prepared a bouillon in an ordinary saucepan with five and a half pounds of beef on the bone, with carrots, parsnips, turnips, leeks, browned onions, a clove and salt. The liquid, which was detectably acid, evaporated to dryness after seven hours of boiling with the meat, left a residue that I decomposed with nitre, water and sulfuric acid, and which, put into Marsh's apparatus, released hydrogenated arsenic.... *If new experiments confirm this result* [emphasis in the original], it will demonstrate that the beef bouillon that we consume every day contains an arsenical preparation.[21]

Actually, it would do no such thing. Although Orfila specifically denied it later in the *Réponse*, sulfuric acid can be con-

taminated with arsenic, as was found when six thousand
beer drinkers in Manchester at the turn of the twentieth
century were poisoned with arsenic, which was traced to
contamination of the sulfuric acid used in the production of   87
the sugar used in the brewing process.* Moreover, it would
be necessary to conduct a control experiment in order to
prove that the arsenic came from the contents of the bouillon rather than from the saucepan itself.

Be that all as it may, Orfila's account is very different,
and intrinsically more likely, than Raspail's, for it is not easy
to imagine the collection of two hundred bouillon for testing. If Raspail was wrong here, he was clearly not an entirely
scrupulous controversialist. He later implicitly referred to
Orfila's supposed finding of arsenic in the bouillons when
he remarked that, using Orfila's methods, he would find
arsenic in the seat upon which the judge sat.

But some of Raspail's scattergun or blunderbuss accusa-
tions against Orfila were justified. To explain the difference
between Orfila's findings and those of the Limoges chemists, Raspail pointed out that Orfila had brought a reagent
from Paris, potassium nitrate, that the Limoges chemists had
not used and that could have been contaminated with arsenic and had not been demonstrated *not* to contain arsenic.†

---

* "The implicated Bostock brewing sugars became thus seriously contaminated by arsenic in the course of their manufacture through the use of
sulphuric acid supplied by the firm of acid makers, Nicholson and Sons,
Limited, of Leeds." *First Report of the Royal Commission Appointed to Inquire
into Arsenical Poisoning from the consumption of Beer and Other Articles of
Food or Drink* (London: His Majesty's Stationery Office, 1901), 2. That sulfuric acid could be contaminated by arsenic was known long before. See,
for example, A. Chevallier et Jules Barse, *Manuel pratique de l'appareil de
Marsh* (Paris: Labé, 1843), 124. The authors say that potassium nitrate is
very rarely contaminated with arsenic.
† That contamination during testing was, and remained, a real problem
and not a figment Raspail's imagination was demonstrated in the famous

Moreover, Orfila did not keep any of his reagents for subsequent analysis, as he should have done, and underlying Raspail's criticisms of him is the implicit allegation that he was acting corruptly and dishonestly in order to dig the prosecution out of an embarrassing hole, even if to do so were risk a sentence of death being passed on an innocent woman.*

Certainly, Orfila seemed to be keen to help the prosecution. When Raspail pointed out that, even if Lafarge's body contained arsenic, which he thought at the least not beyond doubt, it might have derived from arsenical medication that Lafarge could have been prescribed on his visit to Paris, Orfila replied in his *Réponse* that there was no evidence that he had been prescribed such medication. He thus entered a dispute that was not strictly toxicological and thereby revealed his bias; unwittingly, of course, he admitted that Raspail was right, for in saying that there was no evidence that Lafarge had taken arsenical medications, he confirmed what Raspail had argued, namely that Lafarge *might* have taken such medications (commonly used at the time) and the mere possibility cast doubt on the prosecution case, enough to render a conviction unsafe.

Raspail offered other objections, some justified and others fanciful (for example, that a single piece of green paper, whose coloration was arsenical, dropped in the cemetery

---

cause of Dr. Smethurst in England in 1856. The most important English toxicologist of the time, Dr Alfred Swaine Taylor, was obliged to admit (which he did with admirable honesty and frankness) that the arsenic he found in the samples in the case derived from the metal gauze he used in the analysis rather than from the samples themselves. As in the case of Madame Lafarge, the accused was on trial for his life.

* In fact, she was sentenced to life imprisonment, commuted by Napoleon III in 1852, shortly before her death from tuberculosis. This was shortly before Napoleon III commuted Raspail's own sentence. These displays of relative mercy did nothing to dispose Raspail in Napoleon's favor.

might have leached arsenic into Lafarge's corpse through two small holes in the coffin). The fact is that, soon afterwards, Orfila gave up appearing as an expert witness in cases of poisoning, not because he was afraid of Raspail, he said, and as the jingle suggested, but because he was exasperated by having to dispute with unqualified persons, by whom he could only have meant Raspail, pointing out that the courts had always sided with him:

> My refusal to take part has nothing to do, as has been maliciously insinuated, with the fear of new disputes, since all my efforts so far have been crowned by success: no, it must be attributed solely to the invincible repugnance I have had all my life to disputations with men whose incompetence is at least equaled by their bad faith.[22]

Raspail continued his dispute with Orfila beyond the grave – Orfila's grave, that is. In his long essay on Marat, Raspail defends Marat from the imputation that he was once a charlatan who sold quack medicine, by the following irrelevant interjection:

> If public opinion had no other reproach to offer to the late Orfila than that of having been at the beginning of his career a clown and a street musician, I would have been the first to defend his memory.[23]

Raspail was a socialist in politics as well as a republican, but he accorded no important role to the state, which he deeply mistrusted, and did not really devote much attention to the detail of how socialist equality was to come about. He believed that all decisions should be as local as possible and looked forward to a world in which there were no hierarchies or constitute authorities. Insofar as the state should exist at all, it would be easy to ensure that all its expenditure was directed to public and not private purposes such as the upkeep of kings and others. He said that anyone who could run a domestic household could run a state.[24]

90

His penology was simple, not to say simplistic, in theory, and was almost Rousseauvian in its assumption that all bad conduct derived from civilization, or at least from unfavorable social conditions, and could be corrected by kindness and reason. In his time in prison, of course, he met many criminals, including the famous, or infamous, Pierre François Lacenaire, by whose ability to quote long passages of Corneille he was much impressed. Lacenaire was a sometime poet and journalist who was also a swindler and a brutal double-murderer, who was executed at the age of thirty-two. He claimed that his crimes were a form of social protest, and like many a dangerous psychopath, he could be charming. In an article comparing Lacenaire with Wilhelm, King of Prussia, who became Kaiser Wilhelm after the Franco-Prussian War, much to the advantage of Lacenaire, Raspail says:

> Before his stay in Poissy [on the outskirts of Paris where he killed a man called Chardon with an axe and strangled his mother], Lacenaire was cast into swindling, by a need that devoured him who was the son of a high-placed family of ruined bankers, by the need, I say, to eat and above all to drink, (he drank, without difficulty, twelve bottles a day while still standing). In Poissy, all the rage he felt in his heart against society, his enemy, came out.[25]

Raspail wrote:

> Is it not time to transform your ferocious laws against the guilty into good, kind preventive laws to make them better?... Give everyone bread to eat, education to pro-

mote their intelligence. Sow equality everywhere in the face of needs ... that is the idea, more than ever, to support in the interests of the future of humanity ...*[26]

Here are the tropes of one pole of penology, that crime is purely the result of social conditions, to be overcome by kindness and social reform, the other being that man is inherently inclined to wickedness and chooses to do wrong. I am more inclined to the second pole than the first, though not without the need to exercise judgment and mercy, taking account of extenuating circumstances. I find it hard to think of Lacenaire as a victim of society, though one cannot help but wonder whether there was something congenitally odd about him.

I find it harder to summarize Raspail than any man I have ever read about. He was brilliant, gifted, visionary, and silly. He was hard-working and impatient. He was a friend of justice but often unfair. He was a jealous but faithful husband and an excellent father to his five surviving children, all of whom revered him. He was genuinely concerned for the welfare of others but sometimes grotesquely egotistical. He was both modest and grandiose. Whether his grandiosity was the result of his paranoia, or his paranoia was the result of his grandiosity, I am not sure (those who feel themselves persecuted must believe that they are worth persecuting).

I will give a couple of brief instances of his grandiosity. When, at the head of a crowd whose number must forever be unknowable, he broke into the City Hall where the Provisional Government was sitting after the downfall of Louis

---

* I have omitted a clause that shows Raspail at his most mad. "Above all, above all, show the door to that society that parliaments have condemned as infamous, the Society of Jesus [the Jesuits]." Raspail here suggests that this is the most important measure that could be taken, surely a symptom of a paranoid mindset.

Philippe, he exclaimed, "In the name of the French people, I proclaim the republic, one and indivisible."[27] This implies a certain self-belief or self-importance, to say the least; and even after the elections of December that year, in which he stood as President of the Republic and he received 36,900 votes to Louis Napoleon's 5,434,226 (and in which even the far from socialist General Cavaignac received 1,448,107 votes), he never doubted his own effect and importance. [28]

In 1846, his great enemy Orfila sought revenge by bringing a case against him for practicing medicine without a license to do so, as the law required. In his very long speech in his own defense, Raspail said a) that he had always been excluded from all institutions of higher learning; b) that, despite having lectured at the faculty of medicine in previous years, he didn't want their diploma anyway; and c) that he was better than all the other doctors combined, who were merely an impudent rabble of money-grubbing charlatans. This is not the way to win friends and influence people – although, as it happens, his speech was applauded because of the eloquence of the way in which he pronounced it.

For many years content to live in poverty, he said in the course of this speech,

> I studied, like today's doctors have never studied for a single day of their lives.... Do you know that, to arrive at the point at which I am, at which I dominate all these men [the medical profession] and force them, great and small, to transcribe what I write in order that they should appear to know something; do you know that I had to work eight hours a day for ten years, and six hours for another ten years? Do you know that I do not recall during this long period of time ever having gone to bed without a headache … ?[29]

One detects a certain arrogance here.

Raspail was clever but foolish, good but irritating, modest but grandiose. As Whitman might have said, he contained within himself multitudes, and for all his defects an air of greatness hangs over him and he deserves his boulevard.*

---

* Orfila, by the way, has a street named after him in Paris also, the rue (not the boulevard) Orfila. Perhaps it is an irony that the street named after Orfila, a man of the establishment, is in a less chic part of Paris than the Boulevard Raspail, which as it happens very near Père Lachaise wherein Raspail is buried.

Enrique Gómez Carrillo
(1873–1927)

FEW LIVES ARE more extraordinary than that (I almost said *those*) of Enrique Gómez Carrillo. He must have been born under some special star that marked him out from others, for at the age of eighteen he left his native Guatemala to pursue, with almost immediate success, a career in Paris as a writer, intellectual, and bohemian. In his day he was famous, or at least celebrated and partly notorious, but practically nothing is now written about him without drawing attention to the oblivion into which he has fallen, even in his native Guatemala.* It is true that in the 1960s, there was a brief attempt, for nationalist reasons, to have his remains returned to Guatemala, and a monument was erected to him, but his body was not returned, and the nearest to return that was achieved was the spread of some earth from Père Lachaise at the site of the monument. Guatemalan intellectuals were divided on the question of whether his

---

* A typical example is to be found in Paul Webster's biography of his third wife, *Consuelo de Saint-Exupéry: La Rose du petit prince* (Paris: Le Félin, 2002), 52. "Today, Gómez Carillo has rather fallen into oblivion but at the beginning of the century he counted as one of the most influential members of Parisian culture, ever since his arrival in the capital, aged eighteen, in 1891." On a personal note, I stayed for several months in the delightful city of Antigua Guatemala (where Gómez Carrillo was born) in the house of Michael Shawcross, a British seller of books both new and antiquarian, resident in Guatemala, who himself had a vast library on the country, and I never heard him mention Gómez Carrillo, though we talked much of Guatemalan books.

remains should return to Guatemala: the argument for return being that he was Guatemalan, and the argument against being that he lived all his adult life in France and that is where his heart was.[1]

No ordinary person could have made his way so quickly at so early an age and from so provincial a backwater as Guatemala into the heart of bohemian Paris. He became immediately acquainted with Verlaine, the great poet, and later with Oscar Wilde. It is said that he even gave money to Verlaine from the Guatemalan scholarship that he was supposed to use to study in Madrid, a city that he soon abandoned for Paris. Interestingly, though, and perhaps surprisingly, he wrote all his many books in Spanish, not in French.

Mystery and mythology surround his biography. Even the exact number of his books is not known:

> As the astronomers tell us that there are stars whose light has not reached us, so there are works of Gómez Carrillo that remain in the zone of conjecture, that people assert have been published, and that they have read and possess, and yet that have not been listed in any of the bibliographies up to the present day.[2]

Fifty-five years later, in 2011, we read in the introduction to a reprint of his three volumes of autobiography, *Treinta Años de mi Vida* (Thirty Years of My Life), and eighty-four years after his death:

> How many books did Gómez Carrillo publish? Nobody knows for certain. He shuffled his pages, gave different titles to similar contents, and at any time could deliver to any generous publisher a supposedly unpublished work although it had been published only a few days before by another.[3]

One of the strange, almost bizarre, things about his career is the persistent rumor that he was Mata Hari's last lover and that it was he who betrayed her to the French as a spy, thereby becoming partly responsible for her death by firing squad. He took advantage of the rumor to write a popular book about her, *Le mystère de la vie et de la mort de Mata Hari* (The Mystery of the Life and Death of Mata Hari).[4] In this book, however, he denied that he had ever met, or even seen, Mata Hari. He recounts a conversation in Madrid with the disgraced and exiled French minister of the interior Louis Malvy, who had been cast out from France in 1918 for five years because of alleged negligence in the performance of his ministerial duties, and was also suspected of treason, his pacifist newspaper, *Bonnet Rouge*, having received funds from the Germans.

Gómez Carrillo asked Malvy what Mata Hari's true role had been during the war, on the assumption that, as minister of the interior at the time, Malvy must have had inside knowledge. The following conversation ensued:

> "But of the two of us who must know who were the friends of the famous dancer, it is you."
>
> "Me ... why?"
>
> There was a moment's silence, during which the former minister's fine face became worried. In the end, visibly disturbed, he wanted to apologize for his indiscretion, and asked me to talk of less macabre subjects. But I had a great curiosity to know the reason for his enigmatic phrases; and so, serious in my turn, I asked him to explain what they meant.
>
> "It's no secret from anyone," he replied, "and I don't mean only your love affair with Mata Hari."
>
> "My love affair with Mata Hari?"

"Yes, everyone is whispering that you were her last lover ..."

"Me? That's very flattering, after all, because she was so famous a woman," I exclaimed, laughing. "Only, there's nothing to it."[5]

Malvy went on to say to Gómez Carrillo, "delicately," that the rumors claimed that he was not only the secret lover, but the denouncer of Mata Hari. The author denied these charges, using two arguments: first that he was so notoriously a Don Juan that he never hid his affairs, and second that, having written two books on the subject of exotic dance, he had never so much as mentioned Mata Hari. And Malvy went on to say that the rumor spread by Spanish Germanophiles that Gómez Carrillo had been decorated as a commander of the *Légion d'honneur* for his services as the denouncer were absurd, because the republic rewarded the exceptional services of policemen with money, not honors:

"The more grotesque a calumny," murmured [Malvy], "the more it finds people disposed to believe it."[6]

Gómez Carrillo provides another argument as to why he could not possibly be Mata Hari's betrayer. "I remember," he writes, "the first time my name spread beyond the purlieus of the literary world and reached the ears of the general public [in Madrid].... I had been elected corresponding member of the Royal Spanish Academy at the age of twenty-one. The title so flattered my youthful vanity that I put it on my visiting card." But when he learned that one of the members of the Royal Academy, called Cotarolo, had, in order to claim a reward, revealed to the police the whereabouts in Madrid of the notorious French swindler Madame Humbert, who had fled to Spain on exposure of her swindle, he told the permanent secretary of the Academy that unless it expelled Cotarelo he would resign. This raised a public controversy, for and against denunciation of wrongdoers.

Gómez Carrillo wrote, partly as proof of his innocence with regard to his alleged denunciation of Mata Hari, that:

> I who have always felt the most profound horror for all amateur *detectivism*, all dilettante Sherlock-Holmsianism, believe therefore that I behaved nobly.[7]

This seems to capture quite well the self-congratulatory inclinations of many intellectuals when they pronounce simplistically on morally complex issues, making generous-sounding rhetoric stand for real thought.

No one finds informers – those who denounce minor wrongdoers (or even the innocent) to the authorities out of spite, sadism, revenge, or desire for petty reward – attractive. But that, surely, is not the end of the matter: at some point, failure to inform becomes complicity, sometimes with a great crime. In the prison in which I worked as a doctor, no prisoner was more despised, or in danger of attack, than a known informer, called *a grass*, but there was nevertheless an implicit limit to prisoners' fear of or unwillingness to inform on each other. Once, for example, a prisoner secretly murdered his cellmate, who was found dead, apparently by hanging. I was on duty that night, and two prisoners gave me clues that resulted in the apprehension and conviction of the murderer. The informers were more subtle in their moral thinking than Gómez Carrillo: yes, informing was unpleasant and sometimes truly disgusting, but no, there could be no blanket prohibition of it.

Of course, it could be argued that Madame Humbert was a swindler, not a murderess. Indeed, her swindles were so outrageous that they exposed the foolishness, greed, and gullibility of the grandest of grand people in the French Third Republic: the kind of spectacle that we earthlings, prone to *Schadenfreude*, always enjoy and the opportunity for experiencing which, more recently, persons such as Bernie Madoff and Sam Bankman-Fried have provided us – except that Madame Humbert was a far more interesting character, having started out as the illegitimate daughter of two illegitimate parents in rural France.* Moreover, having been once exposed, it would have been impossible for Madame Humbert to have resumed the swindles that allowed her and her whole family to live in the greatest of luxury for twenty years. She was ruined for good, and therefore no further punishment would have served any useful purpose.

Against these arguments that must have sustained Gómez Carrillo in his self-satisfaction might be argued two things. First that though Madame Humbert's swindles amusingly exposed the folly and credulity of the elite, they also ruined thousands of small savers who lost everything in the eventual crash. There were quite a number of suicides as a result of her defalcations, and much suffering beside. Hers was not merely an amusing morality tale, a kind of practical satire on the rich and well-educated; she deprived thousands of people of the fruit of years of hard work and sacrifice.

Second, while it is true that she would never have been able to return to her dishonest activities, and that any harm she was able to do had already been done and would not have been undone by punishment, *not* to have punished her would also have had its consequences, by implying that

---

* For a brief account of the case, see Hilary Spurling, *La Grande Thérèse, or the Greatest Swindle of the Century* (London: Profile, 1999). Although it mentions that Madame Humbert was arrested in Madrid, it does not mention the controversy over Cotarelo's denunciation.

everyone can rightfully escape punishment provided that the harm done by his acts cannot be undone by punishment and that he will be incapable of repeating those acts.

Punitiveness, of course, is another unpleasant characteristic, along with tendency to inform. To punish is cruel, not to punish is generous. And yet this too is simplistic and, in the end, less generous than it at first seems. Let us suppose that the case here were not of swindling, but of murder.* Let us suppose also that the victim was the one man whom the murderer ever wanted to kill, and he was therefore unlikely ever to kill again. Would we say, "Well, that's all right then," and leave it at that? Would this not give license to everyone to kill one person, provided only that it was the person whom he hated above all others?

Furthermore, the harm done by the crimes of someone like Madame Humbert is not over the moment she is exposed. If one has lost one's life savings, one does not have another life in which to recuperate them, and, even if one did, it would impose onerous work on those who had previously saved precisely to be free of it.

And there is yet another consideration. As I know from clinical experience, those who have been victims of serious crimes the perpetrator of which has been dealt with leniently suffer severely from this very leniency, because it implies that what they have suffered as victims is of no great importance to the state by comparison with feelings of the criminals and, more particularly, of the intellectual class which is in favor of such leniency for fear of appearing punitive in the eyes of each other.

---

* Incidentally, as Hilary Spurling's book makes clear, Madame Humbert's swindles were not without their violent aspect. Her brother, Romain, was a violent man and maybe even a killer, who tried to suppress exposure of the swindles by violence towards those who tried to do expose them.

As we shall see, Gómez Carrillo had a considerable capacity for hypocrisy, but let us return to the rumor that he was the betrayer of Mata Hari. Where did this rumor originate? Given that he was a famous lothario and Mata Hari was generous with her favors, it is not inherently impossible that he was her lover.

Trying to find how a rumor originates is often like trying to find the precise margin of a mist. Some authors give the rumors no credit: two lengthy recent biographies of Mata Hari do not mention them,* nor does a novelized account of her life by the popular author Paulo Coelho (and their sensational nature might have been expected to attract the attention of a novelist).† In constrast, Paul Webster, in his biography of Consuelo de Saint-Exupéry, the widow of Gómez Carrillo, implies that the award of the *Légion d'honneur* to the author just after the end of the war is some kind of evidence in the rumors' plausibility.‡ [8]

One explanation of the rumors is that they were the work of Guatemalan authors and others envious of his success. There is another reason why he might have been hated, however, as we shall see. "The rumor began with certain mediocre writers envious of his prestige," said the poet, Miguel Marsicovétere y Durán.[9] Mentioned in this connection is a

---

* Pat Shipman, *Femme Fatale: A Biography of Mata Hari* (London: Weidenfeld and Nicolson, 2007), and Philippe Collas, *Mata Hari: La dernière danse de l'éspionne* (Paris: French Pulp Éditions, 2017). Collas is the grandson of Pierre Bouchardon, who was the investigating magistrate in Mata Hari's case, and was certainly biased against her.
† Paolo Coelho, *L'Éspionne* (Paris: Flammarion, 2016). Would it be cruel or unjust to notice that Coelho published his novel the year *before* the centenary of Mata Hari's execution, when there was certain to be a flood of books about her? If it wasn't shrewd, it was fortunate.
‡ "Whatever the role played by Carrillo in this arrest, after the Armistice he was made Commander of the Légion d'honneur for services rendered to France during the war."

jealous former wife of Gómez Carrillo's, Raquel Meller, also a dancer, though a less successful one than Mata Hari.[10] Admiral Canaris, the head of the German *Abwehr,* apparently claims in his memoirs that it was Gómez Carrillo who betrayed Mata Hari.

Another theory is that Gómez Carrillo, like Mata Hari herself, was a fantasist and liar who was always avid for publicity, and started the rumors himself, of which he then took advantage to write a book. César González-Ruano wrote, "Those of us who knew Carrillo knew that he was a man capable of inventing a story that he pretended hurt him and against which he protested, because his time in bohemian Paris and his desire *épater les bourgeois*, as well as his literary and personal position as an *enfant terrible*," meant that he no longer knew, or wanted to know, where reality ended and fantasy began.[11]

Now to the reason why Guatemalan writers might have hated as well as envied Gómez Carrillo. The curious fact is that this man who demanded the most absolute liberty for himself, and indeed lived largely as if it had been granted him, was a paid praise-singer of Manuel Estrada Cabrera, one of the most thoroughgoing despots of Guatemala's history, a history that is not short of despots. In the year in which Estrada Cabrera came to power (semi-constitutionally, before he revealed his vocation as tyrant), 1898, Gómez Carrillo wrote a pamphlet so sycophantic that only fear or favor could explain it: and since he was beyond Estrada Cabrera's reach, money is the explanation. The pamphlet begins wittily:

A few weeks ago, one of our most illustrious writers asserted that visitors to Guatemala would leave without knowing anything about Estrada Cabrera because of the great amount that has been written about him.[12]

This draws attention to the distinction between information and knowledge in a wider sense, a distinction all the more important in the age of social media. But the tone of the pamphlet soon changes into that of flattery that is redolent almost of high Stalinism: 103

> During the days of solemn silence, when the cheap press left off its vociferating ... the silhouette of the successful liberal candidate stood out clearly. The people could see him, then, in the grave serenity of his office, always serene, always energetic, always concerned for the well-being of the country.[13]

And so on and so forth.

This pamphlet earned Gómez Carrillo the Guatemalan consulship in Paris and a generous salary.

It is not uncommon, of course, for a newly elected head of government to arouse the enthusiasm of his supporters, but the enthusiasm is usually followed more or less quickly by disillusionment.* In the case of Estrada Cabrera, however, the enthusiasm never abated, despite the irrefutable evidence of his increasing tyranny. Gómez Carrillo's dithyrambs continued, and the Guatemalan novelist and essayist, Carlos Wyld Ospina, in his book *El Autócrata* (The Autocrat), published in 1929, two years after Gómez Carrillo's death, says that it was the practice of the dictator to suborn writers, of whom Gómez Carrillo was one, so that they spread propaganda about the magnificent achievements of his regime.[14] In 1913, Gómez Carrillo wrote to the dictator as follows:

---

* "A change of rulers is the joy of fools," goes an old Romanian peasant saying.

My very respected friend: ...

Thanks to you, my you, my young compatriots are going to read me. I have not waited to savor in this life this honor that in general is reserved for the dead. But because it is so unexpected, the pleasure you have given me fills me with pride. In the face of the admirable work of popular education that you have done for many years, I have many times thought of the intimate satisfaction that one must experience to see that, thanks to one's efforts, new generations are being raised carrying in them the germ of culture that one day not very far off our country will be highly placed among the most civilized countries of the world.[15]

Mutual backscratching could hardly go further.

In October 1915, Gómez Carrillo wrote to the president of the National Convention (the parliamentary façade of the regime) as follows, with regard to the forthcoming "election":

Permit me to say that although I am not legally entitled to vote in the next presidential elections, I will do so morally. My vote is that of all Guatemalans: a sincere vote for our great Estrada Cabrera, who has saved the country from a thousand dangers and has given in peace, progress, national dignity and love of culture. Personally, it is not the first time that I say Estrada Cabrera is the greatest politician on the Latin American continent.... In Europe, I pronounce his name with pride and say, "He is a statesman who would do honor to France or England."[16]

By this time, Estrada Cabrera had long been in receipt of money from the dictator and could hardly have failed to be aware of the nature of his regime. Carlos Wyld Ospina described its despotic characteristics, to say nothing of its financial corruption:

> Estrada Cabrera came to be the only important person in Guatemala.
>
> [His] morbid passion for power and control led him to demand of the country adoration, of his name, his words, of the most trivial manifestations of his personality. He tolerated different qualities [from his own] provided they did not rise above mediocrity, or while they remained in a lower sphere, anonymous and hidden.... The quality he most persecuted was independence of character.
>
> ...
>
> The ... collaborators with the autocracy formed an army of henchmen and traffickers.... The informers, spies and official and unofficial hangmen were legion.
>
> ...
>
> Estrada Cabrera required of his servants two indispensable qualities if they wanted to stay in their posts: obedience without question and adoration without let-up.[17]

Finally, all was lies:

> The entire administration was a farce. Like a malign acid, the lie corroded and corrupted everything. It lived by the lie, in the lie, and for the lie.[18]

Interestingly, there is another Guatemalan writer, Miguel Ángel Asturias, who is buried in Père Lachaise and who, like Gómez Carrillo, was the diplomatic representative of his country in France, who took an opposite view of Estrada Cabrera from that of Gómez Carrillo, his most famous novel,

El Señor Presidente, being a fictionalized description of his effects on life in Guatemala. Asturias won the Nobel Prize in the days when a higher proportion of its recipients had literary merit.

Gómez Carrillo's obsequiousness from afar towards Estrada Cabrera might have been one of the reasons he was disliked by some of his less successful compatriots, who therefore spread nasty rumors about him.

Gómez Carrillo died quite a rich man. He had a flat in Paris full of precious objects and a magnificent house and garden in the south. He also owned property in Argentina (he became an Argentine citizen and consul of that country in France, suggesting that his loyalties were fluid). Though dissipated for much of his life, he was a ferociously hard worker, writing fluently and with ease, often publishing several books a year. Yet it is difficult to believe that his wealth derived entirely from his writing. For example, my copy of one of his most commercially successful books, the one about Mata Hari, says on its cover that it is in the thirteen thousandth printed, a very respectable sale, but books in those days were cheaply produced and such a sale could hardly have yielded a fortune. Is it possible that the foundation of Gómez Carrillo's wealth was subvention from the dictator? Even though Guatemala was a poor country, the resources of its dictator were huge by comparison with those of the average, or above-average, writer.

Before leaving the subject of Mata Hari and Gómez Carrillo altogether, it is perhaps appropriate to mention the latter's love life, which was rich and complex. His biographer, Edelberto Torres, claims that "No Don Juan in any age had so many women in his arms during his life as Gómez Carrillo,"[19] and whatever the precise accuracy of this claim, it is certain that the writer was a great seducer (including, sometimes early in his life, of men). His first and short marriage, to the daughter of a rich Peruvian general, ended when, having driven with her to her hairdresser's in Paris, she found him when she returned from the salon drinking in a café with their chauffeur. His wife, anxious to preserve social distance from the servants, said that the chauffeur would have to go. "If he goes, I go," said Gómez Carrillo, and he went.

He was a man of great charm. The famous Nicaraguan modernist poet Rubén Darío said that if one day Enrique decided that he wanted to be a bishop, he was sure that he would succeed in becoming one.[20] His fundamental outlook on life was Wildean, aesthetic rather than moral. He was without scruple in pursuit of what he wanted, and towards the end of his life he said that if he had his time over again, he would want to live as he had lived.[21]

It is said that, in his time in Paris, Gómez Carrillo fought eighteen duels and was the best swordsman in the city. Some expressed surprised that he had neither killed nor been killed (for my part, I am surprised that duels persisted so commonly into the twentieth century). He almost fought a duel with the former lover of his third wife, the Mexican writer José Vasconcelos (whose work is nowadays much more read than is Gómez Carrillo's), who was advised to desist because of Gómez Carrillo's skill with the sword.[22]

His third wife, Consuelo Suncin, to whom he was married, as her second husband, only for the last eleven months of his life, was a Salvadorean woman who in some ways resembled Mata Hari, though not physically. Like Mata Hari, she escaped her extremely constricting provincial life to the bright lights of Paris, where she enjoyed the bohemian life. Even in the eleven months of their marriage, Gómez Carrillo (who said that he could offer her only his syphilitic decrepitude) found the time and energy to be unfaithful to her, as she to him. But perhaps the power or attraction of his personality is testified to by the fact that when she died in 1979, fifty-two years after him, she chose to be buried next to him, though she had remarried and was still the widow of Antoine de Saint-Exupéry, the famous writer and aviator who was lost in an accident in the Mediterranean in 1944.* She might have elected to be buried at sea near to where his plane went down but chose instead to be interred next to Gómez Carrillo. This is reminiscent of Caitlin Thomas's decision to be buried next to her first husband, Dylan Thomas, thirty-seven years after his death, even though she had since remarried and had a son by her second husband. No one, I think, would deny the power of Dylan Thomas's personality.

"Nothing," wrote Carlos Wyld Ospina, "helps to conquer literary fame like a reputation for being an 'immoral writer.' Gómez Carrillo had it and sucked the juice from it with consummate cleverness, in his art and in his life as a bohemian of the purest dye."[23] He goes on to say that Gómez Carrillo started as a novelist but was a bad one. He excelled, however, as a chronicler, essayist and travel writer, mixing frivolity with seriousness and erudition. And, attached as he was to the life of a Parisian flâneur and boulevardier, he was also a great traveler at a time when travel was a good deal more arduous than it is today. His books can still be read with amusement, instruction, and pleasure. He was, in fact, a very good writer, however one assesses his character, and, after all, one judges a writer principally by his writing.

In 1905, for example, in the wake of the Russo-Japanese war, he went to Russia, which then as now, was not an easy

---

* There is a curious distant connection between Gómez Carrillo and one of the other subjects of this book, Eugène Melchior de Vogüé. Gómez Carrillo's third wife's third husband, Antoine de Saint-Exupéry, had a prolonged friendship and affair with Hélène de Vogüé, wife of Pierre de Vogüé, great-nephew of Eugène. See Paul Webster, op. cit.

thing to do. The resultant book, *La Rusia Actual* (The Russia of Today), is an extremely powerful denunciation of the oppressive nature of Tsarism and can now be read as a corrective to the common notion that, because the communist regime was so vastly worse than the tsarist regime, the latter was really not too bad. Gómez Carrillo did not write prophetically of Russia, like Dostoevsky or Conrad, but he was certainly no optimist about its future.

The dedication of the book, to Doctor Geo D. Coen, is interesting in itself, at least for students of Gómez Carrillo:

You remember, dear friend, that afternoon when you advised me severely to renounce my habitual frivolous fantasies and devote myself to social studies? We were sitting on a terrace on a boulevard. It was spring. And while you were talking of serious things, I was ecstatic over the delightful Parisiennes who went rhythmically by. "Never" – murmured the froufrous of the street – "will any problem interest you more than us."

But Gómez Carrillo underwent a change:

There came a day, however, when the deep, the sad, the unpleasant, the dirty, the poor, seduced me. It was my long day in Russia. There under the snow I forgot the frivolous and devoted myself to the serious. I read documents that before would have made me laugh, and I cried; I copied columns of figures, horrible figures; I translated judicial documents. And when I had finished, I said to myself, "This is the study that my good friend Coen always advised me to make." I have it here, my friend. It is a heavy book. It is an archive of cruelties. It is the memorial of a time of blood and pain. Your upright and pious soul will feel on reading it what mine, frivolous but good, felt in writing it.[24]

110   Russia has always been a corrective to lightheartedness.

Gómez Carrillo expresses the same anxiety on crossing into Russia that Custine did in 1839, and which we would probably feel today and people will no doubt feel in a hundred years' time. The first chapter, "The Tsar Who Trembles," is devoted to the fear that the autocrat himself suffers, very similar to that experienced by the last autocrat but one, as described by Vogüé twenty years before:

> In this vast empire of terror, the one who is most afraid is the monarch. In this respect, at least, his supremacy is evident. The fear of others, those who see the image of Siberia before them at every step, results in a simple shiver, if compared with the perpetual shaking that torments the imperial being. What can I say! The very Sultan of Turkey, who in his dreams has the most atrocious visions of death, is an heroic figure by comparison with his neighbor. Abdul-Hamid loves, intrigues, desires, orders, hates, lives. Nicholas II ... hardly breathes. He seeks a distraction, a pleasure, in his long days. In vain. The only thing he does is struggle against the shadows that threaten him. The long hours of meditation, the consultations with dukes and ministers, the prolonged reading, is the response to nothing but fear. Every effort at reform is a product of fear. Fear, fear without end, is what moves and motivates him. Only fear![25]

This is all very different from the sound of dresses passing on the boulevard.

Gómez Carrillo is good on Nicholas's character:

Like every weak and fanatical being, Nicholas is superstitious and attached to occult sciences and experiments.
In the first years of his reign, his intimate adviser was a
Frenchman called Philippe, whose power reached such a
pitch that the Grand Dukes and ministers trembled in
front of him ...[26]

Nizier Anthelme Philippe (1849–1905) was a French healer
of supposedly extraordinary powers, several times tried for
the illegal practice of medicine but eventually having doc-
torates of medicine conferred upon him. It is easier to be a
healer when very few cures exist.

Fear in the tsarist empire was also an opportunity:

This perpetual, horrible fear, is an inexhaustible mine
for the Grand Dukes and functionaries, in which are to
be found honors and advantages. Far from combatting it,
they seek to increase it by diabolical inventions. The
police invent conspiracies; the generals imagine revolutionary projects; courtiers see nihilists everywhere. General Trepov, present Governor of Saint Petersburg, is a
master of this. His history, as everyone knows, is full of
inventions of assassination attempts against Caesar.[27]

Trepov himself was the object of many assassination
attempts, though he died of illness. This was a time when it
was not always easy to distinguish the secret police from the
revolutionaries and vice versa; it is surely rather odd that
Gómez Carrillo did not see the parallels between tsarist
Russia and Cabrerist Guatemala.

Gómez Carrillo is eloquent on the fate of the Jews. He
ends the chapter:

112

In Russia, there is no forgiveness even for the tombs of the Jews. A telegram from Irkutsk says the Jewish cemeteries in which the bodies of the political exiles are buried, killed in the massacres at Irkutsk, present a sad aspect. Two weeks ago, all the monuments were destroyed and the remains of the bodies strewn about.... The cemetery appears to been invaded by barbarians. Invisible hands continue this sacrilege with rancor and hatred.[28]

With a single anecdote, Gómez Carrillo captures the Gogolian aspect of Russian bureaucracy. An English journalist of his acquaintance goes to a government office in St Petersburg to enquire about the revenue from tobacco. Ten people who are obviously doing nothing suddenly try to appear busy. He begins "Could you … ?"

> "Not here," all ten reply immediately without even knowing what he is going to ask.
> He persists, however, and continues, "Could you give me some information on the revenue from tobacco?"
> "Not here," the ten reply.
> On the door of the office were painted the words, "Statistical information about tobacco."[29]

This is the very essence of bureaucracy.

Gómez Carrillo has an ability to capture essences. He doesn't much care for St. Petersburg, which he thinks is grandiose without beauty. He says that it is "an encampment of palaces," which a Russian friend of mine thought a very apt description. It is a city by decree, of decree, for decree, but I think it beautiful all the same.

In the year in which Gómez Carrillo traveled to Russia, he went also to the other combatant in the war, Japan, and published a book in the same year about his impressions. I

don't know whether he was the first Guatemalan ever to
visit Japan, but there surely cannot have been many before
him, and the fact that he even thought to do so is a tribute
to his imaginative curiosity.

There is little doubt that he preferred Japan to Russia,
finding there much to admire (he found nothing in Russia
to admire). But his entry into Tokyo from Yokohama was
disappointing, for despite the vastness of the city, he saw
nothing beautiful there. The streets were muddy and filthy;
the citizens disposed in them of whatever they did not want,
just as they did in Port-au-Prince the last time I was there.
Even in China (according to Gómez Carrillo), despite its
poverty, the streets were at least jollier. Contrary to his
romantic dreams of Japan, Tokyo was wretched. He describes
his journey from Shimbashi station, "vulgar but lively" to
his hotel (one of three European establishments in the city):

> Journey without end, made in tall and narrow vehicles
> pulled by a man who trots like a horse. Oh, the sadness
> of these vehicles! I feel it more here than in China or in
> India, no doubt because of the muddiness of the streets
> and the enormous distances. We went for half an hour
> through sordid little streets, and we were still far [from
> our destination]. The journey generally takes an hour,
> sometimes two. The Japanese [rickshaw pullers] were
> content to smile, happy in to all appearance, resigned in
> reality, and continued to trot through the interminable,
> the incredible, streets of their city. From time to time,
> they stopped a second to dry the sweat of their brow and
> then continue their dreary way, more than dreary for
> those unused to it – anxiety-provoking.[30]

Reading his account of the city, one can only wonder at its
transformation in far less than a century: and for those of us

(who are many) who are inclined to take the present for granted, as if all that exists now has always existed and always will exist, it is a valuable corrective to that shallow view.

One of the things that strikes him immediately is that the entire population seems to wear spectacles. "The soldiers, the tram-drivers, the policemen, the workers, everyone wears them. They are objects of national necessity."[31] Gómez Carrillo thinks that this is a matter of fashion, rather than an expression of a genetic predisposition to short-sightedness. (In North Korea, I was struck by precisely the opposite phenomenon, the complete absence of spectacles, as if the wearing of spectacles were an admission of national weakness. Under the reign of Macías Nguema in Equatorial Guinea, the wearing of spectacles was dangerous, for it implied that the person was educated, and the dictator was very sensitive on the subject of those who were more educated than he.)

Gómez Carrillo was an acute observer, but not of the future. He laments something that makes the streets of Tokyo even uglier:

> Progress, which has not remembered to construct pavements in the streets, or put lights in the public thoroughfares, has, by contrast, added to the horrors that already existed, thanks to the telegraph and telephone networks. Oh! these infinite wires! You can imagine a spider's web like this. In the humblest alleyways there are thousands of wires and hundreds of poles to keep them up. The story of *a telephone in every home*, even in those of beggars, is not a legend. There, where there is neither a bed nor clothes, is a telephone. At the corner of every street you see kiosks which say *Public Telephone*. And it is thereby that Europeanism is reduced to some melon hats and numerous telephones.[32]

Despite the Japanese victory in the Russo-Japanese war, in which they used the most modern weaponry of the time and sank almost the entire Russian Baltic fleet, Gómez Carrillo did not see in this mass adoption of what was then new technology as a harbinger of the speed with which Japan caught up, and in many respects surpassed, European nations: he saw it only as a manifestation of the crudeness and ugliness that westernization brought with it. Indeed, when one looks at the views of Edo (as Tokyo was then called), and the landscapes, of Hokusai and Hiroshige, one cannot but sympathize with the viewpoint of Gómez Carrillo, who was an aesthete above all. How far ugliness existed in those two artists' time, I do not know; what is certain is that Japan's civilization was of the highest aesthetic sophistication and refinement.

It is easy to romanticize previous ages as being more beautiful than our own, and no doubt (after a certain age) we are all prone to do so. But Gómez Carrillo has done his homework, and while he accepts that before the advent of modernization – with the industrialization that brought with it both great wealth and horrible poverty, Japan had a materially egalitarian society – he quotes accounts of the famines that affected the country that are as graphic as can well be imagined: human suffering is not of recent invention. He quotes the eighteenth-century poet Bakin's account of the famine of 1786:

A witness worthy of credence assured me that of five hundred families in a village, only thirty remain: all the members of the others were dead. Eighty *sens* [cents of a yen] were given for a dog and more than fifty for a rat. The dead were eaten ...

A man who had already lost his wife and older son was ready to sacrifice his other son. He went to his neighbour and said:

116

> As [my son] is going to die also, it would be better to kill him and eat him. As his father, I don't have the courage to kill him; if you do, we'll share him.

The neighbor accepted, "but hardly had he killed the child than the father beheaded him with an axe, not out of revenge, but to have the body all to himself."[33]

Japan before industrialisation, then, was not always an aesthete's paradise.

Gómez Carrillo gives an interesting account of Japanese nationalism and sense of superiority, at the same time as its chivalrous conduct towards the defeated Russians (as a man of contradictions himself, he could spot the existence of contrary tendencies in the world). For example, the Japanese preserved the Russian Orthodox cathedral in Tokyo from attack and allowed it to continue to function throughout the war, all the more surprisingly because the cathedral itself was of a scale (and ugliness) designed to dominate the city, whose buildings were still of modest proportions. It also came as something of a surprise to me to learn that there were Japanese converts to Russian Orthodoxy.[34]

But the Japanese, at least the upper class, were so impressed by their own military victories over China and Russia that they fell victim to the illusion of many successful nations, that they were special, unique, providential, destined to be the center of the world. Gómez Carrillo writes:

> In his heroism, in his love of justice, in his cult of loyalty and generosity, the samurai is sustained by pride in being Japanese. You others, you who believe you love and admire your countries; you others, men of Europe

and America, you hardly deserve to be called patriots! The citizen of Japan deifies his country. – Listen: "The civilizations of all countries must unite in Japan; and Japan will transform all these civilizations by its own influence, and give to the world a new and veritable civilization. Such is Japan's special mission, that which will eternalize its influence."[35]

117

The civilizations of India and China reached Japan and could expand no further; the civilizations of Europe went to America, which brought them to Japan, and could go no further. Therefore, Japan was destined to be the center of the world.[36]

Success in war gave the Japanese a sense of invincibility (which before long proved dangerous even to themselves, let alone to their neighbors). The Russians, they said, fought from a sense of duty, the Japanese from a desire for glory and indifference to their own individual lives, and the latter were therefore bound to prevail.*[37] Their sense of anger and disillusionment at the provisions of the Treaty of Portsmouth, brokered by President Theodore Roosevelt, which were relatively favorable to Russia considering its military defeat, was directed at their own diplomats, who were blamed,[38] but neither they, nor Gómez Carrillo, realized that the treaty was relatively favorable to Russia because Russian strength in the Far East was increasing while Japan's position was overextended.

Gómez Carrillo reports, he does not condemn, but he is eloquent on the aesthetic marvels of Japan, which he thinks superior to all others:

---

* One cannot help but notice the parallel with the Islamic fanatics who think they are bound to win because they are attached to death as strongly as their opponents are attached to life.

> Yes, human language is powerless to describe these mar-
> vels of art, grace, light, harmony and sumptuousness.
> Merely to say, for example, that the most grandiose of
> European architecture appears wretched compared with
> these does not suffice. What difference between the
> intensity of feeling that one experiences and the cold-
> ness of the sentence with which one tries to express it![39]

This may appear exaggerated, yet I am not unacquainted
with the response to the art of other civilizations. When I
walk through the gallery of Islamic art in the Victoria & Albert
Museum in London, I think "This is of incomparable beauty,
it is the acme of human creation"; then I walk through the
gallery of Indian art and think, "This is of incomparable
beauty, it is the acme of human creation"; then I walk
through the gallery of Japanese art and think, "This is of
incomparable beauty, it is the acme of human creation."
Finally, I pull myself up short and remind myself that art is
not a team in a sporting league, and that to appreciate one
tradition is not to denigrate another.

Gómez Carrillo, frivolous aesthete turned serious social
commentator in the wake of the Russo-Japanese war, saw
much to admire in Japan and nothing at all in Russia. Were
he to return, would his judgment be very different now?

In the following year, however, he returned to what
many would consider frivolity, the froufrou side of his work,
by writing a book, *Psicología de la Moda Feminina* (Psychology of Feminine Fashion).[40] This was published three years
later in a French version, *Psychologie de la mode* (Psychology
of Fashion).[41] These books are, in fact, so different that they
are almost two – just as Edelberto Torres says.[42] There are
passages that are identical, passages that appear in one version but not the other, and anecdotes that are the same,

except for the identities of the persons involved. It seems that Gómez Carrillo was not obsessional when it came to such detail. For example, referring to the extravagant cost of the female fashions of the time, displayed above all on the stage, he writes in the Spanish version:

> "I'm ruining myself with dresses," said the Director of the *Comédie française* a little while ago.[43]

In the French version, we read:

> "I'm ruining myself with dresses," said the director of a Madrid theater a little while ago.[44]

Obviously, the anecdote means the same thing in both versions, but is either of them true? I would guess that something like this was once said, but it somewhat reduces one's faith in Gómez Carrillo's trustworthiness.

He is always interesting, though. Writing at a time when women wore whalebone corsets to try to squeeze themselves into the shape then considered ideal, undergoing a kind of torture in the process, he tells us that all the arguments are against it; but the makers and sellers of corsets need not worry. He tells the story of

> a woman prisoner who made herself a corset. For a corset was [every prisoner's] dream. Exasperated by the prison tunic's ugliness, she managed to deceive the prison's surveillance, and made a corset as well as she could from the iron wires of the grille of the punishment cell's window. She was so tightly squeezed in it that she fainted one morning during mass. It was thus that the mystery of her incredibly slim figure was revealed. And note that to

obtain all the bits of iron wire, she had to court punishment an enormous number of times so that she should be
shut in the cell with the window with the precious grille.*[45]

Intellectuals might scoff at fashion as a subject of serious
study, but Gómez Carrillo relates an anecdote about the
poet Mallarmé (who wrote articles about fashion for many
years): if *he*, one of the greatest poets of his day, considered
fashion a suitable subject for serious reflection, there was no
reason for Gómez Carrillo to spurn it:

> It is probable that if the very boring Sully-Prudhomme,
> who had just died without ever having understood the
> beauty of a woman's hat, had asked [Mallarmé]: "Of what
> importance is that?" The good poet, always serious, would
> have replied: "The greatest importance!" In effect, there
> are few things in the world that are as interesting as a
> frill, a hat, a ribbon, a flower, anything, in fact, that embel-
> lishes our idols. For poets above all, women's dress ought
> to be of capital importance. Is not a dress a poem in silk?[46]

This was written before the First World War, of which
Gómez Carrillo was to be a chronicler. It has a *fin de siècle*
preciosity about it, something of Oscar Wilde.

Perhaps the most interesting thing that Gómez Carrillo
has to say on the subject of the fashion of his day is that
increasing democracy caused elegance (achievable with effort
by anyone) to become valued more than beauty (a natural
gift).[47] I am not sure whether this was true, but it certainly the
advance of pseudo-egalitarianism in the modern world has

---

* Gómez Carrillo had the story from Paola Lombroso (1871–1954), daughter of Cesare Lombroso, the doctor, criminologist, and anthropologist.

led to the triumph of ugliness as a desideratum.* Ugliness is democratic, within the reach of all without effort; beauty is aristocratic, by nature elitist. In ugliness, then, is virtue.

Gómez Carrillo's contemporary chronicles of the Great War are a world – a universe – away from that of fashion. These chronicles have both the advantage and disadvantage of contemporaneity. What they have in immediacy they lack in historical perspective. Published in the first half of 1916, *Le Sourire sous la mitraille*, "Smiling Under Fire," is as contradictory as life itself.[48] It is an account of the author's guided visit, as a neutral citizen, to various parts of the Western Front in that year, when the war was still less than half over. His military minders naturally tried to ensure his safety, but prudence was no guarantee of it, and the author undoubtedly braved death as the following makes clear when he is in one of the trenches:

> At a turning, a cortege that was coming in the opposite direction, preceded by an officer, forced us to take refuge in a side-passage to let it go by.
>
> "A wounded man," someone said.
>
> The colonel advanced towards the cortege.
>
> "He's dead," a soldier murmured. "A lieutenant ..."
>
> Indeed, there on a stretcher, very pale, as if asleep, as if he had fainted, but still with an expression of life and warmth, was an officer who had received us half an hour before, in his post as a lookout. On his face, between his eyes, we saw a little purple circle. His hands, crossed on

---

* I write this not very long after Sam Bankman-Fried's arrest, who, when he was supposedly worth $16 billion dressed with a kind of deliberate sloppiness, and smartened himself up when faced with the prospect of going to prison for a long time. I also write it soon after Vivienne Westwood, a woman who made her name by the promotion of deliberate ugliness, died.

his chest, stood out on the dark background of his uniform with a macabre whiteness.[49]

122   Gómez Carrillo vividly describes the capriciousness of the damage wrought by the German bombardment of the city of Arras:

> In their cruel caprice, the shells sometimes contented themselves with opening a breach in the walls or breaking the windowpanes in smashing the insides of houses, leaving the façades almost intact. A little open door allows us to see the destruction of a palace. And yet the exterior was not in the slightest damaged. The shell, here as in so many places, entered through the roof. Elsewhere, by contrast, only the external wall was destroyed, the rooms inside remaining intact.[50]

A single incident during a successful attack on a German position captures the absolute horror of war in general and this war in particular:

> A blond Bavarian … seized a leg which had just been blown off one of his comrades, and brandishing it like a mace, he hit everyone in front of him with it.[51]

The contrast between this and the capital importance of women's dress could hardly be greater.

Unsurprisingly, Gómez Carrillo was very pro-French and anti-German, but he recognized the appalling effects the war had on the sensibility of civilized men. Here a cultivated, educated French officer, talking to the author in the trenches, describes an encounter between his men and the Germans:

"What has stayed with me most is the arm movements of a herculean mountain infantryman who thrust through Germans with his bayonet, blessing each one he killed. Ah, what a beautiful memory!" The officer laughed a cruel and magnificent laugh which showed the white teeth of a heathy human beast ...

"What can happen in the depths of a soul is incredible," [he said].

Then, very amiably:

"Let us have lunch, gentlemen, it's getting late."[52]

Gómez Carrillo found the Germans to be a mysterious people, sentimental and savage, innovative and conventional, brave and submissive, polite and vicious (he felt no qualms about writing of national characteristics). He witnessed air raids over the city of Amiens, a city of no military significance, with its most magnificent cathedral:

Heroically, the German aviators destroyed a patisserie with its staff and all its contents. But it was said that what attracted them most was the cathedral.[53]

Later, Gómez Carrillo writes:

Do you know how many lives the morning flights of the German dove have already cost the capital of Picardy? A supplement of the local newspaper tells us of eight dead and nine injured. Among the dead, there is a young Spaniard and a French shopkeeper about forty years old. The other victims were women and children. "An old woman," I read, "was literally decapitated by a bomb."[57]

These figures tell us that aerial bombardment was still in its infancy, but there was no need to despair about future progress in this respect. Gómez Carrillo tells us that:

> Progress is so admirable a thing that a single shell does more damage than all the cannon balls fired by the Spanish during the siege of Cobie in 1636.[55]

Would the war ever end? Gómez Carrillo (who had no way of knowing how or when it would end) says:

> As the war is at present, it is not likely that it will end this year, or next, or ever .... No doubt there will be battles every day, every day we will lose thousands of men, every day we will win yards of terrain .... But what are thousands of men in a mass of four, five or six million, and what are a few yards on a front of over six hundred miles? No, it is not likely that with the methods we have observed for so many months, we shall arrive at a result soon ...[56]

Gómez Carrillo ends the book by describing the brief German occupation of Amiens at the beginning of the war when, according to witnesses, they behaved very well: there were no massacres, no theft, no rapes, no atrocities of any kind. This was in marked contrast to their occupation of other cities. Seeking an explanation as to why there should have been this difference, a civil servant of the city tells Gómez Carrillo that it is because the German commanding officer ordered decency:

> It demonstrates something ... serious and ... terrible. When the Kaiser's troops display savagery, when they burn, when they murder, when they mutilate, when they

Alice-René Brouillhet (1887–1960)

Eugène-Melchior de Vogüé (1848–1910)

François-Vincent Raspail (1796–1878)

Enrique Gómez Carrillo (1873–1927)

Charles Loudon (1801–1844)

Jules Cornély (1845–1907)

Jean-Richard Bloch (1884–1947)

Émile Souvestre (1806–1854)

rape, when they pillage, they are obeying a superior order.... When they are told to be respectful, there is not a Prussian who would utter a peep. Those responsible for the crimes of Louvain, Senlis, Liège, are not the sol-   125 diers, no.... They are the chiefs.... These people only kill, rape, burn when their chiefs order them to ...[57]

I have touched on only a small portion of Gómez Carrillo's work. I find him a protean figure, very difficult to summarize. He was intelligent, bold, brave, charming, talented, cultivated, multifarious, hardworking and unscrupulous. Perhaps he sums himself up best, describing his childhood:

I drank life ... in great mouthfuls, I drank the light, beauty, the joy of growth and enjoyment; I drank from the ardent glass of the tropics, I was intoxicated by the perfume of flowers, by the color of the sky, by the smiles of girls, by the caresses of my mother.[58]

Charles Loudon

(1801–1844)

CHARLES LOUDON was born in Glasgow where he qualified as a doctor, practiced medicine in Leamington Spa, and
retired to Paris in 1841, where he died in 1844 and was buried in Père Lachaise.

Leamington Spa in the days of Dr. Loudon's practice was
a recently established spa town, soon fashionable, elegantly
built of neoclassical white or yellow stucco terraces, where the
rich or prosperous gathered to take the waters supposedly
for the sake of their health. One would not expect a doctor
practicing in such a town to be quoted by both Karl Marx
and Friedrich Engels (in separate works), but such was the
case with Charles Loudon.

Leamington Spa, which was allowed the prefix *Royal* after
a visit by Queen Victoria in 1838 while Dr. Loudon was still
practicing there, declined as a watering place in the 1840s,
but retained its gentility into the 1950s at least. John Bet-
jeman captured the sad gentility in his poem *Death in Leamington*, written in 1932:

> Do you know that the stucco is peeling?
> Do you know that the heart will stop?
> From those yellow Italianate arches
> Do you hear the plaster drop?

It seems that the principal industry of Leamington is now
the development of video games.

The first of Loudon's two books is titled, less than succinctly, *A Practical Dissertation on the Waters of Leamington
Spa; Including the History of the Springs, a New Analysis of
Their Gaseous and Solid Contents, the Rules for Drinking the*   127
Waters, Bathing, Diet of the Patients, and Other Regimen. Published in 1828, it went through three editions by 1831, though
in the last edition Loudon removed all reference to diet.

Almost certainly, Loudon's patients would have been
either those are now called *the worried well*, the aged and
chronically but not dangerously ill or infirm. For the modern reader – certainly the modern medical reader— what is
most striking about this book is the number of *ex cathedra*
statements in it, injunctions and instructions for which not
only is there no evidence, but no awareness that evidence is
even needed for them. In this blithe disregard of such a
need, Dr. Loudon was far from alone, of course: practically
all medical books of the same epoch were the same in this
respect. In fact, it was only very recently in historical terms
that the insufficiency was of such *ex cathedra* statements was
realized, based as they were solely upon the authority of
personal experience or that of other people similarly based,
as in the following example (of which there are scores in
Loudon's short book):

The sulphureous waters are taken in the same doses, in
the same divided portions, and at the same hour of the
morning, as the saline.*[1]

---

* The sulphureous waters were said to be capable of inducing mild nausea.
The price for an entire family to drink them during the whole season was
£2 2s., that is to say about £200 in our money, or £1 1s. for two people of
the same family. This, of course, did not include accommodation, meals,
amusements, etc. See *Beck's Leamington Guide* (Leamington: J. Beck,
1839), 31

What might be called the testimonial era of medicine endured until well into the 1930s and '40s. A glance into any textbook of medicine of the time will show it. Here is the treatment of lobar pneumonia as described in one of the premier British textbooks of medicine in 1941:

128

> The diet should be restricted to fluids and semi-solids, eggs, milk and meat extracts and the various invalid foods being given up to 2 or 3 pints in the 24 hours. Dextrose, in the proportion of 2 to 4 ounces to the pint of lemonade or orangeade, is useful. Too much milk should be avoided, as it is liable to cause indigestion and flatulence.... Hot linseed poultices to the back and side may be employed, but cataplasma kaolini or antiphlogistine applied on lint does not require such frequent changing and disturbs the patient less.... A pneumonia jacket is preferred by some, by others the ice poultice or ice-bag is found soothing. A dose of calomel should be give at the outset.... [Oxygen] should be warmed and may be bubbled through alcohol.[2]

This is not much of an advance on Loudon, more than a century earlier, and in 1972, one of the founders of Evidence-Based Medicine (the movement that, after more than two millennia of medical practice, demanded that treatment should be founded upon something more solid than opinion, tradition, and personal experience), Archibald Cochrane, wrote that the medical profession had hitherto relied on "the uncritical belief in [its] ability at least to help if not to cure."[3]

He continued:

> The basis of this belief was probably the doctor's ability to reduce pain, the general placebo effect, the tendency of many diseases to disappear spontaneously or improve

with time, and the higher education and social status of the doctor in the past.*

The psychology of the doctor–patient relationship was a variant of *folie à deux*.†

Cochrane goes on:

> [The doctor] very earnestly wanted to help. He had a fair number of drugs at his disposal and has read or heard a lot of suggestions that drug X helped in disease Y and that a visit to a spa helped in disease Z.... It was a marriage of two minds – between the desire to help and the desire to be helped.[4]

In some ways, of course, this made things easier for the doctor: for, as Cochrane remarks, he was not blamed for deaths, and he did not have to supply evidence for his assertions, other than "In my experience," or "As such and such an authority states"; impotently watching people suffer or die of common diseases could not, however, have been altogether a cheerful way to spend one's life.

---

* This is not a hundred percent accurate. At the time Loudon was practicing, his social status may well have been lower than that of many of his patients. Queen Victoria did not regard her personal physician, Sir James Reid, though she had knighted him, as quite a gentleman. "The gentlemen *and* Dr. Reid will join us after dinner," she said. No doubt this was because Dr. Reid, like all doctors, had to go to the vulgar expedient of earning his living and being paid for his services. Moreover, many of the treatments of the time were so unpleasant that one cannot help but suspect that it was their unpleasantness that stood guarantor in patients' minds that they were doing them some good. "If I go through so much unpleasantness," they must have thought, "it cannot be for nothing."

† In a *folie à deux*, a person living in close association with another, usually the dominant one of the two, becomes deluded, and the other person takes on the delusion of the first. The second loses the delusion if separated from the first, who likely requires medical treatment.

130

In the first edition of Dr. Loudon's book, the population of Leamington Spa *during the season* (before the 1790s it had been but a tiny village) was given as 5,500; in the third edition, as 6,000, an increase of 9 percent in only three years. Whether this denoted an increase in the resident population or in that of visitors, or was the result of a different way of calculating the population, is not mentioned.[5] But perhaps this change was at the root of Dr Loudon's subsequent interest in the population question, as we shall see.

Dr. Loudon extols the town in which he elected to settle and practice. Whether he genuinely believed his propaganda, or was drumming up business (possibly both, of course), I cannot say. But Leamington Spa, according to him, had many advantages, both natural and man-made. It was possessed of eleven springs of different mineral contents, enumerated with almost obsessional exactitude in the book, and therefore, according to Dr. Loudon, of different medicinal properties. Leamington Spa was far from the Atlantic and German Oceans (as the North Sea was then called), and therefore of "genial" climate and free of excessive winds. Being ninety miles distant from London, the metropolis could be reached in ten hours and "enables residents to avail themselves of those advantages which the celerity of the conveyance so conveniently affords."* [6]

Dr. Loudon's dietary does not sound much fun. It seems to exclude anything remotely appetizing.

---

* That London could be reached from Leamington in ten hours, this being regarded as little, tells us something about the sense of time people had in Loudon's day. Thus a tiny fact may reveal to the imagination something historically and psychologically important. It takes just over two hours by road and an hour and a half by train to make the same journey today, traffic jams and train strikes permitting.

Tea and coffee should not be taken at breakfast.... Chocolate or cocoa is preferable, and by persons whose stomachs cannot bear any of these, milk and water ... bread and milk, or other light spoon-meats, must be substituted. The bread used should be at least forty-eight hours old, and if toasted not eaten while warm; but biscuits made of flour and water simply, are better; and if either of them be covered with butter, the quantity must be very small.... Luncheons are mostly hurtful, and are even unnecessary ...

131

Dinner is not to be delicious, either:

A little beef-tea or broth, when not very rich, may be allowed.... As well as at all other meals, the bread eaten should be stale. . . Fish is to be taken with the greatest circumspection, and in most cases none at all.

Somehow, though, good cheer should be kept up at meals, because "by removing the influence of the mind off the stomach" and because it "necessarily prevents that improper and unwholesome custom of quick eating," it "has a twofold beneficial influence on the habits of the invalid."[7] Personally, I do not find it all that easy to be jolly while dining off a little tapioca washed down with warm water, and it is possible that Dr. Loudon suspected that his recommendations did not attract customers, for he eliminated them in the third edition (the second I have not seen).

In a very surprising development, Dr. Loudon went from concerning himself with the imagined or real minor ailments of the worried well, that is to say the rich,* to reporting on

---

* In their defense, it must be said that the hold of even of the rich in those days was precarious, and what seemed like minor ailments could easily

the use of child labor in English factories. Why he was chosen to be an official reporter for the official commission, I do not know; perhaps he met and impressed government ministers or other important personages taking the waters at Leamington Spa. A man who can recommend stale bread only to his patients must have a certain probity. According to J. T. Ward, the members of the commission were chosen because they were "cool, analytical and unsentimental" men:

> . . . disciples of the great Bentham, believing in the hedonistic calculus and the doctrines of Utility, [who] were unmoved by appeals to moral or ethical standards.[8]

For whatever reason, Loudon was chosen as one of the four medical commissioners on the Commission on Children's Employments in Factories, and was paid £200,* plus expenses, for his efforts. He was allocated what was called the North-Eastern District comprising Yorkshire, Leicestershire, and Nottinghamshire. There were two lay commissioners for each medical commissioner, and one of the directors of the commission as a whole was Edwin Chadwick (1800–1890), one of the great figures of nineteenth-century public health, who had trained as a lawyer rather than as a doctor.

Loudon's evidence to the commission, which takes up twenty-three of the very large and closely printed pages of the

---

transmute into fatal ones in very short order. Anxiety about one's health was therefore justified, or more justified than it is today.

* Perhaps a hundred times more in current money. Of course, all such comparisons cannot be exact. What was the price of a computer in 1833? But £200 in 1833 was something like eight times the annual earnings of a young female hand who worked sixty hours a week in one of Loudon factories he investigated. How long his investigations took him, I am not able to say. For his emoluments, see *Office-Holders in Modern Britain, Vol. 9, Officials of Royal Commissions of Inquiry 1815–1870*, available at http://www.british-history.ac.uk/office-holders/office-holders/pp16-28 .

Second Report to the Central Board of His Majesty's Commissioners appointed to collect Information in the Manufacturing Districts, as to the Employment of Children in Factories, and as to the Propriety and Means of Curtailing the Hours of their Labour, was what attracted the notice of Friedrich Engels to him.[9] In his book, *The Condition of the Working Class in England in 1844*, published in 1845, Engels quotes this evidence several times.

> The commission was set up to moderate or dilute the report on child labor instigated by the radical Tory Member of Parliament, Michael Sadler, who supported a bill to limit labor to ten hours per day, and to which the economist, John Ramsay McCulloch, reacted by saying "I look upon the facts disclosed in the late report as most disgraceful to the nation, and I confess that until I read it I could not have conceived it possible that such enormities were committed." The factory owners thought the report unfair, and demanded another report, which they hoped and expected would be more favorable to them.[10]

The setting up of the new commission was greeted with hostility by the population whose conditions it was set up to investigate. The commissioners, of whom Loudon was one, were the object of obloquy and even threat. "Have you made your wills?" asked one pamphleteer. Referring to their generous emoluments, posters in Bradford (which was in Loudon's area of investigation) said, "Nice pickings! Commissioning is no bad job ... for Idle Lads." The *Morning Herald* said, "Your commission is a farce – a farce after a tragedy, and intended, like the farce, to obliterate the impression of the tragedy." * The commissioners were accused in Loudon's area of

---

* cf. Karl Marx, "Hegel remarks somewhere that all great world historical facts and personages appear, so to speak, twice. He forgot to add: the first

earning their daily bread by a work so dirty that an honest operative, however humble, would scorn to undertake.

134   When Loudon and his other two commissioners went to Leeds, there was a demonstration of three thousand children against them led by Cavie Richardson, the author of *Factory Children: A Short Description of the Factory System, Descriptive of its Effects on the Religion, Morals, Comforts and Health of the Children Employed in the Manufactories of England and Scotland*. Richard Oastler, a radical reformer, accused the commissioners of finding the time "to guzzle wine and to eat and drink to the full" in the home of a mill owner, while having been unable to visit many mills or talk to the workers in them. When the report of the commission was published, *The Times*, hardly a revolutionary publication, wrote:

in order to decide whether infants ought to be killed or crippled by premature and oppressive work, it was not necessary that 12 gentlemen should be sent on a voyage of enquiry and produce as a result of their researches, a large blue book 14 inches by 9 and weighing about 9 lb.*[11]

Nevertheless, Engels quoted Loudon quite extensively (though the English version of Engels's book has an English translation of the German translation of the English original),† in particular Loudon's conclusion:

---

time as tragedy, the second time as farce," *The Eighteenth Brumaire of Louis Napoleon*, https://www.marxists.org/archive/marx/works/1852/18th-brumaire /cho1.htm. It is unlikely that Marx, aged fourteen, read the *Morning Herald*, so this must be taken as the literary equivalent of convergent evolution.

* I can attest personally to the inconvenience of the volumes produced, which if read in bed might crush a weak person.

† My edition of *The Working Class of England* is contained in the volume,

I think it has been clearly proved that children have been
worked a most unreasonable and cruel length of time
daily, and that even adults have been expected to do a
certain quantity of labour which scarcely any human is
able to endure. The result of this has been, that many
have met with a premature death; many have been
affected constitutionally for life; and the idea of posterity being injured from the shattered frames of the survivors is, physiologically speaking, but too well founded ...[12]

135

Few people, I imagine, would now be found to dissent from
this. Much of Loudon's testimony was derived from inter-
views with medical men in Leeds, with much experience of
treating factory workers.

Here is Francis Sharp, for example:

I came to Leeds about seven years ago, and became connected with the hospital immediately afterwards. I
observed early the injuries and distortions which the
children from the mills had who applied for relief at the
infirmary. The general appearance of the children at
Leeds immediately struck me as more pallid, and also
the firmness of the fibre as much inferior to what I had
seen in Scarborough.... Observed also that many of those
who applied for hospital aid to be more diminutive for
their age. comparatively and absolutely, than the bulk of

Karl Marx and Frederick Engels on Britain (Moscow: Foreign Languages
Publishing House, 1953), published in the last year of Stalin's life. He is
therefore quoted in the preface by the Marx-Engels-Lenin-Stalin Institute.
Of the leaders of Britain's Labour Party, he said, "It is certain that these
apologies for leaders are hangovers of the past and cannot measure up to
the new conditions. It is certain that they will be compelled in time to give
way to new leaders who do measure up to the militant spirit and heroism
of the British proletariat." I would like to have heard Stalin's observations
on Mr. Blair.

those people I had seen in the North Riding.... During a period of three months ... I find that eighty-nine different people applied for relief from injuries sustained from machinery; many of those, too, of the most serious description, and two were followed by death. I have known this to occur occasionally in consequence of the machinery not being properly boxed off; and a most serious case of this description occurred about a year ago, when a boy died from his injuries, and his sister had both her arms broken in attempting to extricate him.[13]

Dr. Sharp enumerated other things he had encountered:

I have observed a peculiar twisting of the lower parts of the thigh bone. This affection I had never seen before I came to Leeds, and I have remarked that it principally affected children from eight to fourteen years of age.... I have now seen of such cases ... nearly 100, and I can decidedly state that they were the result of too much labour.... My attention has also been called to other ailments as resulting from factory labour; and I have seen ulcers of the legs in about 100 young persons ... with and without varicose state of the veins, which are not to be observed in other classes of society at the same period of life, and by me have been attributed to long standing at the labour of the factories.... I was present, and knew a case where a boy, who had in-knees [knock-knees] from labour, had so little command of his extremities, that he fell flat on a boarded floor, and fractured both his arms in consequence.[14]

Children as young as five were sometimes employed in factories, and their hours were long. Children had accidents from falling asleep.

John Dawson, a factory worker, deposed as follows:

> Began between six and seven years of age to work in a
> factory. Worked from six to seven [i.e. thirteen hours]
> Had only forty minutes for dinner. Between nine and
> ten years of age felt a weakness and pain in his limbs,
> and they began to bend. They took four or five years to
> be as crooked as they at present. [He was twenty-eight.]

Nevertheless, Dr. Loudon's conclusion did not follow
straightforwardly from the evidence he adduced, because
several of his medical informants were of directly opposite
views. In fact, Loudon himself had inspected factories in
Leicester that were comparatively well-conducted.

Dr. Williamson, for example, said that:

> It has always appeared to me, that the part of the opera-
> tive population which is not employed in factories, espe-
> cially those who have sedentary occupations, such as
> tailors, shoe-makers, and the like, are more frequently
> attacked with disease.

In fact, Dr. Hunter found the factories to be almost a health
resort:

> I have, in several instances, been obliged to recommend
> young men [shoemakers] ... to adopt another trade, and
> have known them go to the mill with advantage.

The pallor of the factory children did not worry this doctor
because pallor was of different kinds, and "I have often been
surprised to see grave arguments founded on such
appearances."[15]

Another of the medical witnesses cited by Loudon, Mr.

138

Baker, said, "I have turned my attention much to the state of the poor, and particularly to the factory population," and that "it has never appeared to me that the factory children were more languid, weakly, or debilitated than the other classes of operatives." "I consider the general labour of children in the mills as light and easy," he said, and he even knew of cases in which the parents had lied about the age of their children in order that they might be employed in factories. William Wadsworth, surgeon, also quoted by Loudon, who had "been a great deal amongst the poor" had as his opinion that "there is no disease which is purely caused by factory labour," and that "the present hours of labour [in the woollen mills] are not injurious even to the younger branches, so far as their health is concerned." In short, only half of the medical evidence was in favor of Dr. Loudon's conclusion.[16]

This, of course, goes unmentioned in Engels's book, and from our current perspective, it is not difficult to see why (incidentally, Engels, as a wealthy factory owner in Manchester himself, would have known about the conditions of the working class firsthand). It seems to beggar belief that doctors could have claimed that prevailing factory conditions were other than disastrous for children's health.*

There is more than one possible explanation for this. The first is that some of the witnesses whom Loudon interviewed were frightened to offend the mill owners who were the principal power in the cities in which they worked. They dared not speak up against their interests. Some of them expressed the view, not untypical of the political economy of the time, that if the hours of work of children were restricted

---

* To be fair, even those who did not object to factory work for young children on health grounds thought that children younger than ten ought not to be employed in factories because ... well, they were children.

in the way envisaged by reformers, the income generated by children would decline and thus the standard of living of their families fall – which would more than offset any advantages derived from shorter hours of work. Conditions may also have varied from factory.

139

At the time of the commission, sampling error was a concept that had hardly been thought of.

Then there was the question of the standard of comparison. With whom was the health of the factory children to be compared? It was no golden age for children before the advent of the factories. Thomas Malthus (with whom Loudon was soon to be much concerned) informs us that "In London, according to former calculations, one half of the born died under three years of age; in Vienna and Stockholm, it was under two ..."[17] Admittedly Malthus does not specify the date to which he was referring, though it appears to have been about thirty years before he wrote this, that is to say sixty years before Loudon, but even if some improvement had taken place in the meantime, a very high infant mortality rate must have been regarded as perfectly normal and perhaps inevitable. What is normal does not shock, and it takes visionaries (like Michael Sadler) to see that the normal is not inevitable.

Karl Marx also quoted Loudon in the *Economic and Philosophical Manuscripts of 1844*, but not Loudon's evidence to the commission: rather his magnum opus, his *Solution du problème de la population et de la subsistance, soumise à un médecin dans une série de lettres*, published in the year, 1842, following his retirement to Paris.[18] There is no edition of this book in English as far as I know, but a footnote in my edition of the 1844 *Manuscripts* says that the book is "a translation into French, slightly abridged, of an English manuscript."[19] On page 328 of his book, Loudon wrote:

> In correcting the proofs, I have noticed several repetitions of wording and facts; they arise because the English manuscript presented more development ... and my publisher limited the contents of my work to three hundred pages. I have acquired, by this shortening, proof so often repeated, that it is a hundred times more difficult to shorten a text that to compose a new one.[20]

In 1836, Loudon had published in Leamington Spa a short pamphlet on the population question, *The Equilibrium of Population and Sustenance Demonstrated, Showing on Physiological and Statistical Grounds the Means of Obviating the Fears of the late Mr Malthus.*[21]

This pamphlet, a mere ten pages of print, dedicated to Princess Diana's ancestor the Earl Spencer, is intended to calm the fears of those who think the earth will one day be so densely population that man will have to resort to cannibalism to feed himself.[22] To this fear, Dr. Loudon applies two calming arguments. The first is physiological. He points out that a woman's fecundity is reduced to near zero by lactation. If women breast fed their children, he says, for fifteen months instead of the then customary ten, they would reduce the average natality from 4.5 children to four, and since a half of children born at the time died before they reached the age of twenty-four, the average age of marriage (in those Malthusian days, being married was taken as being able to procreate, childbirth outside marriage being statistically negligible), the population would remain stable, each couple producing exactly two children to replace itself. Therefore, if mothers would but breastfeed a little longer, there would be no call to fear an increase in population. Strangely, he did not consider the possibility that, in time, the infant mortality rate might decline to a mere fraction of what it was then.

Dr. Loudon provides an interesting argument about psychosomatic ailments. It was apparently often agued at the time he was writing that women in England should breastfeed for ten months for strictly physiological reasons, in the belief that it was unhealthy for them to do so for longer periods. It was claimed that after than time they fell ill with all kinds of weakness. Not so, says Dr Loudon; their weakness was in their mind as a result of their expectations, as women in other parts of the world breastfeed much longer without coming to harm. The slave women of Jamaica, said Dr. Loudon, breastfeed for much longer than English women, and it was for *that* reason, not the cruelty of the slaveowners, that the slaves failed to reproduce themselves so that fresh slaves had to be drafted in.

As to the fear that food would be insufficient to feed a growing population well enough, Dr Loudon calculated that there were fifteen million acres of land in the United Kingdom that could, with improvement, be cultivated. A mere sixth of those acres could produce enough potatoes to provide a population of one hundred millions (four times greater than that of the country at the time, according to him), at a rate of four pounds of potatoes daily per person, *ergo* there was no need to fear starvation, especially when forty-five million acres were already cultivated with other crops.

Ten years later came the Irish potato famine, as if to substantiate rather than obviate the fears of Mr. Malthus.

In his much more substantial book of 329 pages, plus index, Dr. Loudon returns to the task of refuting Malthus, who was widely known as *Population Malthus*. He was one of the most important political and influential thinkers of the early nineteenth century. He influenced Darwin profoundly, for it was only after reading Malthus that the idea of survival by natural selection occurred to him. And while Marx and Engels detested him, calling him an apologist of the

BURIED BUT NOT QUITE DEAD

bourgeoisie, which in their mouths was a terrible insult though they themselves belonged to it, his thought resembled theirs to a surprising extent. Malthus claimed that, while population had a tendency to increase geometrically, the means of its sustenance increased only arithmetically, and since no population could long outstrip the means of its sustenance, population growth must be limited either by positive restraints on its growth such as famine, epidemic, or war, or by negative restraints such as custom or late marriage (birth control and abortion he viewed with horror). According to Malthus, attempts to alleviate the lot of the poor by means of subvention merely put off the evil hour when they would in effect be culled. Therefore, one must, as Hamlet put it, be cruel to be kind: Malthus did not think it a kindness to the poor to have ever more of them.

In general, Malthus has had, and has, a bad reputation among intellectuals, and the adjectival form of his name, *Malthusian*, is almost an insult. Nevertheless, he belongs to that select band of thinkers whose name *has* an adjectival form; Hazlitt wrote of him during his lifetime that "Mr Malthus may be considered as one of those who have attained a *scientific* reputation in questions of moral and political philosophy."*[23] The popular conception of him as a hardhearted man who contemplated the sufferings of the poor with indifference if not with sadistic pleasure is quite mistaken. In fact, he was a kindly man, a clergyman of the Church of England who could never rise in the church hierarchy because he was

---

* With great shrewdness, for it is easier to be shrewd about the dead that the living, Hazlitt goes on to say, "His name undoubtedly stands very high in the present age, and will in all probability go down to posterity with more or less of renown or obloquy. It was said by a person well qualified to judge … that 'it would take a thousand years at least to answer his work on Population.'" On this view, he has still eight hundred years at least in which to be vindicated or refuted.

born with a harelip and a cleft palate, the latter irreparable, such that he could never project his voice and always spoke with an impediment.* A bishop, presumably, needs to be able to address a large meeting or congregation.

Malthus contemplated the sufferings of the poor not with satisfaction but with sympathy and even horror, which in his case was not merely abstract, but deeply felt; nor would he ever have advocated violence with the unseemly relish of Marx, who in his *Eighteenth Brumaire of Louis Napoleon* described the rising number of victims of the guillotine during the Terror as a sign of social progress.

Malthus first published his essay anonymously, in a very slim version, but the second edition bore his name and he expanded it to two volumes. My edition is 1,064 pages long,† not always an easy read; one does not pick it up with anticipation of much enjoyment. And from the very first, his ideas aroused fierce opposition; the number of books written against him was considerable.‡

No matter how many times Malthus is refuted, or is claimed to have been refuted, he refuses somehow to go quietly, and neo-Malthusianism springs eternal in the breast of doomsayers. In 1968, for example, the entomologist Paul R. Ehrlich commenced his book *The Population Bomb* with the following Malthusian warning:

---

* For an exhaustive, not to say exhausting, account of his not very interesting life, see Patricia James, *Population Malthus: His Life and Times* (London: Routledge and Kegan Paul, 1979).

† The best edition, according to the bookseller: the definition of a best edition for a bookseller being the one that he is about to sell.

‡ This is a fact that Marx and Engels, in their eagerness to trap the bourgeoisie in the amber of their ideology, conveniently forget. In fact, it is far easier to find contemporaneous anti-Malthusian books than those in his defense. William Cobbett even wrote a play against Malthus — not a very good one, it is true.

144

> The battle to feed all humanity is over. In the 1970s hundreds of millions of people will starve to death in spite of any crash programs embarked upon now, at this late date nothing can prevent a substantial increase in the world death rate ...*

This prediction was spectacularly wrong; obesity and over-eating is (for now) more of a threat to the welfare of the human race than famine, but, like a Marxist briefly embarrassed by the failure of the revolution to materialize, at least in the right place, Ehrlich was able to stick fast to his essentially Malthusian faith. He simply shifted his concern from the raw numbers of human beings and their ability, or inability, to feed themselves, to their consumption of the world's finite resources:

> When is an area overpopulated? When its population can't be maintained without rapidly depleting non-renewable resources (or converting renewable resources into non-renewable ones) and without degrading the capacity of the environment to support the population. In short, if the long- term carrying capacity of an area is clearly being degraded by its current human occupants, that area is overpopulated.[24]

Some countries are now concerned more about declining that increasing populations, a kind of mirror-image Malthusianism, as it were (it seems there is no size of popula-

---

* Paul R. Ehrlich, *The Population Bomb* (New York: Ballantine Books, 1970). There is something interesting to be written about entomologists who stray into human affairs: for example, Alfred Kinsey and E. O. Wilson, in addition to Ehrlich. Did they see people as insects, or insects as people?

tion that will please everyone), but a declining population is perfectly compatible with environmental degradation, if each individual insists upon or requires an increased consumption of resources. I know young people who are so worried by that degradation that that they say that they will refuse to have children because of it (I take their ostensible reason for their decision to be the real one). The degradation is real enough; species of birds that were commonly seen in my childhood have all but disappeared. This is not unrelated to the decline in the numbers of insects, both as to population and numbers of species.[25]

145

I have been tempted by Malthusianism myself. Forty years ago, I visited Egypt, and concluded that, if its rate of population growth continued, which it almost certainly would, and the fertile land inundated annually by the Nile did not increase in area, which it could not, and the rest of the land surface being desert, a food crisis was inevitable; I wrote an article to that effect.

It cannot be said that everything has gone swimmingly in Egypt since I wrote that, but the population has increased from 47 million to 112 million without my predicted catastrophe having supervened. Like many others before me, and many since, I did not pay sufficient attention to the difference between a projection and a prediction, nor did I take into account the enormous, though not infinitely great, adaptability of humans.*

On the first page of Loudon's text is a table showing

---

* I had just read Thomas P. Anderson's *The War of the Dispossessed: Honduras and El Salvador* (Lincoln: University of Nebraska Press, 1981), which interpreted what is often called the Soccer War in largely Malthusian terms. The massacre of Haitians in the Dominican Republic in 1937 under the dictator Trujillo has been explained in Malthusian terms, as has the genocide of Tutsis in Rwanda in 1994.

what the population of the earth would be if it doubled from a single couple every thirty-three and a third years starting from a single couple. After only 1,233 years, the earth's population would be 412,316,860,416 – clearly an absurdity.* But it was the *tendency to*, not the fact of, geometric growth to which Malthus had alluded, and it was precisely the fact that the tendency was always halted, brief exceptions notwithstanding, that for Malthus required explanation.

I have in my possession a letter from Loudon to Thomas Doubleday (1790–1870), the author of the anti-Malthusiuan *True Law of Population*, published in 1841, which Loudon evidently sent with a copy of his book, saying that "Of one thing I am certain we are the only two writers on population who have treated the doctrines of Mr Malthus on any thing like rational grounds."[26] (He is considerably less complimentary about Doubleday's ideas in the book, refuting his strange idea that the more access a population has to animal food, the slower the growth of its population.)[27] In the letter, Loudon says, "I was obliged to publish my book in French because no English Publisher would take it." Whether he translated it himself into French he does not say, but, in fact, it appears to me both well-written and to say something original, though not necessarily true.

The book is written in a series of thirteen letters (unlucky for some) to an unnamed colleague, all datelined Paris and dated precisely from February 10, 1842, to April 18, 1842. Whether the book really *was* written as a series of letters, and in little more than two months, cannot be known, but certainly, Loudon claims to have been thinking of the subject for ten years, which is by no means implausible, since his first pamphlet was published six years earlier. And when one has been thinking of a subject for a long time, there often

* We are worried about the size of a world population 2 percent as large.

comes a point for an author when it suddenly overflows the mental vessel in which the thoughts have been contained.

Loudon's first task is to contradict himself, even with a degree of irony, for what he said in his Leamington tract. The fact that he does this suggests that he was a man genuinely wrestling with a subject who put truth above pride or ego. There is a tendency for people to defend what they have said just because they said it, and Loudon is not of this ilk, even if his second effort will not satisfy everyone.

He rejects his simplistic idea that one can calculate the possible number of a territory by simply dividing the number of acres of land by the number necessary to support an individual. This is because man does not live by bread – or rice or potatoes – alone:

> It is certain, let us say, that England could feed 120,200,250 and even 300,000,000 inhabitants. But to arrive at such a result, it would be necessary not only to destroy all beasts of burden, but even more all those that serve as food; it would destroy all fish in the rivers.[28]

Moreover, subsistence farming of a single crop conduces to famine. Speaking of Ireland (just three years before the great potato famine began from which the population has not recovered numerically, being still at only two-thirds of its pre-famine level), Loudon says: "the famine to which its sole source of food (the potato) exposes it."[29]

The monoculture of rice in India, he says, explains why that region is also susceptible to famine.

He accepts Malthus' fundamental point, that population has a tendency to grow much faster than the means to support it: "The accuracy and strength of the doctrine of geometric growth advanced by Mr Malthus [is] perfectly established."[30]

Loudon seems a little confused, however, as to "checks" to the growth of population. He tells us that in these enlightened times (1842):

148

> The plague no longer rules, and the almost unnoticed Effect [on the size of the present population] of the cholera in countries that enjoy a certain level of well-being proves the slight influence of epidemics in our homeland.... Moreover, in all of Europe, governments begin to feel that they have, by comparison with the past, a greater responsibility, whether through the intermediary of representative parliaments or the press or, as in Prussia, that of the enlightened, thinking and virtuous part [of the population].... This enlightened part will certainly not diminish, and the countries in which a wise administration rules of internal affairs will not fail, generally speaking, to increase their populations. We see, then, that neither wars, nor epidemics, nor famines, nor the absence of the comforts of life, nor bad governments, will have the destructive influence they once had on decreasing the number of inhabitants of the earth.* [31]

But earlier, he had listed all those factors that acted to curtail the growth of populations (I give here only a sample):

> The unhealthiness of the climate because of the destructiveness of winds, epidemics, dirty wells, unhealthy food,

---

* Loudon, in an earlier passage, had eloquently described the horrors of war, followed by the rather optimistic view that war as an instrument of policy had been superseded by negotiation between reasonable men, an illusion that springs, if not eternal, at least quite often in the human mind. Loudon's grounds for such an opinion were that there had been no general war in Europe since the end of the Napoleonic Wars in 1815, that is to say for all of twenty-seven years.

famines, agglomerations of the population, foreign and
civil wars, bad local and central government, bad laws,
ignorance and prejudice in the matter of political economy, immorality, religious persecution, slavery weighing
on children and adults, excessive work demanded of
children and adults, occupations or work deleterious to
health, large towns, excesses of all kinds, poverty, the
oppression of the poor, unjust taxes, insufficient and
inequitable pay, the lack of fuel, the shortage or lack of
salt, the tribulations to which the human heart and
mind are perpetually exposed and subject to throughout
life, religious exaltation, demoralisation that brings in
its train avarice, pride and vanity, the injustices and
wrongs done by men to women, unhappy events, accidents by land and sea, sterility of the two sexes, female
circumcision, other means of contraception, either direct
or indirect abortion, civil or religious celibacy, castration,
polyandry, polygamy, separation of married couples,
infanticide, exposure of the newborn, the perversity of
the human heart, and all the ordinary illnesses that pre-
maturely decimate and destroy the human race.[32]

Am I wrong in detecting in this litany a certain pleasure, not
quite sadistic – because Loudon would not himself bring
about any of the things listed – but mildly salacious or voy-
euristic? Mankind, after all, is the only species that enjoys
the contemplation of its own misfortune.

Be that as it may, Loudon, having agreed with Malthus
that overpopulation is a problem, at least potentially, finds
a solution that clearly becomes what is vulgarly known as a
bee in his bonnet.

It is well known that Malthus softened his views somewhat as he aged and gave to moral restraint a bigger role that
previously, thus suggesting that famine, war, and pestilence

150

were not the only way the human population might be cut down to size. As a way of achieving equilibrium between population and resources (he, like Marx and most others, had no inkling of the vast increase in human productivity to come), Mathus suggested the postponement of marriage until the age of twenty-eight for women and thirty for men: and it is here that Loudon finds himself in profound disagreement with Malthus. Far from delayed marriage, Loudon is in favor of early marriage, sometime between puberty and the age of twenty or twenty-one, allowing also for a short time for engagement. He sees this proposal almost as a panacea for all of humanity's problems.

Loudon starts from the supposition that the natural laws of physiology, which are also God's laws, form the basis of how we should conduct ourselves, at least in this matter. He says that man's life is divided into natural periods of seven years, the final one, that after the age of seventy, being described in a way not very encouraging to me:

> At sixty-three, the teeth fall out quickly, and at seventy one has arrived at an age at which there is nothing more than death to expect; if one continues to exist, his life is but misery and pain.[33]

A young man speaks!*

Now, according to Loudon, the natural duration of breastfeeding for a human is three years; the child at that age ceases to seek the mother's breast, assuming that it has not been weaned before. And since conception during this period of three years would be very rare, and since, taking everything into account, including the declining fertility of women

---

* Though only two years from death himself.

as they grow older, this would mean that on average women would have four children, and thus a stable population would be reached because of the four two could be expected to die before they themselves reached the age of reproduc-   151 tion. The problem of overpopulation would be obviated.

But this would be only one of the problems that the breast-feeding of infants for three years would solve – according to Loudon. For example, it would raise the wages of workers by taking women out of the workforce. It would reduce, if not eliminate altogether, the problem of prostitution, which Malthus's proposal of delayed marriage would only aggravate, because men would have to seek relief for their urges elsewhere than from a legitimate wife. Indeed, says Loudon, the later the age of marriage, the larger the number of prostitutes. It is one of his passages on prostitution that Marx quotes:

> The average life of these unfortunate creatures on the streets, after they have embarked on their career of vice, is about six or seven years. To maintain the number of sixty to seventy thousand prostitutes [in England and Wales, Scotland, and Ireland], there must be in the three kingdoms at least eight to nine thousand women who commit themselves to this degrading profession each year, or about twenty-four new victims each day – in average of *one* per hour ...* [34]

Prostitutes, says Loudon, did not have children:

---

* I have used the translation of the *Economic and Philosophic Manuscripts* cited above, which seemed to me completely accurate. It says something for Marx's wide reading that he reached as far as page 229 in a book whose underlying piety and belief in a divine providence must have irritated him.

> The late Dr Marc, physician to Louis-Philippe, King of the French, has observed that of 800 or 1,000 of these women, he never saw more than one who had had a child.* [35]

London was no better:

> Such is the state of demoralisation in this respect in London that we have counted in our metropolis two or three hundred individuals who seduce girls from ten to sixteen years, and it is a calamity that at this so tender age a crowd of them present themselves to hospitals and doctors for treatment of the illnesses that are the result of their bad conduct. [36]

One might have thought that it was not *their* conduct that was bad, but let it pass:

> A large number of the advertisements for domestics and governesses in our newspapers are traps to catch those postulants who have the most charms, in order to have the chance to seduce them. [37]

The police of the day reported that girls were transported from Belgium for the same purposes.

The habit of late marriage, which Malthus wanted people to postpone further in order to prevent overpopulation, was the cause of much syphilitic infection:

> Delay in marriage gives rise to a commerce between humans.... The late Professor Richerand thought that, of a hundred men in the upper and middle classes, there

---

* Dr. Marc seems to have had an odd practice, including both king and prostitutes.

was practically not a single one who had not been attacked by this plague, and Dr Ricord, who is one of the most frequently consulted doctors about syphilitic infections confirmed this opinion to me.[38]

153

This may seem exaggerated: after all, a doctor who specialized in syphilis is likely to be consulted by people who suffer from it, and therefore he is likely to look at the world through syphilis-tainted spectacles. But some time ago, while researching three murders that were committed in quick succession on the island of Jersey only three or four years after Loudon wrote his book, I discovered that not only did fifty percent of proprietors or editors of provincial newspapers sell proprietary medicines, but that half of all their advertising was for such proprietary medicines, and that half of those were for preventives of, or curatives for, syphilis. The disease thus had a place – I won't say an honorable place – in the development of British journalism which may even have been financially dependent on it.

Loudon has much to say on the healthiness of prolonged breastfeeding and the disastrous consequences of early weaning, physical and moral:

"In a machine," says Bichat (*Anatomie Générale*),* "in which everything holds or is linked together, if one piece is disarranged, all are." This is also true in physiology as in morality, and is doubly so in this matter which is both physiological and moral, and in which the only way to assure health both physical and moral is to

---

* Marie François Xavier Bichat (1771–1802) was one of the founders of modern pathology, having identified different types of tissue, which led to the notion of lesions in specific tissues and therefore to a new and better way of classifying diseases.

154

observe the law in its plenitude. Irregularity has no limits, a contempt for one thing leads to another. The short-
ening of the period of breastfeeding leads to frequent
births; these require that marriages take place as late
as possible; this delay leads to seduction, fornication,
bastardy, prostitution, adultery and other crimes in relations between the sexes. The failure to obey the physiological and therefore divine law of early marriage and
prolonged breastfeeding* results in many bodily and
moral ills:

I have described how late marriages lead to seduction,
prostitution, and adultery, which in their turn are the
source of infanticide, voluntary abortions, exposure of
children, drunkenness, obscene conversation, swearing,
blaspheming, brigandage, theft, lies, dissimulation, negligence in fulfilling religious duties, and, in a word, many
other causes of demoralisation.[39]

On page 276, there comes a most remarkable passage about
the pecuniary loss occasioned by the early death of children,
of a kind that gave, and gives, a bad name to the dismal science, as political economy was known:

We have already said that the number of children born
annually in the United Kingdom is about a million, of
whom at least a third die before they are capable of earning their bread. We have calculated many times the
pecuniary loss that might result from this premature
mortality. My own observations permit me to give my

---

* The virtues of breastfeeding are now well-known. According to an article
in *The Lancet*, if breastfeeding were universal, the lives of about 800,000
children a year would be saved. *The Lancet*, "Breastfeeding Series," 2016:
387, 475–490.

opinion on this subject, because, from my childhood to
the end of my minority,* I was the owner of slaves, and
from my travels to the West Indies, and by an uninter-
rupted correspondence with friends and relatives in this
part of the world, I am able to assert that a child, before
he can provide for himself, costs 50 pounds sterling. By
supposing, then, average loss caused by each child under
twelve years old is 20 pounds sterling, the national loss
occasioned by these premature deaths would be several
millions of pounds sterling a year.[40]

The book, we ought to remember, was published only nine
years after the abolition of slavery in the British Empire.
Will someone now destroy his distinctly modest tombstone
in Père Lachaise?

I should mention that Loudon's wife, Margracia, who
survived him and eventually died in Cheltenham, another
Regency spa town, was a also writer, both of unsuccessful
novels and treatises on political economy. It may even have
been she who converted her husband to the idea that physiological, moral, and divine law were all essentially one, and
that therefore prolonged breastfeeding was a moral and religious duty. Her economic writings are all but unreadable;
her sentences are often a maze of clauses such that by their
end you have forgotten what they were initially about.† And
yet she sometimes writes almost with eloquence:

> The most ruinous of our monopolies, and therefore that
> which calls the first and loudest for abolition, is that

---

* This would have been in 1822. He does not say how he came to own
slaves, nor whether he sold them or freed them.
† The most significant is *Philanthropic Economy, or, the Philosophy of Happiness* (London: Edward Churton, 1835).

unjust enhancement of the price of grain, occasioned by the operation of the corn laws.* [41]

156   As to her novels, I have looked only into *Fortune-Hunting*, dedicated to her husband, "Charles Loudon, Esq. M.D." Its protagonist is a shameless confidence trickster who calls himself Colonel Trump.[42]

---

* The laws in question prohibited the importation of cheap foreign grain, in favor of that produced by landowners. Whether protection is *always* mistaken is a question still debated.

Jules Cornély
(1845–1907)

THE TOMB OF Jules Cornély in Père Lachaise is imposing, if not beautiful. A bronze bust of him stands atop a granite plinth, which bears the words "To J. Cornély – His admirers and his friends." Below is a bronze representation of a drape, with the names of his last two newspapers, *Le Figaro* and *Le Siècle*, for which he wrote, with the following quotation from him:

> We are aware of having served a great cause, we shall remain the servants of all great causes, and we shall leave open the windows of our abodes so as to hear from as near as possible the cries of the oppressed and the sorrows of victims.

I think these words are not without nobility and are sincerely meant. On the rear of the granite plinth, on another bronze plaque, we are told that the monument was raised by public subscription under the patronage of the presidents of both the senate and the Chamber of Deputies, and among the mentioned subscribers were Alexandre Millerand, once a left-wing socialist and later president of the republic, the Prince of Monaco, and Joseph Reinach, the great historian of the Dreyfus affair. Cornély must have been a person of considerable standing to have attracted such subscribers to his funerary monument.

The bust atop the plinth is by Paul Moreau-Vauthier

158

(1871–1936), a distinguished sculptor who was himself buried in Père Lachaise after he was killed in a car accident. To judge from a photograph, it captures Cornély very well, and not only physically but in spirit also. He had a kind of squarish head that radiates an obstinate probity, both when he was right and when he was wrong. As he looks out ahead, seeking inspiration, his head resting on his bent left arm, he has a feather quill in his hand, and one can almost hear it scratching urgently on the paper below when the right words finally come. The bust makes clear that his work was the most important, or at any rate significant, part of his life.

The great cause to which his epitaph refers must surely have been the Dreyfus affair. Cornély was long a firm Catholic and monarchist, deeply opposed to the republic that followed the defeat of the French in the Franco-Prussian War, and at first he believed in the guilt of Alfred Dreyfus (as did most people of his political opinions), but under the influence of the evidence, he changed his mind and became a Dreyfusard. His last book recounts this change of mind and is a powerful and inspiring reminder that evidence can sometimes affect our beliefs.

Of Cornély's biography I have discovered little. He was born in a tiny village in the Jura called Nogna, which has the distinction of having fewer inhabitants now than it did two and a half centuries ago. He was baptized Jean Joseph, not Jules, and was one of seven children, two, or possibly three, of whom died in childhood. He died in the rue de Clichy in the ninth arrondissement of Paris two weeks short of his sixty-third birthday. He married Marie Clotilde Barbe Warnecke, a painter, who died in 1914 aged sixty-nine.[1] He had two sons and one daughter, Marguerite Marie Cornély, who died in 1945 aged seventy. One son, Michel, died aged thirty-three in 1914, having been a cook in the army. He was buried first in Montmartre Cemetery but exhumed almost exactly a year after his death and reburied in Père Lachaise.[2] I do not know the reason for this removal and reinterment. There were no speeches at his interments.

How Cornély moved from the most rural of rural back-
grounds to the most metropolitan of metropolitan activities, national journalism, I do not know, but in 1878 he published, aged thirty-three, his first book, a romantic historical novel titled *L'Oeil du diable* (The Devil's Eye). It could not have been successful, for he never published another, and in truth it is not very good. His talent was not for fiction.

The book begins as if it is going to be scientific romance along the lines of *Frankenstein*. A mysterious young man called Aubryot comes in 1777 to live near a village near Brest in Brittany. He inspires fear in the villagers. He rents a house near the coast where there is a strange rock formation which Aubryot is able to use as a kind of lighthouse, luring ships to their wreck. Aubryot strips the wrecks of anything valuable but uses the cadavers for unspecified experiments which yield him almost superhuman medical knowledge.

This he uses one day to save the life of the local squire, the comte de Roquetel – in return for the hand of his beautiful daughter, Elise, who, however, loves her first cousin, the vicomte de Roquetel. After the marriage between Elise and Aubryot, the latter becomes Aubryot's hated rival. Disappointed in love, the vicomte goes to America to fight under Lafayette in the Revolutionary War, accompanied by his faithful Breton servant, Nicou. Both Elise and Aubryot, who has refrained from sexual relations with his wife at her request, follow them to America, Aubryot with the intention of killing the vicomte there.

It would take far too long to recount the ups and down and ins and outs of the melodramatic plot; suffice it to say that Elise, Nicou, and the vicomte are so invariably good, brave, honorable, and clever that one comes before the end to hope that the evil Aubryot will triumph (which of course he does not), an excess of virtue being almost as unattractive as any other kind of excess.

Although Cornély was explicitly and even militantly Christian, one does not detect much forgiveness in the fate of Aubryot, but rather a sadistic imaginary death. Tied up so that he cannot move, he is forced for ten minutes to watch a slow-burning fuse progressing towards a barrel of gunpowder near him, before being blown to smithereens.

It is as well that Cornély never returned to the genre, though he did become something of a literary critic. In 1893, he published an interesting review of a novel that began with an essay on the novel and other literature in general:

> It is horribly banal to say that the soul of a people is reflected in its literature, just as an individual's features are reflected in a mirror. However, if all the memoirs and documents left us by past generations which served as the basis of history were to disappear, we should obviously no longer have knowledge either of the succession of great men or of events: we could not know who fought where for what. But a few pages of prose, a few pages of verse, that escaped the disaster would suffice to reconstitute the moral portrait of past generations. We could not say: here is what they ate, here is how they dressed. But we could say: here is what they read, therefore here is what they thought. Later, who knows? New barbarians will arrive. They will not come out of the deep North, nor from the vast spaces of Asia; they will be natives. They will be born in the home, in the homeland, among the rotting remains of decomposing civilizations. They will, perhaps, be the children of free, secular and compulsory

education.* They will all know how to read and will treat
books as badly as the Goths of Alaric and the soldiers of
Omar treated them.[3]

161

Certainly, this seems prophetic of the way many libraries
have been treated in England recently, with the willing
cooperation of the very people, librarians, who were supposed to cherish and preserve them; Virginia Woolf once
expressed the wish that great libraries should be regularly
burnt down, before they could once again become reposito-
ries of past error. Cornély continued:

> The leadership of the Commune overflowed with teach-
> ers and university lecturers. This did not prevent the
> Commune from burning the library of the Louvre and, if
> there had been time, it is probable that the officers of the
> Prussian army ... would have been able to observe the
> volumes of the Bibliothèque nationale go up in smoke ...

It is the elites who welcome the collapse of civilizations,
though it is worth recalling that Gibbon's *Decline and Fall*
covered a period of a thousand years.

Cornély then goes on to imagine a future time, after the
total dissolution of our civilization, when a few sages will
try to imagine from the scraps of the literature of his generation, for example the work of Zola, what our civilization
was like, and the sages will not conclude much good of it:

> The people who lived in those distant times had no
> moral instinct. In peacetime, they behaved a little worse

---

* That education should be free, secular, and compulsory was a corner-
stone of French republican educational policy, though in practice the Catholic Church continued to provide much schooling.

than animals, and in war they fought among themselves much worse than they.[4]

162 In essence, this is the King of Brobdingnag's judgment on Gulliver's countrymen:

> I cannot but conclude that the Bulk of your Natives, to be the most pernicious Race of odious little vermin that Nature ever suffered to crawl jupon the Surface of the Earth.[5]

Pessimism about the human condition and the state of civilization springs eternal, though it is rarely that nothing happens within a relatively short time to justify them.

How Cornély joined the ranks of the Parisian journalists I do not know, but by 1879, he had joined the staff of *Le Figaro*, still one of the two most important French newspapers. By 1881, however, *Le Figaro* had rallied to the republic, and Cornély, a convinced monarchist, left to start his own newspaper, *Le Clairon* (The Clarion). This created enough of a stir for Cornély to be satirized on the front page of *Les Contemporains*,* showing him as him as a youngish man in bourgeois dress clutching a trumpet in one hand and a copy of *Le Clairon* in the other, with the following verses underneath:

> Jean Cornély, the clarion of the king,
> Bravely blows on the tombs,
> The people hear without any fear

---

* Presumably, the first name of Cornély was changed in order to avoid any possible action for defamation. The weekly journal ran for only forty-three issues and ceased publication three months after having satirized Cornély in its fashion. See *Les Contemporains*, September 15, 1881.

Jean Cornély, the clarion of the king.
For the knights are in disarray
Under the shells and under the bombs,
Jean Cornély, clarion of the king,
Bravely blows on the tombs.*

The republic was then only eleven years old and royalism, or anti-republicanism, was still strong, though divided between legitimists (of whom Cornély was one), Orléanists, and Bonapartists. At any rate, he must have been thought sufficiently prominent to be worth satirizing.

Cornely's second book, published by *Le Clairon* in the last year of its existence, 1884, was titled *Le Czar et le Roi: Souvenirs et impressions de voyage* (The Tsar and the King: Memories and Impressions of Travel).

Cornély traveled to Russia to attend the coronation of Tsar Alexander III in Moscow in 1883, on his return visiting the comte de Chambord, whom legitimists considered King Henry V, in his exile in Austria, then returning to attend the comte's funeral shortly afterwards.

Forty-four years before Cornély made his journey to Russia, another Frenchman, the marquis de Custine, had gone there in search of justification for autocratic monarchy as a form of government, not surprisingly since his father and grandfather were guillotined during the French Revolution despite having been sympathetic towards it, and his

---

* Jean Cornély, clairon du roi,
Bravement sonne sur les tombes,
Le peuple écoute sans effroi,
Jean Cornély, clairon du roi.
Car les preux sont en désarroi
Sous les obus et sous les bombes,
Jean Cornély, clairon du roi,
Bravement sonne sur les tombes.

mother having barely escaped the same fate. Custine, however, returned from the Russia of Nicholas I a firm believer in constitutional government.

By contrast, the bourgeois, or even petit bourgeois, Cornély went to Russia predisposed in favor of autocratic monarchy and returned more than ever convinced if its benefits. He stayed less than a month, whereas Custine stayed three, but it is not because of the length of time that they spent that their books are so widely different. Custine's book is vastly the more profound, but Cornély's is not therefore without great interest.

Cornély was dazzled by the palaces of St. Petersburg and the polychrome and greatly varied grandeur of the Kremlin. "He who has not seen the Kremlin lit up," he says, "has seen nothing."*[6] The magnificent ceremonial that he witnessed, the clockwork efficiency of displays, never gave him pause, as they did Custine, who pointed out that tyrannies demand immense sacrifices to bring forth trifles. Cornély skates the surface, but surfaces are interesting (and important).

His account of what he saw in Russia strikes me as a Tsarist equivalent of the journeys made in Soviet Russia by Western intellectuals in the 1930s, when they saw precisely what their guides wanted them to see and nothing else. The surveillance and control was less strict, of course, but it was there. Despite being well-disposed to tsarism, as the authorities must have known, all his dispatches, like those of the other correspondents, had to pass through the censor. According to Cornély, the censor never even read them, and just waved them through, but, even if that is true, surely the mere fact of the censor's existence (and that he could have become less accommodating at any time, according to

---

* The Spanish say, "Quien no ha visto Sevilla, no ha visto maravilla": "He who has not seen Sevilla has not seen the marvelous."

whim) could, indeed must, have exerted a dampening effect on writers less well-disposed than Cornély.[7] He lets his favorable predisposition get the better of his imagination.

Only once does Cornély even hint that all may not be well behind the "fairyland" façade of the ceremonial he has come to report upon.* It is true that, as he describes it, it must have been so impressive as to overwhelm most critical faculties. The huge variety of resplendent uniforms worn by thousands of people, the gorgeous ecclesiastical robes, the chiming of hundreds of church bells, the mysterious ceremonies in the Orthodox cathedrals, the displays of jewelry, the massed choirs and orchestras, the waiting for the tsar to appear as if Messiah for the day, the hundred-and-one-gun salutes, the cheering and throwing in the air in unison of the caps of thousands of soldiers, the magnificent trains of horses, the apparently adoring crowds and mass acclamations of hundreds of thousands of people, the firework displays – who would not be taken in, or at any rate affected, by it all? I think I would have found it difficult to resist the conclusion that the tsarist empire was on solid foundations and loved by the people.

All the same, Cornély had noticed that posted every hundred meters along the railway line from St. Petersburg, which he took himself, stood a soldier to prevent any possible attacks not only on the tsar himself, but also on the dignitaries en route to his coronation. This precaution was not the manifestation of irrational paranoia; after all, the coronation was necessary at this time only because Alexander III's father, Tsar Alexander II, had been assassinated in 1881 – possibly, as I have said, the most disastrous assassination, together with that of the Archduke Franz-Ferdinand, in the

* *Féerique*, he calls it more than once.

history of the world.* But Cornély did not enter into the question of whether the assassination signified something more than the existence of a few ruthless malcontents such as are to be found in all places at all times.

166

He recounts with admiration and almost wonderment the provision of free meals (free to the recipients, that is) provided for half a million Muscovites immediately after the coronation. Whether this figure was accurate, I cannot say; Cornély, I suspect, is not entirely to be trusted with figures. Describing the persecution of Catholics under the Tsar Liberator, Alexander II,† he says that two hundred Catholic priests were deported to Siberia, that any employee of the government, from highest to lowest, had to convert to Orthodoxy if he wanted to keep his job, that any Catholic wishing to marry an Orthodox had to do so in an Orthodox church, likewise with any foreigner, but above all, that at the start of his reign, there were twenty-nine million Catholics in the Russian Empire and only fifteen million at the end of it.[8]

This latter assertion seems *prima facie* unlikely for, if true, it would have meant that a third of the population had been Catholic. Even allowing for the Poles and the Lithuanians, this seems impossible.

Be the exact figure what it may, there can be no doubt that enormous numbers of people were fed after the coronation, and that to do so required a miracle of organization that was completely at odds with the shambles that one usually associates with Russia. The great success was in a way

---

* Like George VI, who never expected (or wanted) to be king, Alexander III, the second son of Alexander II, had not expected, until the death aged twenty-one of his older brother Nicholas in 1865, to be tsar.

† So called because of his emancipation of the serfs in 1861, nearly two years before the Emancipation Proclamation in the United States. Both emancipations went off in practice at half-cock, as it were.

unfortunate: it encouraged the repetition thirteen years later after Nicholas II's coronation, when more than a thousand people were killed in a stampede.*

Alexander III, though normally regarded as reactionary by comparison with his murdered father, was more tolerant of Catholicism than he. His empire was, of course, multiethnic, multicultural, and multi-confessional, and Cornély makes much of the attendance at the coronation of the prelates of various religions and sects:

> After an army of metropolitans, archimandrites, and multicolored [Orthodox] priests, came two Catholic archbishops, enveloped in purple. Then came Armenian priests, then Lutheran ministers, Calvinists and a superb mullah, someone like the bishop of the Ottoman subjects of His Majesty.[9]

Cornély here omits to mention that there was no rabbi at the coronation to represent the Jews. He was not to know that, later in his life, he was to be appalled by the anti-Semitism displayed in the Dreyfus affair.

As a royalist and supporter on the union of church and state, he compared Alexander's religious policy (and, indeed, that of every other country) favorably with the French Republic's:

> There is only one nation where the Church is hunted down, humiliated, impoverished and persecuted. That nation, alas, is ours.[10]

---

* The disaster following the coronation was widely regarded as a bad augury for Nicholas's reign, not least by Nicholas himself. See, for example, Orlando Figes, *A People's Tragedy: The Russian Revolution 1891–1924* (London: Jonathan Cape, 1996), 18–19.

At the time Cornély wrote, the division between the clerical and anticlerical parties in France was strong, and the total victory of the latter was not taken as a foregone conclusion.

Cornély draws another comparison with Russia unfavorable to France. He compares the perfect state of preservation of the Kremlin with the destruction during the Commune of the Palace of the Tuileries:

> It is by these exterior signs that the health or illness of nations are recognized, as the health or illness of individuals is betrayed by the temperature of the skin, the movement of the eye, or the shade of the complexion.[11]

As insight into the future course of history, this was less than prophetic.

Cornély was much impressed by the patience, the almost fatalistic mansuetude of the Russian common people, who waited for hours without complaint or disturbance for the tsar to arrive or for their free meal to be distributed:

> The multitude here is admirable. It waits, motionlessly legs crossed for days, without uttering a murmur. One felt one was approaching the Orient, where immobility and patience are the foundation of human character.[12]

When Cornély observed this to a general, he heard but did not really listen to the general's reply:

> Do not bank on it [he said]. It would take nothing to transform all these sheep that one leads by a string into unchained tigers.[13]

The general then said that a false alert, a panic, would lead to incalculable disorder – which is precisely what happened at the coronation of Nicholas II, and which some historians claim irretrievably besmirched his reign.

Cornély, true to his monarchist convictions, believed that Alexander III was loved by his people, except for a few violent malcontents:

> On the very day of the coronation ... I met General Kaslov himself, who indicated by his hand the room where the imperial repast was taking place, with the casualness that one traveler would employ on indicating to another the door to a table d'hôte. And it is absolutely certain that the little silver medallion that I wore [as an accredited journalist] signified nothing, for the most stupid of the nihilists could have procured a similar one.
>
> No, what protected the Emperor and his family during these days [of the Coronation] was the love of his subjects![14]

And who, he asked, could not or would not love Alexander III?

> [He] whose exterior one could depict in three words, "a valiant man." A grave goodness, tranquil, sovereign, a little placid perhaps, but profound and mysterious, spreads over the features of Alexander III and commands sympathy.[15]

This is very similar to what was written about Stalin by visitors to the Soviet Union fifty years later.

For Cornély, Alexander III was a moral exemplar:

> Above all, His Majesty Alexander III is of an extreme simplicity, almost bourgeois and a model of domestic virtue.... As for morality, his subjects say that he is the only Russian who is faithful to his wife.[16]

Apart from his dithyrambs to the tsar, there is one other respect in which his account resembles reports of later visits to the Soviet Union: he praises the authorities who have made his visit so agreeable.

> To end this account of our stay in Moscow without cordially thanking two people who, in different capacities, were concerned with the press during the festivities, would be an act of ingratitude. First, His Excellency the Minister of the Imperial Household, Count Voronstov. This great personage, in inviting the press to the coronation, in opening all doors to it, in treating us all a thousand times better than we would have been treated in a so-called liberal nation proud of its press, gave proof simultaneously of a real, enlightened liberalism and an exquisite courtesy.
>
> He entrusted the practical details of our reception to Mr Vaganov. Mr. Vaganov established his headquarters in the Hotel Moscow, at the very gate of the Kremlin [and where the journalists were put up], and stayed there during all the celebrations, bending over backwards, sacrificing himself, present at all times, ready to answer all our questions, and eager to anticipate all our wishes.[17]

Unlike Custine forty years before him, Cornély did not recognize all this as an elaborate attempt to pull the wool over the eyes of the foreign visitor, a great tradition that continued well after Stalin's time and which might even be said to persist into the present day, when the former KGB colonel covers his regime and country with a patina of state religiosity.

But we should not be too hard on Cornély, who was not the first, and certainly not the last, to be deceived. After all, he saw what he saw, and the devotion of the multitudes to the tsar was real, even if it could switch as the perception of the candlestick can change suddenly to that of two old crones in the drawing beloved of psychologists to prove that perception is a gestalt and not a deduction from an accumulation of individual data. The magnificence of the ceremonial, of the costumes, above all of St. Petersburg and the Kremlin, were real. It was hardly surprising that, on a visit lasting three weeks, and with a predisposition in favor of tsarism, that Cornély did not penetrate deeper, as did Custine.

He does, however, make one observation that is pregnant with meaning in the modern world. Remarking on the military bearing and deportment of Russian and Cossack soldiers, he writes of the Russian soldier: "this soldier, so strong, costs five times less than a French soldier and seven and a half times less than an English one."[18]

How often does one read of raw military expenditure, raw military numbers, raw military display, as being a true reflection of relative military power! Serried ranks and immaculate display are supposed to translate into actual military prowess; this is like supposing that the film, *Cleopatra*, was a contribution to classical scholarship.

Cornély's next book, published in 1888, was, in a way, a repetition of the performance, though at half the length. It was titled *Rome et le jubilé de Léon XIII: Notes d'un pèlerin* (Rome and the Jubilee of Leo XIII: Notes of a Pilgrim) and was published by *Société Générale de Librairie Catholique*. Coincidence or not, my copy when I obtained it remained uncut, and I was the first person to have read it in its 135 years of existence.

The book, unsurprisingly, concerned Italy rather than Russia, but was infused by the same dislike of secularism and preference for an almost theocratic polity, or at least one in which the Church was a partner of the secular power.

The historical context is important in understanding

Cornély's book. Italy had been unified under the crown of Piedmont only eighteen years before, and the papacy despoiled of its secular power in the Italian peninsula. The pope was virtually a prisoner in the Vatican, which had not yet been recognized as a sovereign state. Cornély, a fervent Catholic, was of the opinion that the papacy needed secular power as well as spiritual; he saw the Piedmontese, now Italian, monarchy as a malign force for secularization. His Catholicism trumped his monarchism, though his ideal was that they should be united. Of course, the Papal States did once unite the two: the pope was pontiff *and* king.

Cornély's aim was at the secularists of his own country, who had not yet secured their total victory. He despises them for what he considers their ignorance of history. The Catholic Church, he says, is at the root of all European culture and even science, and to pull a plant up by the roots is to kill it.

His book is a series of dispatches from Rome. The first, dated January 1, 1888, begins with what is surely an exaggeration: "The civilised universe is at this moment present at a unique and grand spectacle."[19]

The place is Rome and the occasion is Leo XIII's Jubilee, that is to say the fiftieth anniversary of the first Mass that he pronounced. Of course, it depends what you call the civilized universe, but I think that this event might have gone unnoticed by quite a large proportion of it: unless, that is, you make the assertion true by definition by making the criterion of civilization is attendance at the Jubilee.

It must be remembered that, at the time that Cornély was writing, anti-Catholicism was a good deal stronger than it is now. It was only shortly before that Bismarck had given up the *Kulturkampf*, the struggle against Catholicism in the newly established German Empire, that Protestantism was still strong as was its feeling against Catholicism, and that even in the United States, with its official secularism, it was a moot point as late as 1960 whether a Catholic could be elected president (or successfully steal an election). In Britain, it was only recently that open Catholics could be members of the elite, and to many theological and doctrinal questions still seemed of immense importance. The long, melancholy withdrawing roar of religion to which Matthew Arnold drew attention in his most famous poem* was not yet complete.†

Cornély then indulges briefly in what might be called a Whig interpretation of Catholic history, enumerating all the benefits wrought by the Church – among which, rather surprisingly, is the invention of gunpowder by the monk Roger Bacon and of bombs by the Bishop of Munster.‡ [20] Not only did the Church save Europe from barbarism, but Cornély also attributes every achievement by a Catholic to his Catholicism: for example, he says that it was a Jesuit who founded the first gas factory, in Preston, Lancashire, in 1815. [21]

Cornély unites his clericalism with his nationalism. France is the oldest daughter not only of the Church but of the Pope. He says:

> Suppress … the work of the great geniuses who emerged from the Church … and say if you do not also suppress the magnificent work of constituting French unity, as well as the most imperishable monuments of the national language. [22]

---

* "Dover Beach," 1851.
† In 1898, Cornély briefly reviewed a book about Nietzsche, *La philosophie de Nietzsche* by Henri Lichtenberger, in *Le Matin* of February 21, without remarking on Nietzsche's profoundly anti-religious attitude.
‡ Cornély does not mention the claim of the Chinese to have invented gunpowder. Of course, invention, like living organisms, may display convergent evolution.

This is, to say the least of it, a highly schematic history of France, omitting mention, for example, of the Wars of Religion that were responsible for up to three million deaths. At this stage of his intellectual development, Cornély appears to suggest that the only real French are Catholic, and that anyone and everyone else is some kind of unwelcome foreign body.

Cornély compares the foolishness of republican France in religious matters unfavorably with the cunning of Bismarck. The latter was anti-Catholic, but he was above all a German nationalist and saw the unwisdom or impossibility of persecuting the Catholic Church to which so many in the newly established German Empire were attached. He wanted to retreat with honor from his previous anti-Catholic stance, and an occasion to do so presented itself.

A dispute occurred between Germany and Spain over the Caroline Islands in the Pacific, over which both countries claimed sovereignty. The claim of Spain was historic, that of Germany economic. The two countries were almost on a war footing over slivers of land that were of vital interest to neither of them, and Bismarck feared that, in the event of war, France might side with Spain, revenge for the defeat of 1870 still being uppermost in many Frenchmen's minds. Bismarck therefore had the brilliant idea of appealing to the pope as arbitrator of the dispute, to which he knew that Spain could not but agree, and which would at the same time reconcile Protestants and Catholics in Germany. He knew that the pope was more likely to be sympathetic to Spain than to Germany, but the compromise agreement suggested by the pope nevertheless secured Germany's economic interests. Bismarck had killed two controversies with one suggestion.

For Cornély, Bismarck's resort to the pope to solve his problems was evidence of the continued moral authority of the Church and a harbinger of the future. In the light of history, this now seems to us absurd, but Cornély thought that in the struggle between the papacy and the fundamentally secular Italian kingdom, the former would win in the end, both because of its spiritual force and its popularity with the people. The pope might for the present be a virtual prisoner in the Vatican, but Cornély imagines what would happen were he to leave his prison and walk the streets of Rome:

> The Pope leaves the Vatican and appears in Rome: there would be a delirium of enthusiasm to make the Coliseum shake on its ancient foundations. On that day, there would not be enough flowers in all Italy to carpet the road over which the horses of the Pope's carriage passed. And that evening, the intoxicated Romans would go to bed thinking that it was enough for the Pope to have shown himself to put – may I be forgive for the vulgar expression – His Majesty Humbert [the King of Italy] in the pocket of his white soutane.[23]

But what of France, which has allowed Germany to steal its thunder where the Vatican is concerned?

> Will it [France] leave all to its conqueror? will it cede it to the Pope as it has ceded its provinces [Alsace and Lorraine]? Will it, on the contrary, get rid of its sectaries who are killing it, throw into the abyss all that morbidity of atheists and free-thinkers that is determined to mutilate its history? will it put in the same bag the hypocrites who are underhandedly preparing the separation of Church and State and the violent proponents of it who want to do it straight away?
> Will France think of all that?
> France? she is still relying on the rotten fluid in which

the electoral bacilli are agitated. She examines the infu-
soria. When the culture is finished, she swallows the
nauseating soup. And she inoculates herself once again,
perhaps, with the disease that will carry her off.[24]

These are hardly words of religious tolerance or political
pluralism, nor are they those of someone who one would
have expected later to be a defender of Captain Dreyfus, but,
however rarely they do so, minds can change.

Most of the rest of the book does for Leo XIII what his
previous book did for Alexander III. Cornély is susceptible
to the grandeur both of ceremonies and surroundings, to a
degree unusual in a modern intellectual. Beauty can dilute
critical faculties just as critical faculties can vitiate if not
beauty itself, the impact of beauty. *Pace* Keats, truth is not
beauty, nor is beauty truth: but the search for both is necessary to a life well-lived.

Cornély ends his book as follows:

I will be satisfied if the reader, in reading my book, experiences the emotions that I felt: for, having no pretense
to have written a literary work, I have hoped to write a
work of Catholic faith and religious propaganda.[25]

I think even believing Catholics today will find Cornély's
book somewhat embarrassing, but in its defense (I surmise)
might be urged the violence of anti-religious and anticlerical propaganda of the time. Church and state were not formally separated in France until 1905, and I have in my
possession a book published on the centenary of that event,
reproducing the anticlerical propaganda of the time. What
surprised me about this propaganda was that, if I had
looked only at the graphics, I might have concluded that it
was a book about anti-Semitic propaganda of about the

same era. The same visual tropes were used by the anticleri-
cals and the anti-Semites, for example of an evil looking spi-
der floating over the world, its thin legs encompassing it in
its grasp, or a hook-nosed man (a priest rather than a Jew)
enticing small children into the false shelter of his cloak.
Conspiracy theory breeds conspiracy theory.

Whether Cornély had changed before the Dreyfus affair,
or whether the Dreyfus affair changed him, I do not know,
but there is no doubt that it was a turning point in his life
and that he subsequently played an unexpected (and honorable) role in it – unexpected by me, that is.

In 1894, Alfred Dreyfus, the scion of a wealthy Jewish
family from Alsace, who was a captain in the army, was
arrested on a charge of spying for Germany, the charge
based upon a forged document found in a wastepaper
basked in the German embassy in Paris. The real author was
a Major Esterhazy, a louche and unprincipled man, always
in need of money and ready to do anything.

Dreyfus was found guilty by a miliary court and sent for
life to Devil's Island, off the coast of Guiana. There he rotted
for several years, while a campaign was mounted by intellectuals, journalists, politicians, and one notable supporter in
the army, Lieutenant-Colonel Picquart, to overturn the
unjust conviction. This took years, and Dreyfus was not
fully rehabilitated until 1906. In the meantime, the whole of
France – or that part of it which read the newspapers – was
transfixed by the affair.* Even until relatively recently, *l'Affaire* meant the Dreyfus *affaire*: every other *affaire* has to
have a name appended to it.†

---

* What agitates the educated or intellectuals does not necessarily agitate
everyone else. After all, everyday work must continue to be done.
† *L'Affaire* is a book by the Academician Jean-Denis Bredin (Paris: Julliard-
Fayard, 2nd ed., 1993), the author obviously not thinking it necessary, even
at that later date, to say *which* affair.

For fourteen years, Cornély had written for *Le Gaulois*, the conservative journal owned by Arthur Meyer, an Alsatian Jew who believed in Dreyfus's guilt, which had incorporated Cornély's failing *Clairon*. Whether Meyer truly believed in Dreyfus's guilt, or appeared to do so to emphasize his primary loyalty to France, is impossible to say, but there was a parting of the ways between Meyer and Cornély in 1897, when the latter published an article favorable to the case for Dreyfus's innocence. Cornély left *Le Gaulois* (which in its time had published work by such famous authors as Maupassant and Octave Mirbeau) to return to *Le Figaro* as political editor.

Cornély's departure evidently created a minor stir in the little world of Parisian journalism and was written about in the way that journalists are still inclined to take storms in their professional goldfish bowl as being newsworthy in themselves. Meyer wrote an article in *Le Gaulois* which, while appearing to defend Cornély, was less than complimentary to him, saying, or implying, the very opposite of what it appeared to say:

> There was never, I repeat, a shadow of disagreement or misunderstanding between M. Cornély and me. Hardly had the small cloud of this unhappy Dreyfus case sown trouble everywhere that I had to respect the doubt he had about the guilt of the former captain.... This could not have been the reason for his decision [to leave *Le Gaulois*]. I do not want to believe, whatever he says, and according to his own words, that he wanted to assure his independence in his last years.... I would rather believe that in becoming the political director of *Figaro*, he was tempted by the idea of "monarchizing" the newspaper that he now entered.[26]

Of course, by "securing his independence," Cornély could have meant either his financial or his editorial independence, or both.* Meyer insinuates that Cornély could have continued at *Le Gaulois* while writing pro-Dreyfus articles, but this seems to me improbable, given the firmness of Meyer's opinions, and by writing that he *preferred* to think, rather than that he straightforwardly *did* think, that Cornély was motivated a desire to change the editorial policy of *Le Figaro*, Meyer implied precisely the opposite. In essence, Meyer was accusing him of financial greed – a motive completely unknown to later generations of journalists, of course – and the ambiguity of his wording preserved him from the possibility of an action for defamation.

In 1900, Cornély published his last book, *Notes sur l'affaire Dreyfus*. This book, 646 pages long, consisted of his articles on the case written for *Le Figaro*. Apart from the first two articles, written in 1894 and 1897 respectively, the articles (on my count, 240 of them) were written between August 2, 1898, and September 20, 1899, that is to say twenty per month. This in itself is testimony to the degree to which the case gripped, if not the imagination of the country, then the imagination of the literate part of it.†

In the preface, Cornély again disclaims any great merit for his work:

> Journalists write for the next day.... Once [their articles] have lost their freshness of topicality, it is very rarely that

---

* "His last years" is a phrase of some interest in this context. When Cornély went to *Le Figaro* from *Le Gaulois*, he was fifty-two. What is considered old age varies with life expectancy. He had ten years almost to the day to live.

† "Apart from Paris the country was little interested. As yet the provincial bourgeoisie were immune.... The provincial artisans and the peasants were never roused." Guy Chapman, *The Dreyfus Case: A Reassessment* (London: Rupert Hart-Davis, 1955), 199.

they are worth much. That is why the idea of reprinting in book form the prose that I have scattered through the press for almost thirty years never occurred to me. But numerous friends have asked for the lines that I have devoted daily to the Dreyfus affair in a convenient and permanent form. I hope this has been done according to their wishes![27]

The effect either of age, or of the affair itself, moderated Cornély's views. He remained a monarchist, but a much less strident one, pouring far less scorn on those with whom he disagreed than he had done formerly. Perhaps he realized that the republic was there to stay and that monarchism in France was a lost cause, like a glass shattered into a hundred fragments. Moreover, his attachment to France was greater than to any political dispensation under which it was ruled.* He was above all a patriot.

The book has the virtues of its defects. For those who know little of the affair, it can have scant meaning. The affair itself was simple in outline but of byzantine, or soap-opera, complexity in detail, so that the cast of characters is immense and changing in the way that a kaleidoscope changes. From the beginning of the affair in 1894 to the time of the end of the book, there were seven prime ministers, eight ministers of the interior, and eleven ministers of war. You would have to be a specialist academic historian, or someone suffering from Asperger's syndrome, to follow all the permutations. And that is all without following the intricate intrigues of all the other characters, louche, cowardly, heroic, upright, equivocal, as the case might be.

---

* President Sarkozy, not generally regarded as a deep thinker, felt it necessary more than a century later to point out that the history of France and of its achievements was longer and greater than that of the republic.

The virtue of the book is its immediacy. It is history in the making, as it is made. The writer does not have the intellectual luxury of hindsight or of knowing the denouement of the events he describes – if, indeed, events can be said to have a denouement, for their effects may reverberate down the ages, and history will have no end until the final extinction of mankind. To read a book like Cornély's on the Dreyfus affair is a valuable reminder to purist contemporary judges of our predecessors that life is lived forwards rather than backwards and that wisdom (or goodness) after the event is but a poor type of wisdom (or goodness). One man's view of present events is no more than that, of course, is inherently very partial, and can serve only as one piece of a vast mosaic if we wish to know history as "it really was," that is to say in its totality: a vain hope but one to which we constantly aspire. We all have a view of history founded on a larger or smaller number of pieces of the mosaic.

Cornély emerges rather well from the book. He describes the fevered atmosphere of the time, at least among the newspaper-reading and polemic-susceptible class, and he tries constantly, and unexpectedly in view of his book about Rome, to act as a febrifuge. He wanted his compatriots to fix their minds more narrowly on the questions at issue: was Alfred Dreyfus guilty of espionage or not, and was he justly condemned or not? (These questions are related but not identical: a man may be guilty but unjustly condemned, as well as unjustly exonerated.) He comes across as coolheaded, while everyone around him is losing his head – but it is easier to preach moderation than to practice it.

As a patriot, Cornély was anxious that the honor and prestige of the army – almost the only institution that united the country after 1870, notwithstanding its catastrophic defeat – should be preserved. He therefore tried to walk down a middle path between those who said that if

Dreyfus were innocent, the army was rotten to the core, and those who said that, whether he were innocent or guilty, the army's initial condemnation must be maintained because the morale of the army was more important than the fate of any individual (especially a Jew).

182

Cornély knew that Dreyfus was innocent, that the case against him depended entirely on a document that had undoubtedly been forged. A "secret dossier," which allegedly contained further evidence against Dreyfus that could not be revealed in public for reasons of national security, and whose existence was an argument employed by those who believed in Dreyfus's guilt, was also bogus; it contained nothing. During Dreyfus's initial court martial, this secret dossier had been available to the prosecution, which used its alleged contents as a reason for Dreyfus's conviction, but the documents in it (which were juridical nullities) were not made available to the defense, which could easily have shown their vacuity. The failure to disclose the contents of the "secret dossier" was enough by itself to show that the conviction of Dreyfus by the military judges was unsafe because it self-confessedly relied on a total violation of elementary legal principle. Cornély draws a comparison with what Lady Bracknell called "the worst excesses of the French Revolution":

> Certainly no member of my family was condemned by the revolutionary Tribunal, even if this tribunal sent cobblers and marquises, coachmen and counts, domestics and duchesses, pele-mele to the guillotine. But if the profound and lowly humility of my ancestors protected them against contact with judges who condemned with no warning, I have all the same a horror of these barbaric practices, and I leave to some of our gentlemen,

great-grandsons of their victims, the sublime virtue of praising them.[28]

This is very strong and obviously refers to the fact that some of those who insisted on Dreyfus's guilt, believing in the value of the "secret dossier," whose evidentiary value they took on trust, were aristocrats.* This marks something of a change in Cornély's attitude to aristocrats, whom previously he had treated as if, simply by virtue of the possession of a title, they were superior persons not only socially but morally. (Of course, the opposite view, that titled persons are inherently corrupt, is equally prejudiced and unjust.)

183

Over and over again, Cornély describes or alludes to the state almost of delirium to which the affair has reduced Parisian society. On their invitations to dinner parties, hostesses would add that they desired that the *Affaire* not be brought up during the evening for fear of it destroying the pleasure of the event.† In many ways, what he describes is reminiscent of contemporary America, where people of differing views – there being only two possible – can barely inhabit the same room for a short while without, at least

---

* Including the Marquis Melchior de Vogüé, uncle of one of the writers who is the subjects of this book. He is also mentioned in Cornély's book *Le Czar et le Roi* as having attended the funeral of the Count of Chambord, otherwise known as King Henri V.
† There was a famous cartoon in *Le Figaro* in 1898, titled *A Family Dinner*. In the first panel, a large extended family sits round the dinner table with the paterfamilias at its head, raising his index finger and saying, "Above all, let us not talk about the Dreyfus affair!" In the second panel, we see the table completely wrecked, an intellectual-looking gentleman strangling a female relative, a gentleman with a black eye, a lady trying to stick a fork into the neck of an old gentleman she is holding face down on the tablecloth, the paterfamilias violently haranguing a young man, etc. The legend is "They talked about it."

metaphorically, coming to blows. The dichotomization of opinion was almost complete.

The affair had the effect of destroying critical faculties: almost everyone took up a position and stuck to it, employing any old argument to defend it:

> We all resemble – practically all of us – the old dyspeptic captain who drank his milk wearing spectacles with green lenses so that he could think he was drinking absinthe ...[29]

At the end of this piece written on November 6, 1898, seven or eight years before the complete rehabilitation of Dreyfus,* Cornély says: "Therefore, we must wait, smiling sweetly, for the end of this strange illness that is to intelligence what colorblindness is to sight."[30]

It would take a very literal-minded person not to notice some analogies with our own fevered ideological disputes that are about empirical matters only to a slight degree, mere facts being grist to our ideological mill rather than the foundation of our ideology.

The controversy was destructive of pleasure. There was a lull in it while the appeal court decided whether there should be a retrial, those both for and against such a retrial saving up their energies to attack one another once the appeal court's decision was known. "That is why, nothing interesting having happened, I savored for some days the pleasure, of which we shall soon be deprived, of not talking about the affair."[31]

Perhaps the most impressive thing about Cornély was

---

* Perhaps not quite complete. I dine sometimes in Paris with a man, a *Polytechnicien*, a statistician and musicologist, very erudite, who believes still in Dreyfus's guilt.

his ability to change his mind, for no reason that I can find
other than the effect of the subsequent evidence upon him.
We should like to think that, as the rational animal, this is a
commonplace phenomenon among us, but the fact is that it
is rather rare. Here is what Cornély wrote at the outset of the
affair, after the court unanimously found Dreyfus guilty:

> Without doubt this affair is very disturbing to the mind.
> It shows us that a highly educated man [Dreyfus], whose
> frequention of intelligent people, familiarity with what
> is purest and most elevated in French society, possession
> of a fortune with a straight path in life without obstacle,
> was unable to prevent him from committing the lowest
> crime.[32]

At this point in the affair, December 23, 1894, the danger
seemed to Cornély to be that people would conclude from
Dreyfus's guilt that the French army was rotten with spies
and traitors:

> That there has been a traitor in the French army proves
> nothing against the French army. The Apostles were
> infinitely less numerous than artillery captains, all the
> same, there was a Judas among them, and his treachery
> did not prevent them from conquering the world.[33]

Initially, belief in Dreyfus's guilt was then almost universal.
It is worth remembering that at this time the socialist leader,
Jean Jaurès, after whom there is almost no town in France
without a street named, was outraged not by the unjust conviction of Dreyfus, but by the fact that he was not shot, which
leniency he took as evidence of unfair discrimination in
favor of the rich. As a deputy in the Chamber of Deputies,

instead of contenting himself with the facts, he attacked the court-martial and the Government, which could have ordered Dreyfus's execution but had refrained merely because he was a rich bourgeois.* [34]

186

The other deputies were outraged by this, and "Jaurès rushed back to the tribune roaring abuse at a Government which protected cosmopolitan speculators and liars masked as patriots." [35]

This brings to mind the Stalinist anti-Semitic slur that Jews were "rootless cosmopolitans," and as far as I can tell Cornély never wrote anything that came near to it in anti-Semitic connotation; Jaurès, moreover, seems to have adapted slightly Hamlet's moral aperçu: treat each man after his desert and who 'scape the firing squad?

It is only fair to point out that Jaurès also changed his mind, though if his original wish had been granted, it would have been too late for Dreyfus.

As the affair progressed, Cornély became more and more scathing of the injustice committed:

Everyone knows that ever since Dreyfus was sent to Devil's Island and entrusted to the paternal surveillance of M. Lebon [a notorious sadist], the organizers of this voyage remained astonished at the fragility of the means they had employed to obtain this magnificent result. Laubardemont, I believe, said: "Give me two lines of a man's writing, and I will have him hanged." This sweet

---

* Actually, the difference between a death sentence and incarceration on Devil's Island, or in the other French penal settlements on the coast of Guiana, was not very great, given the life expectancy of the prisoners once transported. It might well have been that Dreyfus's determination to survive was strengthened by the injustice done him. If he had been guilty, he might have lain down and died.

judge has been outdone, since we have deported and dis-
honored Dreyfus with a few lines of Esterhazy's
writing.* [36]

There is magnificent, controlled rage here, the irony more
devastating than a dagger-thrust. I think Cornély deserved
his noble tomb.

---

* Laubardemont was a judge under Louis XIII who sent at least seventy-
five supposed witches to the stake and was notoriously willing to find
whatever his political masters wanted him to find. He plays a role in French
history similar to that of Judge Jeffreys in English.

Jean-Richard Bloch

(1884–1947)

IN PÈRE LACHAISE there is a little area or corner set aside for dead communists, as if communism were a religion separate from that of everyone else buried there and believers had a different kind of afterlife from the bourgeois dead. Among those interred in this corner are the traitor, deserter, fugitive from the justice, apologist for mass murder, dictator-in-waiting, leader of the French Communist Party, and deputy prime minister of France, Maurice Thorez.*

Near his tomb is that of Jean-Richard Bloch, novelist, essayist, travel writer, newspaper editor, and playwright. He was widely published and well-known during his lifetime, but in the preface to an anthology of his work published in 1948, the year after his death, the great poet (and fellow communist) Louis Aragon lamented that he was already less and less read, that he had become "more a name than a writer, more a political being than a human being."[1] Thirty-three years later, a book by Jean Albertini was published with the title *Avez-vu lu Jean-Richard Bloch?* (Have You Read Jean-Richard Bloch?), to which the obviously expected answer was "No." Albertini's book begins:

---

* At the end of the war, Thorez had his French nationality — which had been removed because of his traitorous conduct and desertion — restored, and de Gaulle included him in his government for the sake of social peace. The communists were then the largest single party in France, and there was the real possibility of a civil war, which the inclusion of the communists for a time in the government obviated.

To publish and present a choice of Jean-Richard Bloch's work is first to try to contribute to a reparation. For his whole oeuvre has suffered the scandalous punishment that is inflicted by the bourgeoisie and its institutions (the universities, publishers, newspaper, etc.) on those who take the part of the people: that of *organized* silence.[2]

189

This paragraph is itself interesting, for it is clearly written by someone of the orthodox communist mentality that subsisted in France right up to the second year of Mitterrand's presidency (at least). For the writer of it, the bourgeoisie and people are two clearly defined species, four legs good and two legs bad; moreover, there is a distinct flavor of conspiracy theory about it, as if a directing committee of the bourgeoisie were engaged upon a plot to prevent the republication of Bloch's work. Be that as it may, the essential point is that, by 1981, his work was forgotten even by the reading public. There was a slight revival of interest in him at the end of the last and the beginning of the present century, with a colloquium in 1997 at the Bibliothèque nationale, whose proceedings were handsomely published five years later.[3] The editors in their foreword say:

Few of his books are easily accessible to the ordinary reader,* and despite a recent revival, his rediscover has not participated in the more or less successful publishing "coups" of these last years of authors either forgotten or little known.[4]

---

* This is not strictly true. The last time that I looked on a secondhand bookselling site, AbeBooks, there were 511 copies of his books for sale. Of course, if he suddenly became very popular, they would soon be exhausted.

There was even for a number of years an active association for the study of Jean-Richard Bloch's life and work, but it ceased activity for good in 2015, and must surely have had very few members.* Whether the oblivion into which Bloch has again fallen is definitive, I cannot of course say.

190

Bloch had an interesting but tragic life. Like Dreyfus, he was born into the Alsatian Jewish bourgeoisie and grew to adult consciousness in the heyday of that affair. He was thus simultaneously privileged and subject to adverse prejudice.

He studied unsuccessfully at the École normale supérieure and then performed his military service for a year in the company of, among others, the future Nobel prizewinner for literature Roger Martin du Gard. He returned to study at the Sorbonne, where he failed literary studies and switched to history and geography instead. After graduation, he taught for several months in Poitiers, but, with the help of family money, he abandoned teaching for the life of letters and founded a small magazine, *L'Effort*. In 1907, he married Marguerite Herzog, the sister of the writer André Maurois.

In 1912, he published his first book, a volume of six stories titled (after the first of them) *Lévy*. He completed his first and most celebrated novel ... *et Cie.* (... & Company) while in Florence and volunteered for the army in 1914. He was wounded three times, suffering from the after-effects, both physical and psychic, for the rest of his life. He was one of twenty-five survivors of a company of one hundred soldiers.

After the war, thanks to inflation, his private income evaporated and living by his pen became difficult. He published another novel, *La Nuit kurde*, "Kurdish Night," but most of his work now consisted of political and social essays

---

* Its headquarters was in the rue Stendhal, in the Twentieth arrondissement, where my wife and I considered buying a flat, instead buying one about two hundred yards away.

and travel books, of which he published several. Always a socialist, he moved further to the left and joined the French Communist Party. He spent several months in the Soviet Union in 1934 and visited Spain at the outbreak of the Civil War. In 1937, he founded and edited, with Louis Aragon, the newspaper *Ce soir*. After the occupation of France, while the Soviet Union was still allied with Nazi Germany (supplying it with war matériel right up to the invasion), he managed to obtain a safe conduct across Nazi Germany to Moscow. He stayed in the Soviet Union until 1944, broadcasting in French from there. He returned to France in that year.

One of his daughters, who had joined the Resistance, was caught by the Gestapo, taken to Germany, and there beheaded. His son-in-law was likewise caught and tortured to death. His mother, aged eighty-six, was deported to Auschwitz and gassed there.

In his last years, Bloch became a complete and uncritical apologist for Stalin. His last book, published posthumously, was a hagiography of that terrible man.

One might have thought that the eponymous first story in his first book, *Lévy*, was exaggerated or melodramatic, had it not been so prophetic. Twenty-six years before the Kristallnacht in which Jewish-owned shops in Nazi Germany were vandalized and destroyed by anti-Semitic mobs and Jews were attacked in the street, all at the instigation and with the complaisance of the authorities, Bloch's book describes a similar event that took place in Poitiers in 1898, in the immediate wake of Colonel Henry's suicide during the Dreyfus Affair.*

---

* Henry cut his throat in his prison cell after having been forced to admit that he had forged a document that was vital in Dreyfus's conviction. There was widespread anti-Semitic rioting in France immediately after Henry's suicide. I have not found any specific reference to riots in Poitiers, but it is likely that such riots, or such a riot, took place.

The protagonist of the story is a traveling salesman of bicycles, Valentin Loubatié, recently given the west of France as part of his pitch. Lévy has a bicycle shop in the city, and his family are the only Jews there, apart from the newly appointed teacher in the lycée. When Loubatié visits Lévy for the first time, Lévy asks him to stay to dinner with his family. Lévy and fastens the door to the living area behind the shop with a chain and appears fearful. Loubatié soon discovers why: a distant growling noise becomes the sound of a mob outside, shouting "Swine! Swine! Death to the Yids! Bastards! Pigs! Sell-outs! Traitors! Death to the Jews! Death to the Jews! We'll have the guts of Lévy and the ass of his slut! Yids! Swine! Prussians!"[5]

The rioters beat on the shutters and a heavy object smashes a window and lands on the table. "For God's sake, these animals are going to kill us!" exclaims Loubatié. "What have they got against you, then?" he asks.

"It's the suicide of Colonel Henry this evening.... Haven't you heard?" comes the reply.[6]

The face of one of the rioters appears at a broken window:

> Above the entrance, the ugly face of a thug rose up cautiously at the broken window.... He blinked in order to make out something through the dark of the shop. The entrance to the dining room was a rectangle of light. The thug looked in with caution. Then he burst out laughing.
>
> "Ha! The pigs are at the back in their sty. We only have to set fire to it. We'll get them as we wanted!... Set the fire! We'll get the Yids and the bicycles they've stolen!"

Other voices shout that they'll burn the guts of the Yids and "take back" the bicycles. The thug has climbed to the window on a ladder held by two companions, but the ladder begins to move. He shouts, "Hold it, you below, you piles of shit!"

> He lost his balance, and instinctively grasped the rest of the glass that was still in the window frame, cut himself, swore and disappeared, like a puppet at a puppet show.[7]

This was almost exactly the scene that I once witnessed myself at a literary festival in Lewes, when Antifa demonstrators prevented the speaker who was scheduled to speak after me from speaking. The demonstrators were not anti-Semitic – at least, not at that precise moment – but they were driven by the same type and degree of hatred. This hatred is a kind of beast in the lair of the human heart, waiting its occasion to be unleashed and frolic in the ruins that it produces.

The mob continues to threaten, bang on the doors, throw things. Loubatié saves the day by taking out the pistol he has with him and declaring firmly: "I'll put a bullet in the head of the first of you who enters, the first who throws something. I'm not a Jew, but I'm not just going to die like a dog."

Interestingly, Loubatié contrasts himself, an Aryan (the term he uses) with the Jews:

> The tall man [Loubatié] with a neat black beard, brown eyes and clear skin, felt himself to be truly of a superior race. The word Aryan came back to him. He did not know what it meant. But he understood that he did not want to die and that these people [his hosts] would let their throats be cut like sheep.*[8]

---

* This notion, of course, caused a controversy when Hannah Arendt published her account of Eichmann's trial in Jerusalem.

When the riot is over and the shop wrecked, Loubatié departs and takes the first train out of Poitiers. He returns only ten years later, to find Lévy has in the meantime become an important commercial and political personage there. His son is a student at the École normale supérieure in Paris, giving him sure entry into the French elite, Lévy's only regret being that he has abandoned altogether his Jewishness (which amounts, in Lévy's case, only to adherence to a few rituals, not to any profound religious belief). Loubatié finds Lévy at a café with all the political notables of the Radical and Socialist parties of the town. Bloch writes with a certain detachment: "These gentlemen were of every physical form: but the French *Homo politicus* is of a type whose uniformity has already attracted the attention of zoology."[9]

Lévy's rise to prominence and prosperity (the last line of the story informs us that he has taken over his competitor's store) only ten years after a near-pogrom is a sign of moral progress, but there is within the story a caution against facile optimism. Within the Lévy household is an old man, a furrier called Davidowitsch, who fled first Russia, then Poland, arriving in France as a country of asylum, only to experience a near-pogrom soon after. During the anti-Semitic disturbances, Lévy says "Can we stay here … ? We so believed that this time it was for good." Davidowitsch replied: "There is nothing lasting for the people of God. When they flee from here, then they flee from there, and from everywhere, in a life that is a flight without end."[10]

Loubatié, at that time, suggested that they leave for the Argentine and return when things have calmed down, but Lévy tells him that it is impossible, he has loans to repay.

Ten years later, when he returns to Poitiers, Loubatié meets Davidowitsch again:

"You haven't left, then, Monsieur?"

"Left?"

"For Buenos Ayres?"

"I am naturalised French ..."

"So you're going to stay, permanently?"

Davidowitsch did not think it worthwhile to answer a question about permanence. It was a category for which his brain had no place.[11]

In view of the author's subsequent family history, the story "Lévy" has great poignancy.

Another story in the book, "Le Vieux des routes" (The Old Gentleman of the Road), relates an imagined outbreak of plague in Poitiers. Plague is the most literary of all epidemic diseases, and the theme was taken up again by Camus thirty-five years later. Like Camus, but less successfully, Bloch invests the outbreak of the disease with metaphorical, and not just literal, medical meaning.

Having recently experienced enforced isolation as a response to epidemic illness, readers of Bloch's story today – if there were any such persons – would no doubt find resonance.

At the outbreak of the plague, a symbolic punishment of the city for having been ungenerous towards a tramp, Poitiers is cut off from the rest of France.

A cordon sanitaire forbade all communication between the affected area and the rest of the Republic. You could return there, but not leave. Those who tried to flee were pushed back into the circle of death by the flash of bayonets. The stations were closed, the roads cut off, the post suppressed, an embargo pronounced on all persons and things coming from the epidemic's area. The telephone remained the only link by which the two worlds communicated. In the interior of the circle [of death], the houses were burnt, the cadavers incinerated, the survivors washed down in formol, and thirty militarized doctors patrolled the four affected boroughs to the sound of a drum, in the name of the Public Safety. The troops of the cordon sanitaire used their cartridges; four certain executions, with an implacable savagery ... crushed the vestiges of resistance. A Deputy [of the National Assembly] protested that one couldn't prevent him from taking the grievances to Paris of the population that was still unaffected; he was incarcerated, and as he tried to escape, he was deliberately shot dead with a revolver by a doctor who knew that he was himself infected and who succumbed the next day.[12]

Law and order breaks down; the poor pillage the rich, and the rich wreak their revenge on the poor. But the epidemic ends, as epidemics always do, and four men among the eight hundred survivors discuss what they have just lived through. "No one will ever understand us again, we are alone on Earth," says one. "These hundred and thirteen days have emptied all the days to come of their savour," says another.[13]

These indeed are the sentiments of many people who have survived some extraordinary catastrophe.

Will the world after the epidemic be better, the same, worse? The four men have the discussion that was commonplace even before the end of the COVID epidemic – the French novelist Michel Houellebecq combining two possibilities by saying that it would be the same, only worse.

The last book that Bloch prepared for the press, *Moscou–Paris* (Moscow–Paris), was published in April 1947, the month after his sudden death in March of that year, and thirty-five years after his first book was published.

By then he had turned himself into an apologist, if not an actual mouthpiece, for Stalin. There are probably few more striking examples of the individual voluntary servi- tude of an intellectual than that of Jean-Richard Bloch, and the reasons for it are of some psychological interest. He was, after all, a gifted, highly intelligent, cultivated man of many personal virtues. After his death, the novelist and essayist Georges Duhamel, like me a doctor, pronounced a eulogy for him in the Académie française (to which Bloch was never elected), despite the deep disagreements with Bloch that Duhamel had had. He said of his that he was happy, friendly, and profound, noble and exemplary, pure and serene.[14]

Even allowing for the convention that one does not speak ill of the (recently) dead, but also taking into account the fact that Duhamel could have remained silent and that Bloch had severely criticized a recent book of his, these words of praise seem to me sincerely meant and probably true.

How, then, do we account for Bloch's support of a regime that suppressed freedom to an extent unprecedented in recent times and was responsible for the deaths of millions of people, a question all the more pressing because Bloch had personal experience of that regime, hiving lived under it for nearly five months in 1934 and for forty-four months between April 1941 and December 1944?

The answer, I think, is that Bloch was a religious man without a religion. He therefore sought transcendence in the secular field or plane. His search was strengthened, but not in the last analysis determined, by his personal suffer- ings. He was a socialist before the First World War, when he witnessed not the decimation, but the near-extinction of his own generation, in a war that was suicidal on all sides. Suf- fering is reduced by explanation and meaning, which makes it at least bearable: so Bloch was susceptible to finding an explanation and a meaning in life, the more total the better.

Marxism and faith in the Soviet Union (which at the time meant faith in Stalin) answered the call. It also must have made his losses in the Second World War somewhat more bearable: they did not die in vain.

198

Unfortunately, there is also a less flattering explanation of his slavish adherence to the Stalinist regime, namely the human weakness of vanity and the gullibility that it can induce. Bloch's vanity, and that of his wife, were necessary conditions of their voluntary enslavement to the regime, which had become expert in deceiving intellectuals such as they.

Bloch was invited to the Soviet Union, as a fellow-traveling sympathizer and possible agent of influence, in 1934. In France he was tolerably well known as a writer and intellectual (and two of his novels had been translated into English), but in the Soviet Union he was positively lionized and treated as if he were world famous. He was completely taken in, and he never realized that he had been so deceived:* probably it would have been too destructive of his self-esteem if he had realized it.

The fact is that he was very easily deceived because he wanted to be deceived. By 1934, the Soviets were experts in manipulating the impressions of Western intellectuals who were at least halfway there already, and who were (often justifiably) critical of their own societies.†

The Soviet methods were both crude and subtle. The Soviets understood the vanity and easily flattered self-importance of Western bourgeois intellectuals. The crude

---

* Unlike Gide.

† The classic work on the deception and self-deception of western intellectuals who visited the Soviet Union, and later other communist states, remains Paul Hollander, *Political Pilgrims* (New York: Oxford University Press, 1981).

method was to put them up palatially and feed them royally. Because they consorted with Soviet intellectuals while being so royally lodged and fed, they swiftly came to the conclusion that such intellectuals were very well-treated by the regime, which therefore must have esteemed intellectuals highly (when, that is, it wasn't killing them), unlike Western governments which left such intellectuals to eke out their existence as best they could, which often wasn't very well.

In her chapter in the book about Bloch published in 2002 by the Bibliothèque nationale, Ludmilla Stern makes the technique abundantly clear, drawing her information from the letters of Bloch and his wife at the time:

> The visit of the Blochs was organised by the Soviet government, and they were received in luxurious conditions. The newspapers emphasized the importance of the visit of "the illustrious French writer," and his portraits were numerous. "They perform marvels for their guests," wrote Marguerite Bloch of the "comrades" who arranged everything: their journey across the USSR, the welcome at the station, the whole stay. Their room at the Hotel Metropole was a "real nabob's place, with sitting room, piano, bathroom." "We have never been so well-treated while paying nothing." They lived their voyage to the Caucasus in a private carriage like "a fairy tale," while their companion, Louis Aragon, was taking a cure on the Black Sea coast "that his own money would not allow him to do in France." All the same, the Blochs [who would normally have felt guilty about such luxury] enjoyed "a situation unimaginably comfortable, we are less disturbed by it than elsewhere," for they were persuaded that the Soviets – and above all writers – enjoyed similar privileges.[15]

As for the food, the plenty and quality of it: "They were daz-zled by the sumptuous party of "an incredible luxury and abundance," organized in honor of the writers at Gorky's."[16]

200

This was written, be it remembered, in the year following the worst of the Ukrainian famine (in the territory through which Bloch traveled). Bloch persisted in his view that there had been plenty in the Soviet Union because he had never personally experienced any shortages. But he knew full well that they existed: in a letter to Romain Rolland dated December 2, 1934, he wrote, "The big event of the day ... was the suppression of [ration] cards for bread and flour.... It is the prelude to the progressive suppression of the coopera-tives, norms, and limitations of sales, the lowering of prices on the open market; visible sign of the abundance that is not for today, but for tomorrow ..."*

In 1947, he could still allow to be published the follow-ing, describing his arrival in Moscow shortly before the Nazis invaded the Soviet Union: "Only a few days were left for us to marvel at splendors of peace, of a brilliantly lit cap-ital, of shops bulging with groceries and other goods ..."[17]

Bloch's account of his arrival in Moscow is sketchy, to

---

* The source is Roland Roudil and Antoinette Blum, *Romain Rolland et Jean-Richard Bloch Correspondence (1919–1944)* (Dijon: Éditions Universi-taires de Dijon, 2019), 381. I hesitate to criticize so painstaking and schol-arly an edition, but I could not help but notice something distinctly odd that perhaps was intended to exculpate slightly, or at any rate mitigate the guilt of, these two writers' Sovietophilia and their de facto approval of the murder of millions. When posting footnotes about Soviet figures of the time unknown to most readers, and all within a handful of pages, the edi-tors delicately refrain from mentioning that they were shot, as if execution were too trivial a fact to be included in any potted biography: for example, Andrei Bubnov, Vsevolod Meyerhold, Alexander Arosev, Sergei Dimanov, and Mikhail Koltsov (and two of their wives into the bargain, presumably just be on the safe side). That Bukharin was shot is mentioned, perhaps because it is so widely known a fact that to omit it would have been noticed. Bloch knew or had met all these executed men.

say the least. In the memoirs of Jean Cathala, a diplomat, literary scholar, and translator of Solzhenitsyn, who also spent the war years in Moscow, the author recounts his meeting with Bloch after the latter's arrival in Moscow. Cathala having told him that, when he was twenty, he had liked one of his novels, Bloch replied that he, Bloch, remained a writer, certainly, but he now wrote only to serve: "articles for *Sovinformburo* diffused in the foreign press ... etc."[18]

Bloch told Cathala that on the way by train from France to Russia, he had stretched his legs in Berlin station and was able to see the effectiveness of the RAF's bombing raids, from one of which the opera house was still smoking. Cathala says:

> I swallowed the questions that I was burning to ask: one doesn't go through Germany to the Soviet Union without passing through Poland; one doesn't see the Berlin Opera from the platform of the station; the protection of the [Soviet] Union of Writers does not exonerate one from having to present oneself to the Occupation authorities ...[19]

Cathala says that on the Frenchman's arrival he abstained from any demonstration that might infringe the neutrality of the country that had offered him asylum, and that the Hitlerian aggression had astounded him as it had astounded everyone else.*[20]

As far as I am aware, Bloch never published a single word in public alluding to the repressive nature of Stalin's regime,

---

* It is almost certain that Bloch's decision to leave France for the Soviet Union saved his life. He was refused a visa to the United States, but he could have gone to Chile, where one of his sons had fled. He preferred the Soviet Union as a destination.

though he was aware of it from early on. In 1936, he wrote to Romain Rolland, with whom he carried on a correspondence for forty years:

> I keep quiet out of respect for the admirable work accomplished in the USSR, because the positive outweighs the negative so greatly that one must say or do nothing that can be used against the socialist state.[21]

The Molotov–Ribbentrop Pact caused some French communists to have doubts about the Party, with its strict allegiance to Stalin and the Soviet Union, the official line being that, up to the invasion of the Soviet Union, the war has simply been between two competing imperialisms and therefore a matter of indifference to communists. By then, Bloch's adherence to the Party, to Stalin, and to the Soviet Union was of mystical intensity, and like a Stalinist Tertullian he wrote: "It is when you will believe that you understand least that you will be the nearest to understanding."[22]

This attitude rendered his faith compatible with absolutely anything; indeed, it was the only way such a faith could survive knowledge of the most evident realities.

The first third of *Moscou–Paris* is taken up by a travelogue of his journey from Moscow back to France by DC-3 aircraft, a journey that took eighteen days, with the author arriving in Paris in January 1945. As the war was then continuing in Eastern Europe, the route had perforce to be circuitous. Planes flew much lower in those days than they do now, of course, but even nowadays something instructive can sometimes be seen from the air: for example, the border between the Dominican Republic and Haiti on the island of Hispaniola is clearly demarcated from 30,000 feet, being green on one side and brown on the other. Perhaps Bloch's most surprising observation en route is his contrast between

Italian and French colonialism in North Africa, to the advantage of the former. In Tripolitana, under the Italians, the land was colonized by men, in small parcels; in Tunisia, under the French, the land was colonized by capital, in large holdings.[23] For Bloch, capital and men were locked in a struggle that only the Soviet Union had overcome.

That Bloch, despite his intelligence, erudition, and talent, was – or at any rate became – as credulous as any Latin American peasant in the presence of a miracle-working Virgin is proved by the subsequent essays in this book. To take but one example of his credulity: he describes how in 1937 he attended in Moscow a congress of "progressive" writers, among them Aragon and Malraux, and how, when Malraux was returning by air from the Caucasus to Moscow, the aircraft in which he was flying had to make an emergency landing in a field at an obscure collective farm on the way:

> The peasants ... ran to give assistance to the crew in distress. One of them looked at the passenger, approached him and said "Comrade Malraux, I think."

By comparison with this, Stanley's meeting with Livingstone was quite by chance. Bloch continues:

> This peasant of a farm lost in the immensity of Russia recognized the young foreign writer at first sight by having seen a photograph of him in one of the innumerable newspapers that had published the debates of the Congress, day by day, in all their details.

The moral is clear:

> Transpose the event to our Western world, so proud of its level of culture, so disdainful of Soviet barbarism.

204

> Imagine young American writer, aged 30 to 35 years,
> forced to land near a farm in the Auvergne or the Limou-
> sin, a few weeks after our International Congress of
> Writers in June, 1935, in Paris. How many of our peas-
> ants knew of this Congress? How many would have fol-
> lowed the debate from far off? How many would have
> been made familiar by photograph with the faces of the
> foreign participants? * [24]

What a voluntarily deluded baby Bloch (at the age of sixty-two) must have been not to have realized by 1947 that all spontaneous meetings for foreigners in the Soviet Union were highly organized and orchestrated!

Two and a half years after his death, Bloch's projected book about Stalin was published in *Europe*, the French liter-ary magazine founded by Romain Rolland, and a little later in book form. It was his testament from the grave, so to speak; how far the published version departed from his wishes, or what would have been his wishes had he lived, is something that cannot be known.

Nevertheless, the sycophancy towards the figure of Sta-lin was far from unusual among French intellectuals of the time. Paul Éluard, in his *Ode à Staline*, written on Stalin's death, wrote:

> Stalin rewards the best of men
> And gives back to their labor the virtue of pleasure

---

* This kind of delusion persisted for many years after Bloch's death. In 1989, I accompanied a group of young British people, all highly educated and all admirers of North Korea, to Pyongyang. We were taken on a tour of what was alleged to be a maternity hospital. It was quite clear that, spot-lessly clean, noiseless, and with no medical staff, patients, or babies in view, it was nothing of the kind. Yet the group was very impressed by the level of maternity care in North Korea.

For to work to live is to act on life
For life and men have chosen Stalin
To symbolise on earth their boundless hopes.*

Two days after Stalin died, the other great poet of the time, Louis Aragon, attended a meeting at the National Conference of the French Communist Party with "the news within me like a knife":

> Every time someone shook my hand, he and I ... feared to look each other in the eye, to see there the tears which would have made it impossible to contain our own.... It was stupid, this shame.[25]

Bloch died six years, less ten days, before Stalin, so he was deprived of the opportunity to contribute to this edifying literature. He did not, however, require death to give the impression of a life, Stalin's, without blemish. For him, Stalin was simple, human, full of humor, but unbending in pursuit of the interests of the working class:

> He is the author of the Constitution of 1936, one of the wisest and most balanced in the world; he caused interior peace in a sixth of the earth's surface and all the prosperity possible in the circumstances to reign there; ... and if one adds that a year and a half after the end of hostilities and the victory over Germany the reconversion of the efforts of war to those of peace, such that abundance is in the process of being reborn there and

---

* Staline récompense les meilleurs des hommes
Et rend à leurs travaux la vertu du plaisir
Car travailler pur vivre est agir sur la vie
Car la vie et les hommes ont élu Staline
Pur figurer sur terre leurs espoirs sans bornes.

that being born there also is one of the only countries
which knows no unemployment, no anxieties and no
social problems; that he has created a country where, as
he has said, life has become better, life has become more
joyful; a country where work, as he has said, has become
a matter of dignity, heroism and glory; if we think of all
this, we can imagine the stature that history and posterity will confer on the man about whom this is said.[26]

According to Louis Aragon who published a long memoir of
him six years after his death, Bloch underwent something of
a conversion experience when they visited the Soviet Union
together in 1934.[27] Here I think Aragon was right, because a
book of Bloch's published only the year before, in 1933, was
not only *not* communist, but was implicitly anti-communist.
After the end of the first war, he became a prolific essayist,
and *Offrande à la politique* (Offering to Politics) is the third
of his series of collected essays, its subtitle being "Third
Essays Better To Understand My Times."*

The book begins with an *Avertissement*, something like a
preamble and warning:

No dogma, no party affiliation, no obedience [to a doctrine or party], if it not intellectually honest. A man who
applies himself to difficulties, insofar as they appear to

---

* My copy is inscribed by the author "*à Charles Nicolle, son ami qui l'admire,
J-R Bloch, oct.* 1933" (to Charles Nicolle, his friend who admires him, J-R
Bloch. Oct. 1933). Nicolle was one of the greatest figures of the heroic age
of bacteriology and parasitology, rightly winner of the Nobel Prize for his
extremely important discovery of the transmission of typhus by the body
louse. He made several other important discoveries also. Though I am not
a strong believer in graphology, I may here admit that Bloch's handwriting
suggests a man of strong character who valued clarity very highly. His correspondence was vast, that with Romain Rolland filling two long volumes.
His private letters are extremely legible.

him, does not impose on them a preconceived order, and does not bend before a pre-established conclusion.

He then quotes Vauvenargues to the effect that "few errors would persist, if expressed clearly."[28]

The first essay in the book is titled "La guerre est en nous" (The War is Within Us). This is an analysis of the causes of war that is about as un-Marxist as it is possible to be. It is not Freudian either, though it is psychological. It consists of an address to university students who were members of an association in support of the League of Nations, the trial run of the United Nations, and about as effective in the prevention of war. By suggesting that war answers to certain deep-seated human needs or propensities, Bloch implies that permanent peace, however desirable, is unlikely. Whether he is right or not in this, he has not yet succumbed to the fatuous utopianism of Marxism, according to which there will (inevitably) come a time when all human conflicts will be dissolved in the acid of the dialectic.

Bloch speaks as a man who has known war, not as an armchair theorist. He has known in his own flesh and blood the horror, but also the excitement, of war. He could be said to have been an enthusiast for it, insofar as he was the survivor of a unit nine-tenths of which had been killed, and yet he insisted on going to the front not once, but three times, and was wounded on all three occasions.

Do not believe that the accounts of former combatants, not even those who are most vehement again war are of a nature to persuade their hearers. Let us be wary of memory! Human memory is a dangerously optimistic faculty, foolishly moved. It has a strong propensity to efface disagreeable memories and increase the importance, the shine, of pleasant events. Examine yourself, consult your own experience. Do not bad memories play a much smaller role in your mind than good ones? Are they not surrounded by a much less luminous halo? [29]

208

This passage might be of interest to future historians of mentalities, for certainly the propensity to remember happy events at the expense of unhappy ones hardly seems to be the predominant psychological characteristic of our own times, when dwelling on misfortunes, real or imagined, seems to be much more prevalent, the better to be able to pose to be a victim, victimization being the heroism of the age. In a way, this would not have surprised Bloch, for heroism of one kind or another, in however perverted a form, as well as excitement, is for him (at this stage in his intellectual development) a fundamental human need. This is very far from Marxist analysis, which declines to speculate on human nature, preferring it to be infinitely malleable so that a utopia would be possible.

Far from being a timid creature whom danger terrifies, man is so constituted that danger calls to him, attracts him, excites him, overexcites him. Far from being a natural coward, man is courageous. Man is the most courageous animal in the world. I would even say that he is a prodigy of courage, that he is a monster of courage. [30]

When I consider my own life, I realize that Bloch is right, at least if I am not an outlier as far as the rest of humanity is concerned. For quite a number of years, I sought out danger, partly as a diversion from psychological tribulations that had come to bore me. There is nothing quite like danger to help you to forget yourself and the unpleasant flutterings of your emotions. In my case, it was politically dangerous situations that I sought, not unusual feats of physical endurance, and I persuaded myself that it was to some higher purpose than merely courting danger. It is true that it provided me with a fund of memories on which I have drawn in the rest of my life, but it was the danger itself that was the immediate attraction.

209

Bloch goes on to give examples. Everything he says in this regard has the mark of common sense rather than of ideology.

> Hardly had social life been purged of the last vestiges of the ancient coarseness of manners – the feudal combat among the rich, arguments settled by fistfights among the people – than sport was needed to provide ardent young men with a substitute heroism. Sport requires a courageous indifference to certain types of pain and fatigue, a combative spirit, self-mastery. He who motorcycles, skis, or bobsleighs, even non-competitively, risks, if not his life, at least severe injury. I think equally of those intrepid young men who, on the faintest pretext, leave to cross the Sahara. I think of those who join polar expeditions. I think of the early aviators, of the crews of submarines. They are, all of them, far from being exceptions.[31]

Bloch goes on to cite the autobiography of Amundsen, the first man to reach the South Pole. He died in an air crash in an expedition in the Arctic Circle to rescue the Italian explorer General Nobile:

> He was the son of a petit bourgeois; his mother wanted to make him a doctor; he was fourteen when his father died. At that precise moment, the books of [Sir John] Franklin fell into his hands. This reading impassioned him. It influenced him for the rest of his life. Of all the

heroic Englishmen who, had, for four centuries, devoted fortune, audacity and the spirit of enterprise in courageous attempts to open the North-West Passage, none displayed more endurance than Franklin. "The description of his return from his expeditions moved me as much as everything I had read until then," says Amundsen. "He recounted how, for three weeks, he and his little band had fought against ice and storm, with no food other than some bones found in an Indian camp, and how, before reaching the outposts of civilization, they were reduced to eating the leather of their shoes to avoid dying of hunger. Stranger to relate, the passage in Sir John Franklin's account that struck me particularly was that which told of the sufferings that he and his men endured. I felt a burning ambition to endure the same suffering. Perhaps the idealism of youth, which often does not recoil in the face of martyrdom, caused me to consider an expedition in the Arctic Sea to be like a crusade. I, also, would suffer in the interest of a cause, not in crossing burning desert, on the road to Jerusalem, but in the glacial regions of the North, on the road of discoveries, in regions unknown!"

It is worth adding that Amundsen knew that, during his next expedition, Franklin disappeared forever, and that his bones were not found until many years later. This catastrophe itself only stimulated his determination to throw himself on the same perilous paths as the great Englishman.[32]

This has more in common with Freud's so-called death instinct than with dialectical or historical materialism, though it does not quite coincide with Freud's idea either. Franklin and Amundsen may have been extreme cases of the psychological tendency to which Bloch draws our attention, but some form of it is common and would explain the enthusiasm, and even joy, with which the outbreak of the First World War was greeted in Paris, Berlin, Vienna, and London, as if daily life in increasing prosperity were not ful-filling. Bloch himself was enthusiastic about it,* lost no time in joining up, believed that the war must be won,† and returned to the front even when not obliged to do so.

Bloch's book was published not long after Hitler's ascent to power. His analysis of this ascent is not Marxist. He says:

> The racist Germany does not want to be said to be a people among peoples. She is no longer an empire among empires. She does not look on itself any longer as liable to be bound to her neighbours by a game of contracts that suppose equality between the contracting parties. She is the chosen people. She is the only and remaining pure race in the world. She incarnates the only valuable accomplishment of the human species. She deifies and adores herself as the living receptacle of the Creative Will and Witness of the Divine Word on earth.[33]

Bloch points out the inadequacy of Marxism to explain all this:

> Hitler forces us to go back to Mohammed when we seek a predecessor and a model. It is by the example of the Arab tribes that the Germans allow themselves to be fanaticized. And the ethnic pride, the psychic passions, the will to power, the magic, the cults, the prophecies,

---

* As, at first, was the subsequently ardent pacifist and internationalist Stefan Zweig.

† As evidenced in the first volume of his correspondence with Romain Rolland, *Cahiers Romain Rolland No. 15: Correspondence entre Jean-Richard Bloch et Romain Rolland (1910–1919)* (Paris: Albin Michel, 1964).

even the idols, play a part in this tragedy as great as the famous material realities with which the pupils of Marxism content themselves. If one takes the Marxist theses to the letter and in their literal meaning, as all the strictly orthodox socialist parties have done for the past half century, it must be admitted that an event of this nature has left them far behind. The course of history and social development, such as the two Fathers of *The Communist Manifesto* had prophetically traced, has been diverted, and in ways and on matters that one could easily foresee.[34]

Indeed, by capitalizing the word *Pères*, Fathers, in the text, Bloch is surely expressing a certain contempt for them and their followers, suggesting that Marx and Engels were religious figures rather than the scientists they claimed to have been, and that their followers were devotees of a religious cult.

He adhered to that cult the following year, and surely Aragon, himself another adherent, was right in depicting Bloch's change as a *conversion* (though of course not naming it as such, for fear of tarring himself with the same brush).

It would be grossly unfair, therefore, to reduce Bloch's work or career to the level of the ill-written groveling to a totalitarian dictator that one might be tempted to do if one knew only his last works.

Inasmuch as he is remembered at all by literary historians, which seems hardly at all, it is mainly for what they think is his best book, the novel ... *et Cie.* It was written before the First World War but first published in 1918, and then in a definitive edition in 1925. It was translated into English by the first translator of Proust into English, C.K. Scott-Moncrieff, and published in the year of the translator's death, 1930. In his introduction to the novel, Romain Rolland compared Bloch with Balzac:

I make bold to say, without any reservations, that here is
the only French novel I know which is worthy to takes
its place among the masterpieces of the *Human Comedy*.
It is in the tradition.[35]

Since Scott-Moncrieff translated only works of high quality,
he must have had a high regard for the book too.

I am not of this opinion. I think the book too long and
overwritten, though this is not to say that it has no merits.
Some of its descriptive passages seem to me redundant and
obstruct the progress of the story. But let the writer who is
without faults cast the first stone!

Bloch returns to a theme similar to that of his "Lévy."
The novel is the story of the Simler family, Alsatian Jews
who, after the annexation of Alsace and Lorraine by the
Germans in the way of the defeat in the Franco-Prussian
War, chose French citizenship rather than German and
moved to the west of France to pursue their business as
cloth manufacturers.

The two sons of the Simler family's patriarch buy a disused factory in Vendeuvre in the west of France (it cannot
be the actual town of that name, which is not in the west of
France). The whole family then moves there from the little
Alsatian town of Buschendorf where they have a woolen
mill. Vendeuvre is ugly, dirty, and industrial, but deeply set
in its ways and resistant to new ways of working.

At first, the Simlers are scorned by the local manufacturers. There have never been Jews in the town before, but that
does not prevent the inhabitants from having prejudices
against them. When the Simlers try to join the club of town
notables, mostly cloth manufacturers or retired cloth manufacturers, the proposal is discussed by the members, all but
one of whom, Monsieur Le Pleynier, are opposed. Monsieur
de Challieres says, in response to Monsieur Le Pleynier:

Can you imagine Madame de Rauglandre, Madame Pommier, Madame Morindet, Madame Pierrotin, Madame de Challieres, receiving on their [visiting] days Mesdames – ahem! – Simler, and going to return the civility in their little parlor? Eh, you would not allow Mademoiselle Le Pleynier to call there, my friend! I am indeed losing my temper, but I have good reason. Anyone who has seen, as I saw, those bundles of old muddy shawls, those boots, those slimy parcels carried at arm's length, all those signs of sordid rapacity, would not even ask what Vendeuvre can mean to these people, except a halting-place on their road. They are tramps, gentlemen, and nothing more. It is regrettable, I say it aloud, that they have managed to insinuate themselves into the Poncet works [the disused factory that have bought]. Let them keep to themselves, and let us keep to ourselves. When they go, which will not be long, we shall cross ourselves, cross off their names, and continue as before. In the meantime, let us regard them as a foreign body that has found its way into our town, as though we were carrying a bullet in a wound.[36]

This reads both unpleasantly and realistically, and clearly has some kind of bearing on our present travails with immigrants, though it is not easy to specify what bearing. Is all and any feeling against immigrants, no matter their numbers or the culture they bring with them, to be regarded as a variation of Monsieur de Challieres' unpleasant and ungenerous speech? Is it always and everywhere wrong for the inhabitants of towns to wish to remain as they are? Immigrants themselves often turn against further immigration on grounds not very dissimilar from those of M. de Challieres.

The Simlers, however, establish themselves in the town,

and by dint of hard work and adaptability, soon become prosperous and then rich. They begin to swallow the competition. When the fashion in cloth changes, they – unlike the other manufacturers – change their production. One of the patriarch's sons, Joseph, even falls in love with M. Le Pleynel's daughter, and she with him, but because of prejudice, marriage between them is impossible. Interestingly, Bloch does not depict the prejudice on one side only: if anything, the prejudice against the marriage on the Jewish side is stronger even than on the Catholic. The love affair is abandoned, and Joseph marries a Jewess whom he does not love. The son of this marriage is a brilliant boy, Justin, who is offered a place at the École normale supérieur, but he turns it down after carefully calculating that he will make much more money by going into the family business. Bloch's depiction of the son's mentality might have strengthened the prejudice of Jewish mercenariness, but the calculation is hardly one than no one else ever makes. Indeed, it is not uncommon to read articles about which students from which universities make the largest salaries after graduation.

Interestingly, there is nothing very anti-capitalist about the book, at least not doctrinally so. One of the Simler relatives has immigrated to America and returned a multimillionaire. There is no suggestion that he has done so by chicanery or that he is a bad or cruel man. On the contrary, America is praised for its openness and energy in the creation of wealth.

Normally, doctrinaires become less so with age and experience. With Bloch it was the other way around. His travel book on Senegal, *Cacaouettes et bananes* (Peanuts and Bananas) is all but apolitical and has nothing of the ferocious denunciation of French colonialism of the books by Albert Londres or André Gide, for example.[37]

216

What accounts for, not to say excuses, Bloch's transformation into a mouthpiece for a regime that murdered millions and developed a form of oppression as great as any in human history? He grew up during the Dreyfus affair, which had a special salience to a young Alsatian Jew; he witnessed firsthand the slaughter of the First World War and was thrice severely wounded, living with the consequences of his wounds for the rest of his life; he lost his money in the post-war inflation; he saw the effects of the Great Depression; he saw the rise of Hitler. Perhaps he thought (or felt) that it was time for a bulwark against total despair, and instead of turning to a real religion, he turned to the ersatz one of Soviet Marxism (to which his political views already inclined him somewhat). Having made his choice, he could not face a further disillusionment and so twisted all evidence in order to preserve his faith.* This is not admirable, but perhaps it is understandable.

---

* So closely did he cleave to the Soviet line, which for ideological reasons made nothing of the anti-Semitic and genocidal aspect of National Socialist atrocities, that in a speech in 1946 on Nazism he did not mention it, although his own mother aged eighty-six had been consigned to the gas chambers. Michel Dreyfus, *L'Antisémitisme à gauche: Historie du'paradoxe, de* 1830 *à nos jours* (Anti-Semitism on the Left: History of a Paradox, from 1830 to Our Times) (Paris: La Découverte), 193.

Émile Souvestre
(1806–1854)

In his introduction Émile Souvestre's posthumously published last book, *Souvenirs d'un viellard: La dernière étape* (The Memories of an Old Man: The Last Stage), his secretary and son-in-law, Eugène Lesbazeilles,* quotes his father-in-law's estimate of his own literary worth:

> I know better than anyone what is lacking in what I write. The persistence of ideas and the rightness of sentiments do not at all suffice in art; something *flowing and diverse*, which I have always sought in vain, is necessary. I belong, in spite of myself, and whatever I do, to that Celtic land [Souvestre was Breton by origin] where the monuments are of rough stone…. A style of goodwill does not suffice to stamp a book with that seal that will make it live. In this regard, my ambitions have long since evaporated; I am convinced that for daily needs, water carriers are also needed, whose merchandise has no pretension to be bottled and labelled for use in distant consulates.

Lesbazeilles writes:

---

* His wife, Émile Souvestre's daughter, Noëmi, is now remembered principally for having been the first French translator of *Jane Eyre*. Souvestre's other daughter, Marie, was an early feminist and educator, who ran a school first in France and then in England, where she died. Eleanor Roosevelt was among her pupils.

Thus, his only ambition was to feel himself useful. All his efforts would be repaid, he would feel refreshed from all his labors, if he obtained the approval, with that of his own conscience, of good people, if on his solitary path he met kind opinions from time to time to encourage him. He had nothing more to wish for, his heart was filled with the pleasure of triumph, if he had won sincere affection, if he had received the testimony of some precious sympathy, if he had made himself loved.*[1]

It seems that Souvestre was unusually modest for a successful man of letters: and he *was* successful, even if his fame has not endured. Lévy published his complete works well after his death comprising fifty-four volumes, not including his plays, and for which there must have been a market.† In addition to novels and plays, he wrote literary criticism, essays, anthropological studies of Brittany, and history. Some of his books were translated into English or German, and he was possibly the most prolific French author of the nineteenth century apart from Balzac, Hugo, and Dumas. He did not, however, live the life of a celebrated man, as he might easily have done. According to his biographer, David Steel, he left no archive:

> There is no question of a biographer not considering his books, of not judging them. They are ... the only evidence of his life in many of its stages, a succession of rough menhirs – the metaphor is his – without under-

---

* Souvestre's modesty is reminiscent of Somerset Maugham's in *The Summing Up*, in which he places himself at the top of the second division of writers.

† Souvestre first appeared in print in 1829, when he was twenty-three. Thus, his literary career lasted twenty-five years, which means that, on average, he produced work filling two volumes a year.

growth, and encircled by silence as far as the daily existence of their author is concerned.[2]

The author of the biography continues: 219

> Audacious would be he who claimed to have read all of
> Souvestre, or even identified all of his work.... To read all
> of Souvestre is an impossible task (and sometimes, let us
> be frank, not worth it) that I do not claim to have
> fulfilled.[3]

If a man who must have devoted a considerable part of his
professional life to studying Souvestre says this, and if what
Lesbazeilles says is true, that Souvestre was principally a
teacher and a moralist, it might be thought – certainly,
I thought it – that he would not be much fun to read.

I was therefore pleasantly surprised that I found reading
Souvenirs d'un viellard interesting and (though not all the
time) amusing. To an unexpected extent, it speaks to our
times; I think it might even bear commercial republication.

Souvestre is a moralist, but one does not feel harangued
by him in an uncomfortably moralizing way. His novel is
episodic and has no overall plot; his protagonist and narrator, the *viellard* of the title, relates various experiences, none
of them very remarkable in themselves, and the moral that
is pointed is implicit in them, being on one occasion turned
against himself. The protagonist is neither saint nor sinner,
but an average man of his time and class. This doesn't sound
very promising, for we like protagonists to have a strong
character, but Souvestre is sufficiently good a writer to render the ordinary interesting.

Georges Raymond is a sixty-eight-year-old retired
teacher of law. He is widowed, lives alone, and has two children distant from the town in which he lives. Here it might

be worth mentioning that we should not nowadays call a man of sixty-eight *un vieillard*, but at forty-eight, Souvestre considered himself an old man and was preparing to retire to the country when he died suddenly. When, as I shall relate, Raymond has a college reunion, only five of his contemporaries are still alive, and though we do not know how many of them there were, we can assume that the majority are dead.

In the second scene, Raymond is at home when his servant, Félicité, enters after a knock on the front door.

"Monsieur," she says, "it's a monsieur ... who's asking for monsieur."

Raymond/Souvestre says she is the best servant in France – active, economical, faithful – but whose vocabulary contains "fewer words than the smallest pocket dictionary." Her entire "rhetoric" consists of tears or laughter that accompany her incomplete sentences.[4]

There is nothing critical in this, or condescending, there is only affection – just as there is nothing critical or condescending but only affection in "Barkis is willin'."* In fact, one of the themes, or targets, of Souvestre's book is intellectual snobbery that, at heart, is a form of pride. To be inarticulate is not to be a bad person, though it is not to be a good one either, but the evil that the articulate do is probably greater in scope that that done by the inarticulate.†

Later in the book, Raymond/Souvestre says:

---

* Charles Dickens, *David Copperfield*.

† It is worth remembering here Solzhenitsyn's words: "The imagination and spiritual strength of Shakespeare's evildoers stopped short at a dozen corpses. Ideology — that is what gives evildoing its long-sought justification and gives the evildoer the necessary steadfastness and determination." And there is no ideology without articulacy.

In general, we educated men don't understand much about purely practical people; whenever it is necessary to classify them, we always start with ourselves, we suppose that everyone must be like us; we judge the intelligence of our cook by her spelling.[5]

This is very well put; and I have to confess to having been guilty of this kind of error myself.

Raymond/Souvestre tries to deflate his own importance, for self-importance is the besetting sin of those who write:

Also, see what indignation arises when one of these vulgar [practical] activities leads to fortune or influence! With what proud irony we point the finger at these parvenus! What recriminations against a society in which a corner grocer enriches himself more certainly and quickly than the artist, the scholar, the writer! – As if this society lived only by books, [intellectual] problems, or statues, and had no need above all of ordinary workers! As if those most favored by chance ought also to be the most favored by men ...*[6]

Like most intellectuals, I am inclined to overvalue eloquence and sophisticated use of abstract ideas. Raymond/Souvestre brings such as I down to earth:

What strikes me is this cult of the word and the taste for saying everything well. Who gives to nations the leisure to sculpt and polish language? Where was the unlettered

---

* The truth of Raymond/Souvestre's point must surely have been revealed to many an intellectual during the COVID lockdowns, when distribution staff and others continued to go to work while the intellectuals stayed at home, where they would have starved had it not been for the low-paid.

class of that people whose herb-sellers recognized Theophrastus as a foreigner *because he spoke too well*? Who
ploughed, cut stone, forged iron, behind those who
applauded Sophocles or listened to Cicero? – Ask
Spartacus.*[7]

222

Raymond/Souvestre is worried about what he will leave
behind him. The merest mason or tiller of the soil leaves
something tangible behind, of use to his successors: but
what will a teacher of law leave behind?

The author and his protagonist are egalitarians, but not
of an ideological kind. Rather, he is a dust-thou-art-and-to-
dust-thou-shalt-return kind of egalitarian, though this does
not mean that it is without practical consequences.

His excellent servant, Félicité, falls in love with René, the
valet of his neighbor and friend Roger, and she tells him
that she wishes to leave his employ. He tries hard to dissuade her, using arguments which appear rational enough.
René, the valet, wants to open a shop:

> "And have you thought about the income from this shop,
> the insufficiency of your funds to make it prosper, and by
> what worries and privations you will be reduced little by
> little at complete poverty?"
>
> "In the name of God, sir, who has told you this?"
>
> "Experience! Look at all the poor girls who have given
> up comfort and security that they enjoyed in a good mas-
> ter's home to run the risk of a marriage. Just remember
> our neighbor Marguerite, abandoned by her husband ..."
>
> She interrupted me briskly.

---

* Theophrastus was a Greek philosopher born on the island of Lesbos who
was known for the beauty of his expression. Spartacus was a gladiator who
led a slave revolt against the Roman Republic.

"Ah! But René's – René's a good man."

"That's as maybe. But look at the little haberdasher on the corner, who has nothing to complain of in her husband, but can't feed her six children …"

"And such beautiful children!" Félicité said, her eyes dampened …

"But one day sooner or later, she will give them up to the workhouse," I replied cruelly, "because that's the ordinary fate of those brought into the world to suffer."

And the better to convince her, I called statistics to my aid…. I tried to put the Malthus's principal arguments to her in a way that she could understand…. The poor girl understood nothing of what I said, except that I disapproved of her marriage with René, and she began to sob.

At this point, Raymond tries to console her, saying that they would talk about it the next day.

"I'm sure Monsieur must be right," said Félicité, "but all the same I have faith in the goodness of God. He wouldn't have have forbidden the poor to be happy, and for that they must have the right to love each other."

"And who will guarantee the future for you?" I asked; "others have a family, a position, sufficient savings: but you?"

"We'll have Providence," she said, fervently joining her hands together.[8]

Raymond then reflects bitterly, as I am sure did others in such a situation:

Used to her submission, I was wounded by this sudden rebellion; I found ingratitude in the ease with which this type of association was broken which had united us for fifteen years; I said to myself bitterly that the most devoted and faithful of our servants cared only for the guaranteed bread and roof over their heads. By good treatment and trust, we believe they take root in our lives, to bind them to our destinies like humble friends. Illusion! at the first opportunity, the disguised slave breaks his chain. Nothing unites us with them, nothing attaches them to us; we hoped to make a great leaf of the family's tree, but they are nothing but birds hidden in the branches that fly at the first rays of the sun.[9]

If Souvestre himself had not experienced what used be called "the servant problem," this was a convincing attempt at imagining it from the inside. The misanthropy it expresses is intense, but it soon proves shallow, for, shortly afterwards, Raymond goes through the contents of his desk, and in the last drawer he finds the letters to and from his late wife, Louise, from the earliest days of their engagement and marriage. There are also the letters to and from his fiancée's uncle, whose ward Louise was:

Here are the drafts of my pleas to the uncle, in which the exclamation marks are as close together as the bayonets of an advancing column; then the uncle's replies, short, dry, fortified by unbreachable walls; a difficult discussion which can be summarized in this vulgar dialogue,

THE UNCLE: Sir, my [XXX] has no dowry.

ME: I know, sir; but I love her.

THE UNCLE: You also are without any fortune, sir.

ME: Sir, I admit it; but I work and I love her.

THE UNCLE: Think, sir, of all the trials and tribulations that the future might inflict on you.

ME: Oh sir! God will help us, and I must have courage; I love her! I love her! I love her!...[10]

The uncle has used precisely the arguments against Raymond's marriage that he himself employed to try to dissuade Félicité from hers. Raymond then reconsiders his attitude and in atonement for his unkindness to her agrees to pay for the marriage, though he is rich only by comparison with Félicité and René. Raymond reflects,

> Who knows if what I believed to be in her interest was not mine in disguise, or if I weren't horrified by this marriage because it left me without a servant, with all the nuisance of finding another? Alas! our own heart is a theater whose actors are the same as all the others: only good-for-nothings who play the role of hero.[11]

When Raymond was arguing against Félicité's marriage, he had all the appearance of sincerity, and believed himself to be sincere, and yet a short time later realizes that his supposed sincerity and his emotion were bogus. Here is a valuable lesson in self-examination, growing out of a plausible fictional situation. The lesson is pointed, but not with the kind of irritating directness that arouses our opposition. Surely, there cannot be many of us who, on looking back over their lives, have never played the part of a Raymond, and we needed no Marx or Freud to tell us that we often argue for our interest rather than for truth.

Raymond has indeed to find another servant (in that era it was unthinkable that such as he should be without one), and a man called Baptiste, who has been the servant of the late conte de Feral. The count was a disciple of Rousseau and has imparted his egalitarian principles to Baptiste. Raymond describes the count as having been a little bizarre, but with all the great virtues.

Baptiste comes to Raymond's apartment to be interviewed for the position. "He was a little thin old man, very

neat but formal. He wiped his feet three times before crossing the threshold of my study." That he wiped his feet three
times suggests a tendency of to obsessionality that is desirable in a servant. He introduced himself as "Monsieur Baptiste," and this soon proves to be of significance, for when
Raymond later addresses him as Baptiste, having agreed to
take him on, Baptiste corrects him by saying gravely, "Monsieur Baptiste."

> "Ah, you insist that I don't forget the word?"
> "For the same reason that I will never forget it in
> speaking to monsieur."

Raymond smiles at this. It is not what was expected of a servant seeking employment.

> "That might seem strange to monsieur," he [Baptiste]
> added calmly, "but I have my reasons."
> "And without being indiscreet, may I ask what they
> are, monsieur Baptiste?"
> "Certainly, if that would interest monsieur."
> "Very much."
> "Well, then. I believe that language influences habits,
> and that too great a familiarity in terms of address ends
> by becoming a lack of regard."[12]

Raymond asks him whether this was his own idea, and with
admirable candor and honesty Baptiste admits that it came
from the count, whom he regards as a sage, though he says
that experience has proved it true.

I think it still true. Where there is no formality, there can
be no distinctions, and no special regard for anyone. This
heightens social tensions rather than reduces them, for dis-

tinctions will be made one way or another, and when we live in a soup of informal and supposedly friendly equality, we find other less socially lubricating methods of imposing them. I am no uncritical admirer of President Macron, but when he insisted that a young man addressed him as *Monsieur le Président* rather than by his first name, he was absolutely right to do so. When my local Member of Parliament in England addressed me in a letter by my first name, he was absolutely wrong.

In England, at least, the social significance of different modes of address has not quite been lost. Some time ago, the Prison Department sent an edict to prisons to the effect that, henceforth, male prisoners (the overwhelming majority) should be addressed as *Mr.* Smith or *Mr.* Jones, as a means of expressing respect for them. Meanwhile, nurses and doctors were taught to address their patients by their first names on the grounds that it was friendlier. In fact, this default informality towards strangers already in a vulnerable and often humiliating position vis-à-vis others is an exercise in power rather than in friendliness. One might go further: the contrast between the way in which prisoners and hospital patients were to be addressed was an instance of Nietzsche's transvaluation of all values, or perhaps a fulfillment of Samuel Butler's satire *Erewhon*, where crime was treated as disease and disease as crime.*

Baptiste – Monsieur Baptiste, I now feel obliged to call him – elaborates on his, or the Count's, ideas.

---

* I used to tell the few medical students whom I taught that not only were they not to call or address elderly patients by their first names, they were not even to *think* of them by their first names. Admittedly, there is an awkward age between childhood and adulthood when it would be stilted to address people formally, but the liminal should not be made central.

"In ordinary domestic life, it seems that the master has only rights, the servant only duties; from which the former tend always to abuse, the latter to revolt."

"And what do you see as the remedy to all that?"

"Monsieur le Comte gave me to understand that there was only one: reciprocal respect. When the order is polite, there is nothing that can cause revolt. I didn't realize this before; I only found it hard to submit. Then, domestic service appeared humiliating for an old man. Monsieur le Comte taught me how to overcome all that."

"How?"

"By asking more for respect than for promises, and by making my services so useful that they are feared to be lost. When, as a servant, one's hair begins to go white, it is necessary to preserve one's dignity."

"You are right!" I exclaimed. "May God forgive me, monsieur Baptiste, for having smiled just now ..."[13]

Monsieur Baptiste does not demand material equality. He does not demand an equal, or even a greater, share of Raymond's wealth (which in fact is not very great). What he wants instead is full recognition as a human being, as a person with feelings, and not just an animated tool or domestic animal to be given orders like an obedient dog. There is nothing like disdain to provoke anger and fuel resentment, and the unfulfilled need for recognition in mass society is surely at the root of much morbid behavior, such as the covering of walls with graffiti. The demand for respect can, when frustrated, easily turn to violence and intimidation, when fear becomes mistaken for respect, and the demand for uncritical affirmation of whatever the person demanding it does. It is this deformation that monsieur Baptiste's insistence on being called *monsieur* is intended to obviate.

Being episodic, the book has no climax or denouement.

Of course, Souvestre did not live to complete it, but there is
no logical progression in it that could have led to a climax.
The last words that he wrote before his death were Raymond's blessing on a character, Armand, a young man, who
is about to set out on a journey:

> "Go, my dear child," I said to him, folding him in my arms,
> "I give you my blessing. May God keep you."[14]

Our loss of religious belief causes us to think that such
words must always have been unctuous and without real
feeling, at best a mere form of words. Reading Souvestre
reminds us that this is not so. The past really was another
country, where they not only did, but felt things differently.

Raymond was very happily married: the price of which
was deep and lasting grief when his wife died. The immediate period of grief is well, accurately, and movingly described:

> Before I was in her care, and she in mine: each of us was
> concerned only for the other; now I was going to be
> under the sad necessity of thinking only of myself. Oh!
> who could speak of this doleful household change in the
> hour of bereavement! It is above all once the first despair
> eases, once you regain possession of yourself and can
> look around you and understand; it is when your foot-
> steps echo through the empty rooms, that your eyes con-
> stantly meet some memory of the deceased; here a basket
> containing uncompleted work, there her favorite book
> still open at her favorite page; a little further, clothes
> that bear her imprint and recall her gestures; everywhere,
> what she has seen, what she has touched. Her memory
> floats around you and over all the furniture and on all
> the walls; it seems that she has gone out only for a few
> hours and will soon return; at every sound you cock your

ear, every time a door opens you look round as if she were going to appear; you cannot believe in the finality of this absence that has left everything in its place as though for a swift return. It takes a long time for the reality to penetrate your mind, for you to understand the irrevocability of this abandonment. It is then that your courage fails, that you collapse in a grief that has no other object than itself. Oh! how sweet memories are transformed into tortures! With what relentless persistence you go over, room by room, the deceased treasure! How you regret the days lost, the fugitive quarrels! How many regrets at having caused unhappiness to her whom you cannot now cause happiness! Ah! why doesn't the idea of this separation come to us during those wretched times, when our patience is at an end, when we lack understanding? Why, at the moment of causing a tear to fall, do we not tell ourselves: I am stealing from happiness a moment that will never come again; I am striking someone who is condemned to death.[15]

The answer to these last questions, perhaps is simple: that we live life forwards rather than backwards. But this is a very fine description of bereavement and grief, its despair and regrets. Souvestre must have been through it himself, for his first wife died after only a year of marriage, and their child too. Even someone who has not yet been through such bereavement can sense the truth of what he writes and knows that – unless he is completely free of all deep relationships – he will inevitably suffer something similar one day. Curiously enough, and for reasons that I cannot quite analyze, this realization, far from being depressing, is consolatory, and Souvestre, as he wished, performs a service to those who read him.

He is not an ideologist, however, drawing universal conclusions for the whole of mankind from his own experience. Raymond's friend Roger has had quite a different experience of marriage from his:

> Roger's widowhood did not at all resemble mine. Married to a woman who compromised his name, thwarted him in his tastes, he only began to live when he found himself alone: he forced himself never to look back.... This long trial had dampened neither his enthusiasm nor his good will; all that could be useful to humanity interested him. Arts, letters, science, nothing found him indifferent, nothing was foreign to him.[16]

The most amusing episode in the book is when Roger and Raymond have a dinner with the remaining three of their college friends (all the others having died). Raymond/Souvestre allows Roger to describe them:

> Beaulieu is a judge, a former Alcibiades, who thinks his wig conceals his sixty-seven years, wears a frill, and continues to show off the calves that he once had; then Lafort, an excellent man, who thinks he was born for literature because he has been found unfit for any other profession, and who speaks of Horace as if he were his contemporary, although he's only seventy; and last Hériot, younger by a year, but graver by ten, who believes himself profound because he takes snuff.[17]

There is division between these three and Roger about whether the old days were better, a form of the perpetual argument over the ancients and the moderns. Roger is a defender of the present; the others (Raymond being merely an observer) defend the past. Beaulieu, the judge, who according to Roger has read only one book by a lawyer, Brillat-

Savarin's *The Physiology of Taste*,* says as they sit down to dinner:

232
> We still feed, but we don't know any more how to eat, dinners have become simple shows of luxury or a pretext for a meeting; for us they're not an end but a means: what decadence!... Find me a man who, like Commander de Souvré could recognize sixty-four wines just by their bouquet, and distinguish the petits pois of Clamart from those of Épinay.

Roger says he hopes to God that there are no more like him, while Hériot agrees that there are not, as he rummages in his snuffbox "with the air that Newton might have had in searching for the laws of physics."[18]

Beaulieu sounds as if he is parodying me when I lament something that I claim was better in the old days, the old days being when I was young, or sometimes even before I was born. The discussion continues:

> "But," the judge began again, leaning back on his chair and throwing one leg over the other, "I maintain, my dear friend, that everything is disappearing in our world; that the dinners are less refined, women less beautiful, men less amiable ..."
>
> "How can it be otherwise?" interrupted Lefort. "We learn mathematics, foreign languages, and we forget Latin! which means that we don't know French. Our authors of today don't know the great precept of the law-giver of Parnassus:

---

* Jean Anthelme Brillat-Savarin (1755–1826) was a French judge who wrote the greatest treatise on gastronomy.

In short, the divinest author without his tongue
Will ever hold the lowest rung."*

And, all three uniting in a kind of plaintive choir to the
glory of the past, they began to regret its happy suppers,
its gavottes, its tragedies, its bouquets of Chloris,† its
guilds, its local assemblies and its tax-farmers ...
　　Lefort stood up, and taking the floor, proposed a
toast to all that had been and was no more.
　　"Never!" exclaimed Roger, at the end of his patience ...
　　"Devil take these retrospective elegies! Make your
homes in the ruins, if you like; me, I prefer new roofs."[19]

Such discussions, in essence, are not unknown today, a hundred and seventy years later, and will not be unknown in
another hundred and seventy.‡ In fact, I have had many
such discussions myself with my friends.
　　In another meeting between the old college contemporaries, they discuss a subject of perennial inquiry, that of
historical inevitability. Roger, the rationalist, is a determin-
ist. Whatever happens was bound to happen, as he explains
to Raymond:

He explained to me how the evolution of peoples was
subject to providential laws, and I believed him; he
showed me how society was like a permanently worked
field, whose harvests were proportional to the labor
employed, and again I believed him; he told me that

---

* A very loose translation of:
　Sans la langue, en un mot, l'auteur le plus divin
　Et toujours, quoi qu'il fasse, un méchant écrivain.
　　　　　　　　Nicolas Boileau (1636–1711), *L'Art poétique.*
† Chloris was the Greek goddess of flowers.
‡ Assuming that mankind has not destroyed itself.

geniuses are the expected forerunners who instinctively harness themselves to the direction in which they must drag the world, and I did not wish to contradict him. He showed me that wars were the most powerful agent of civilization; he declared that human affairs marched independently of individual efforts, of the revolts of consciousness, and that the victors were on the path of God, since they were successful, and I could not have been more silent: I rebelled against this providence that, like the Fate of the ancients, deprived man of his liberty and always made of the victim an enemy of the gods.

Raymond/Souvestre sums up this view of history very succinctly:

You look at which way the wind is blowing and you set your sails. Wasted effort! the vessel has its own inherent law which will direct it with or despite your help! – Therefore, no more admiration for fruitless devotion; no more pity for the defeated!

As to Roger:

The study of the Germans [the philosophers] had led him to a sort of providential fatalism which made him look at history as a great poem whose scenes were written in advance without our being able to do anything other than recite the role which had been allotted us.[20]

These passages could scarcely have been more pregnant with the disastrous history to come. It is unlikely that Roger/Souvestre had heard of Karl Marx* – they were probably

* Souvestre wrote these passages after Louis Napoleon's coup d'état, and

referring to Hegel – but they summarized to perfection the
Marxist view of history that was responsible for, or at any
rate accompanied, some of the worst massacres in history
and allowed, or encouraged, men to kill, maim, and torture
in the supposed knowledge that they were acting in accor-
dance with providential laws, and that therefore it was not
really they who committed the atrocities, but History.

One of the compensations of reading in old age is that,
having lived through much more than in youth, books reso-
nate in the mind much more also. This resonance is pleasur-
able even if the events brought to mind were once painful,
and what might once have seemed merely fictional, arbitrary, insignificant, or unimportant, takes on in age a depth.
"For a schoolboy," says Raymond/Souvestre, "an atlas is a
schoolbook. For an old man, it is a magic lantern."[21]

One passage, or episode, in *Souvenirs d'un vieillard* recalled
me to an episode from my own early life. Although Souvestre was what one might call an existential egalitarian – he
did not overvalue the intellectual side of life at the expense
of all others – he was certainly not anti-intellectual or
opposed to erudition. He has his narrator tell a story of his
schooldays that is of an honesty that suggests that it must
have had some autobiographical basis.

The beginning of the episode brings to mind *Madame
Bovary*, published, but not written, the year before *Souvenirs
d'un vieillard*:

I think I can still see him crossing our playground for the
first time, led by his mother, a poor pale-faced woman
with sloping shoulders, dressed in widow's mourning.
Although he was already big, he gave her his hand by

therefore after Marx wrote his tract on that event, but it is unlikely that
Souvestre ever read it.

childish habit, and we, who had interrupted our games to look at *le nouveau* [precisely employed by Flaubert], exchanged an ironic smile. On seeing the care given to the least details of his school uniform, the elegance of his manners, and the solicitude that impregnated all the movements of she who seemed to treat him as a treasure, the jester of our group exclaimed: "It's the Dauphin [crown prince]!" And we never called him anything else.[22]

But by the sweetness of his character and his seemingly effortless brilliance which he does not vaunt, being but the gift of God, le Dauphin wins the hearts of his peers. Alas, when it is time to take the final exams, he falls mortally ill. His delirium is movingly described:

he believed that he was under some solemn questioning that was going to decide his fate; he replied to imaginary questions, he explicated out loud the passages demanded, he commented on them with anxious hesitation.... All hope was obviously lost.*[23]

The last discernible words he utters – his dying voice stuttering – are a line from Virgil's Tenth Eclogue, given in French in the text:

Assez; l'ombre est fatale à ceux qui chante.

Enough; the shade is fatal to those who sing.†

---

* The memorizing and parsing of Latin and Greek classics, of course, took a preponderant part of the education of the day, at least in the upper echelons of society.

† In Latin, also given in the text: *Surgamus; solet esse gravis cantatibus umbra. Surgamus* means "let us arise"; *solet* means "usually," omitted from Souvestre's translation. Presumably, the Dauphin spoke his last words in Latin.

After these words, the patient "soon fell into that convulsive somnolence which precedes the final separation; another night passed, but the next day the rattle was gradually extinguished, and when the doctor arrived, all was over."[24]

How could this not take me back to the death of my friend, a kind and gentle boy, a year older than I and the same age as the Dauphin, who was a naturally brilliant scholar who, I am sure, would one day have made a real contribution to learning, but who suffered from severe asthma and a form of scaling of the skin called ichthyosis? His chest was deformed by asthma, and he often struggled horribly to perform that most elementary of tasks, to breathe. It was not long after a new bronchodilating aerosol, isoprenaline, had become available. It provided immediate relief but, as it turned out, at the cost of an increased death rate.

One day, after a short absence, I went to his house and asked for him. His mother opened the door.

"He's dead," she said, and told me the circumstances. He had had a severe attack and she called the ambulance service, which insisted bureaucratically on taking details, while in the background he uttered what were to be his last words, not those of Virgil, but "Don't you understand that I'm dying?" The ambulance arrived just as he died.

As it happened, he had a handsome, ne'er-do-well older brother, and she said something terrible that I have never forgotten, at least in the sense of being able to call it to mind: "Why couldn't it have been him?" she said. "Why did it have to be ... ?"

I fled, my legs shaking with emotion, and I never returned. The subsequent passage in Souvestre was painful, salutary, and consolatory reading:

The days following were sad.... I could not get used to this departure; but at last time did its work. More than a month went by: a new boy replaced he who had gone, and everyone resumed his activities.[25]

238   This is common human experience, a guilty necessity. Several times in my life, I have tried to keep the memory of a dead person foremost in my mind, but it never endures very long, as it will not endure after our own deaths. As Souvestre says, in another book of a very similar genre to *Souvenirs d'un vieillard*, *Un philosophe sous let toits: Journal d'un homme heureux* (A Philosopher Under the Roof: Journal of a Happy Man):

> We do not understand that other men live their lives for themselves. Each of us resembles the earth in the old system of Ptolemy, and wants the universe to revolve around himself.[26]

This book, published in a tumultuous period of French history, disdains to notice politics, as though great events were but the froth or spume on the surface of the ocean of life. The same is true of the *Souvenirs*. Consider the narrator-protagonist of the latter: he lived through the great French Revolution, the Napoleonic Empire and its wars, the monarchy of Louis XVIII and Charles X, the 1830 Revolution, the monarchy of Louis Philippe, the Revolution of 1848, the Second Republic, and the coup d'état and establishment of the Empire of Napoleon III, yet none of these great events is mentioned, even by implication, in the book. What get instead is the following, when the census taker visits the protagonist near the beginning of the book. The census taker asks him:

> "[You are] a former teacher of law?"
>> "Who thinks now only of teaching himself."
>> "Property owner?"

"Of a pension of two thousand francs that he has acquired after forty years of service."[27]

Thus the three revolutions, the several regimes, the two empires, the three reigns of two royal houses, the two republics are of less significance in his life than the pension he eventually receives, having loyally served under all of them. (The pension, though very small, nevertheless allows him to keep a servant, which would now be considered an immense luxury by the vast majority of people.) And thus beneath the revolutions, something more permanent persists; the revolutions are not total, and service in one regime confers obligations on the next. Moreover, for him to have been a teacher of law for forty years implies that there was continuity in the law, political revolutions notwithstanding. An advocate of 1820, say, could still practice in 1854, two revolutions and a coup d'état later. And yet at the same time, the great affairs of the world may affect us whether we are interested in them or not, or even if we think that the affairs of the heart and of daily life are vastly more important to us.

In *Un philosophe sous les toits*, Souvestre displays the same genuine sympathy for the poor and downtrodden as in the *Souvenirs*. His protagonist and narrator is a humble clerk in an office, a man of no great account, but of studious disposition, who lives in a mansard. One holiday, the Sèvres porcelain factory opens its doors to the public, and the narrator decides to go. In the train on the way, he shares a compartment with two sisters, and soon learns their history:

They were two poor girls orphaned at fifteen, since when they had lived as do all working women, with economy and in privation. Making fastenings for the same firm for twenty or thirty years, they had seen ten owners succeed each other and enriching themselves, without any change in their own condition. They still lived in the same room, at the end of one of those cul-de-sacs where the air and the sun never reach. They start to work before daylight and continue until after nightfall, and see the years succeed one another without any other event than the Sunday service, a walk or an illness.[28]

240

Such a life is (to us) incredibly circumscribed or constricted. They had never before been anywhere or done anything: by the time they reach Clamart, a suburb five miles from the center of Paris, they cry that "they didn't believe that the world was so large!"* [29]

The sisters had never been on a train before: it was for them what, perhaps, be a journey into space for most of us. "You should have seen their amazement, their fear, their courageous resolution!" Souvestre does not mock this absence of worldly knowledge, this lack of sophistication, in them. On the contrary:

Was there not something saintly in this ingenuousness that the absence of joys in life had preserved in them? Ah! Cursed be the first who has the miserable courage to attach ridicule to the name of spinster, which implies so many painful disappointments, so many difficulties, such loneliness. Cursed be he who finds in involuntary misfortune a subject for sarcasm ...[30]

This may be a little didactic for modern taste, yet I think it is deeply felt. Moreover, while we may suppose that no one

---

* I was reminded of the time when I hired a car in Colombia and gave a lift to a young peasant in the countryside. He asked me where I was from, and I told him that I was from England. "How long did it take to drive from there?" he asked.

lives the life of these two sisters anymore, surely you have only to look around you to see lives of quiet desperation such as theirs and people who must have suffered cruel mockery on account of their "involuntary misfortune" (a term that implies, incidentally and quite correctly, that people sometimes bring misfortunes on themselves, not blindly, but knowingly). I think Souvestre met the two sisters, or their like; he intuited the nature of their lives.

241

Their experience in the train is so well and sympathetically described that we all but enter their minds:

> The sight of the trees that ran past on both sides of the track caused them endless admiration. The encounter with a train that ran in the opposite direction, with the noise and speed of thunder, made them close their eyes and utter a cry; but all had already disappeared! They looked out, reassured themselves and marveled. Madeleine [one of the sisters] declared that such a spectacle alone was worth the price of the journey, and Françoise [the other sister] would have agreed if she hadn't thought, with a little dread, of the hole that such an expense had made in her budget. Those three francs spent on a single outing were their entire income for a week's work.[31]

This is the raw reality of poverty, not seen through any ideological lens but with the eye of genuine compassion.

At the factory, this narrator and the sisters come across a courtyard in which broken pieces of porcelain are thrown. One of the sisters finds a saucer that is almost unbroken and is decorated somewhat gaudily, but she is delighted to take it as a souvenir of what is possibly the most memorable day of their lives. She thinks that the saucer was destined for the king, forgetting that France is now a republic and that the Sèvres porcelain factory in effect mass-produces the stuff. The narrator says:

242

> I did not want to correct her by telling her that the factory's products were sold to everybody, that her saucer, before having been chipped, was the same as those in shops at twelve sous! Why destroy the illusions of this humble existence?... most often things are nothing in themselves; the idea that we attach to them is what gives the value. To correct innocent errors to return to a reality that is useless is to imitate the scholar who sees nothing in a plant but the chemical elements of which it is composed.[32]

This is full of humane feeling, and much more profound than Nietzsche's shallow view that life could and should be lived without illusion.

Un philosophe sous les toits is interesting from a modern perspective: among other things, it reminds us that Paris was cosmopolitan well before multiculturalism was thought of as a doctrine, and perhaps more surprisingly that even in those days power and celebrity was desired by many despite the high price paid for it, the constant exposure to the public eye and the risk of calumny, envy, hatred, and moral corruption. Visiting an old acquaintance, a high official in a ministry, the narrator concludes of the very powerful:

> They are but men, and if the exceptional life they have made for themselves is an insult to the dignity of others, it is a torture for them![33]

This is well known, but it has never inhibited men – or *some* men – from seeking fame and power.

These books are not great literature, perhaps, but they

can be read with pleasure and are rich in instruction whose
didacticism does not offend because it grows out of real life
situations and the lessons are not simplistic moral principles, as if the author were a moral Euclid. Souvestre calls
us to the exercise of judgment as well as to principle and is
therefore not a simple, boring drillmaster.

Considering these two books, the author's *Le monde tel
qu'il sera* (The World Such as It Will Be), published in 1846,
comes as something of a surprise. Two young people, Maurice and Marthe, are leaning out of their mansard window
one evening in Paris, when Marthe expresses the wish that
she could see the world in the year 3000, by which time all
the problems of humanity will have been solved. Maurice, a
young man of philosophical disposition, had previously
been trying to figure out how best to live:

He started as a result to study the works of those who put
themselves forward as the serious thinkers and sages of
their time. The first to whom he addressed himself were
the philosophers. The explained to him dogmatically
what was the relative and the absolute, the me and the
non-me, the causal and the phenomenal, by means of
formulae that had all the appearance of algebra without
its precision.... Philosophy concerned itself with nothing but grand principles, that is to say those that render
you neither happy nor better.

Maurice, little satisfied, turned to the legal theorists,
the historians, the jurists. They analyzed for him, in
their turn, the different constitutions, they commented
on the different [legal] codes! But under all these constitutions, the greatest number died of hunger while the few
died of indigestion; all the constitutions were deceptive
seas, on which perished the poor boats of the smugglers

while the great pirates went full sail ahead! This wasn't at all what Maurice was looking for; he turned then to the statistician and the economists.

These, who devoted themselves seriously to the question, led him for six months through their columns of figures, then they finished by telling him that all was the best it could be, and that all that was necessary was to leave all as it was ...

Maurice studied the socialists: Robert Owen, Saint-Simon, Fourier, Swedenborg! According to them, each had the obverse of Pandora's box: it was sufficient only to open it for all the joys of life to take wing among men; misery would remain at the bottom [of the box].

All this left Maurice confused: Able neither to accept nor reject all, he remained poised between half a dozen contradictory systems ...[34]

This is not very different, fundamentally, from our moral, intellectual, or spiritual situation today, notwithstanding the tremendous material advance that we have undergone since Souvestre's time. But Maurice, like his young wife. still believed in a glorious future, and that time and human ingenuity would solve all problems.

Having heard Marthe's sigh for the future, an elf, who has a visiting card marked John Progress, sitting on a contraption not very dissimilar from H. G. Wells's Time Machine, arrives and grants her her wish, transporting them to the year 3000. The world government has become the "United Interests," and its most important centers are in Tahiti and Borneo, now called respectively the Island of the Black Animal and the Island of the Budget (the latter being where everything is decided).

The ageing powerful races gave way to younger races. Civilization, transmitted like the lighted torch of a Saturnalia, passed from hand to hand, leaving bit by bit the point of its departure in the shade. New interests called human activity to different skies. Neglected Europe fell slowly into inertia and solitude, while America, then a younger country, absorbed into itself all the elements of life. The old world was nothing but a savage land, whose ruins modern societies exploited.[35]

This is out-Spenglering Spengler, and many years in advance of him too!

Like most imagined futurities, *Le monde tel qu'il sera* is not an attempt so much to guess in literal fashion what the world will be like, as it is a criticism of the present and a *reductio ad absurdum* of current trends. It cannot be said that Souvestre has a clear horrific vision, such as that of *Brave New World* or *Nineteen Eighty-Four*, and his book is therefore much less memorable. His criticisms seem more scattergun than clearly focused. Nevertheless, he sees the future as both deeply collectivist and radically individualist, which is an important insight.

In his year three thousand, for example, motherhood will have been abolished as primitive and babies will grow in hatcheries. The two time-travelers are taken by their guide, M. Atout (Mr. Asset) to a building with "the aspect of barracks, college and hospital."

"And this is where all the wet-nurses live?" asked Marthe.

M. Atout smiled.

"Wet-nurses," he repeated, "you're speaking of a custom of the barbarous centuries!"

"Then," replied Marthe, "the infants are raised by their mothers?"

"Hah!" interrupted [M. Atout], "that would be even worse. Civilization has made us understand the madness of such a waste of time and care. Here, like everywhere, we have replaced people by machines ..."[36]

At the entry to the building is the following notice:

UNIVERSITY OF UNITED PROFESSIONS
Institute for young boys and girls not yet weaned
FEEDING BY STEAM

Inside, the babies are located according to their position rather than by name, such as "Hall Jean-Jacques Rousseau, fourth row, compartment D,"* and are in tiny cages rather like those of battery farm chickens.†[37]

A steam pump sent artificial milk to each little cage at a regular time. The artificial milk called *supra-lacto-gune* or *perfected mother's milk* consisted of 15 percent gelatin, 25 gluten, 20 sugar, and the rest water. It was known to be excellent for babies because those babies, who were many, who refused to take it soon died. The regularity of the suckling by a system of tubes was intended to instill regularity of habits in the infants.

It must not be supposed, however, that by this method of raising babies that the society was an equal one. On the contrary, the growing children were given privileges according

---

* The choice of name is surely not a coincidence, given that Rousseau abandoned his five children.

† The book is amusingly illustrated by three artists, named on the title page as Messrs Bertall, O. Penguilly, and Saint-Germain. The picture of the battery farm for babies — which strongly resembles the only battery farm for chickens that I have ever visited — was by Bertall. Bertall, whose real name was Charles Albert d'Arnoux, Viscount d'Arnoux, was a well-known illustrator and a protégé of Balzac.

to the wealth of their progenitors, and their destiny was also fixed by phrenologists who determined their future profession by feeling the bumps on their heads almost as soon as they were able to walk. The values of the society were entirely commercial: profit was virtue and virtue was profit.

M. Blaguefort (Mr. Completejoke), a merchant, explains to the two visitors that he has "a fault, a very great fault in business," namely that he is too honest in his dealings. Maurice catches sight of a paper on which M. Blaguefort has written the recipes for the products that he sells:

> Recipe for pure chocolate: Take a third part red beans, a third part of bad sugar, a third part lard, flavor the whole with shell of cacao ...

> Recipe for honey: Takes some molasses and flour of rye, flavor with orange flower composed of salts of zinc, copper and lead.* [38]

The contradictory tendency both to a radical egalitarianism and an inflamed individualism and economic inequality is something that Souvestre foresaw, but through a glass darkly. His talent was not great enough, perhaps, to fashion his insight into one of the memorable dystopias of literature, but literature needs its foothills as well as its mountains.

---

* Lead acetate, called sugar of lead, which has a sweet taste, was once used as a preservative and sweetener, though it is toxic. There has recently been a scandal regarding fake honey imported into Europe from China — that is to say, honey adulterated with other syrups much cheaper to produce. One has only to look at the contents on the labels of highly refined and industrially produced foods to realize that Souvestre was hardly exaggerating.

Envoi

There is no end to what is worth reading.

1   Alice Brouillhet, *Sous le ciel africain: 52° à l'ombre (reportage)* (Paris: André Delpeuch, 1931).

2   Ibid., 9–10.

3   Ibid., 12.

4   Ibid., 12.

5   See André Gide, *Voyage au Congo* (1927), and Albert Londres, *Terre d'ébène* (1929).

6   Brouillhet, op. cit., 83.

7   Ibid., 83.

8   Ibid., 96.

9   Ibid., 68.

10 Ibid., 57–58.

11 Ibid., 7.

12 Alice Brouillhet, *Yamunâ le solitaire* (Paris: Éditions "Athena," 1922), 13.

13 Ibid., 33–34.

14 Alice Brouillhet, *La Dame de jade* (Paris: André Delpeuch, 1930), 9.

15 Ibid., 9.

16 Ibid., 10.

17 Ibid., 10.

18 Ibid., 20.

19 Ibid., 21.

20 Ibid., 21.

21 Ibid., 20.

22 Ibid., 20–21.

23 José Ortega y Gasset, *La Déshumanisation de l'art* (Paris: Éditions Allia, 2019), 10–12.

24 Brouillhet, *La Dame de jade*, 71.

25 Henry Bidou, preface to *La Colombe blessée* by Léone Devimeur Dieu-donné (Paris: Albin Michel, 1922).

26 Alice Brouillhet, *Les Héros sans gloire* (Paris, Limoges, and Nancy: Charles-Lavauzelle et Cie, 1927), preface.

27 Ibid., 30.

28 Ibid., 31.

29 Ibid., 32.

30 Ibid., 34, 37.

31 Ibid., 40.

32 Ibid., 36.

33 Ibid., 39.
34 Ibid., 39.
35 Ibid., 40.
36 Ibid., 40.
37 Ibid., 40.
38 Ibid., 40–41.
39 Ibid., 86.
40 Ibid., 89.
41 Ibid., 86–87.
42 Ibid., 87.
43 Ibid., 89.
44 Ibid., 89.

EUGÈNE-MELCHIOR DE VOGÜÉ

1   Anna Gichkina, *Eugène-Melchior de Vogüé: ou comment la Russie pourrait sauver la France* (Paris: Harmattan, 2018), 176.

2   Léon Le Meur, *L'Adolescence et la jeunesse d'Eugène-Melchior de Vogüé* (Paris: Éditions Spes, 1932), 30.

3   Ibid., 23.

4   Ibid., 22.

5   Ibid., 65.

6   *Journal du Vicomte Eugène-Melchior de Vogüé: Paris, Saint-Pétersbourg 1877–1883*, ed. Félix de Vogüé (Paris: Grasset, 1932), 12.

7   Le Meur, op. cit., 69.

8   Ibid., 70.

9   *Journal*, 173.

10 Ibid., 148.

11 Eugène-Melchior de Vogüé, *Syrie, Palestine, Mont Athos: Voyage aux pays du passé* (Paris: E. Plon et Cie, 1876), vii.

12 Ibid., viii.

13 Ibid., 8–9.

14 Ibid., 13–14.

15 Ibid., 14.

16 Ibid., 16.

17 Le Meur, op. cit., 75.

18 Eugène-Melchior de Vogüé, op. cit., 34.

19 Ibid., 89.

20 Ibid., 49.

21 Samuel Johnson, *The History of Rasselas, Prince of Abissinia* (London: R. and J. Dodsley in Pall-Mall and W. Johnston in Ludgate-Street, 1759), ch. 21.

22 Eugène Melchoir de Vogüé, op. cit., 58.

23 Ibid., 96.

24 Ibid., 98.

25 Ibid., 84–85.

26 Ibid., 235.

27 Ibid., 178.

28 Ibid., 182.

29 Ibid., 235.

30 Ibid., 109.

31 Ibid., 333.

32 Ibid., 211.

33 Ibid., 212, 213.

34 Ibid., 219.

35 E. Melchior de Vogüé, *Le Fils de Pierre le Grand* (Paris: Calmann Lévy, 1889), 3.

36 Ibid., 136.

37 Ibid., 198–99.

38 Ibid., 198.

39 Ibid., "Un changement de règne," 293.

40 Ibid., 294.

41 Félix de Vogüé, *Journal*, 225.

42 Ibid., 226.

43 Emily Dickinson, "Tell all the truth but tell it slant—," *The Poems of Emily Dickinson: Reading Edition* (Cambridge: The Belknap Press of Harvard University Press, 1998), 1263.

44 Eugène-Melchior de Vogüé, *Le Roman russe* (Paris: Plon-Nourrit, 1886), 112.

45 Jule Lemaître, *Les Contemporains*, sixième serie (Paris: Lecène, Oudin et cie, 1896), 328.

46 Eugène-Melchior de Vogüé, *Le Roman russe*, 293.

47 Ibid., 270.

48 Ibid., 270–71.

49 Ibid., 263–64.

50 Ibid., 282.

51 Alexander Boot, *God and Man According to Tolstoy* (New York: Palgrave Macmillan, 2009).

52 Eugène-Melchior de Vogüé, *Le Roman russe*, 266.

53 Eugène-Melchoir de Vogüé, *Les Morts qui parlent* (Paris: Nelson, n.d.), 5–6.

54 Ibid., 103–04.

55 Ibid., 110.

56 Ibid., 111, 116.

FRANÇOIS-VINCENT RASPAIL

1   Dora B. Weiner, *Raspail: Scientist and Reformer* (New York: Columbia University Press, 1968), 236, 263.

2   Jules Wogue, *Raspail* (Paris: Fernand Sorlot, 1939), 7.

3   Daniel Ligou, *François-Vincent Raspail ou le bon usage de la prison* (Paris: Jérôme Martineau, 1968), 8.

4   Weiner, op. cit., 1.

5   Georges Duveau, *Raspail* (Paris: Presses Unversitaires de France, 1948), 5.

6   Eugène de Mirecourt, *Raspail* (Paris: Gustave Havard, 1856), 23.

7   Ibid., 33.

8   Weiner, op. cit., 140.

9   On this, see F.-V. Raspail, *Médecine des Familles, méthode hygiénique et curative par les cigarettes de camphre, l'eau sédative etc.* (Brussels: Société Typographique Belge, 1845).

10 Mirecourt, op. cit., 88.

11 Ibid., 42.

12 F.-V. Raspail, *Reformes Sociales* (Paris: Bureau de Publications de M. Raspail, 1872), 35. This section, through page 58, contains an account of Raspail's trial and subsequent imprisonment.

13 Ibid., 35–36.

14 Victor Coste, *Lettre de M. Coste à M. Raspail sur l'Embryogénie* (Paris: Imprimerie de Casimir, 1830), 8.

15 Raspail, *Réformes sociales*, 19.

16 Ibid., 19–20.

17 F.-V. Raspail, *Mémoire à consulter, à l'appui du pourvoi en cassation de Dame Marie Capelle, veuve Laffarge, sur les moyens de nullité que présente l'expertise chimique, dans le cours de la procédure, qui vient de se terminer par l'arrêt de la Cour d'assises de la Corrèze, du 19 septembre 1840 ; rédigé, à la défense* (Paris: Bureau de la Gazette des Hôpitaux, 1840), 3–4.

18 Matthieu Joseph Bonaventure Orfila, Antoine Alexandre Brutus Bussy et M. Ollivier, *Réponse aux écrits de M. Raspail* (Paris: Béchet jeune et Labé), 1840.

19 *Procès de Madame Lafarge* (Paris: Bureau de l'Audience, 1841), 493.

20 See *Procès et Défense de F. V. Raspail* (Paris: L'Editeur des ouvrages de M. Raspail, 1846), 57.

21 Orfila, Bussy et Ollivier, op. cit., 20–21.

22 M. J. Orfila, *Traité de médecine légale, contenant en entier le traité des exhumations juridiques*, 4th ed. (1848), quoted in Roger Teyssou, *Orfila: Le doyen magnifique et les grands procès criminels au XIXe siècle* (Paris: L'Harmattan, 2015), 73.

23 Ligou, op. cit., 45.

24 Ibid., 50.
25 Ibid., 245.
26 Raspail, *Mémoire à consulter*, 86.
27 Ibid., 93.
28 Weiner, op. cit., 215
29 Raspail, *Mémoire à consulter*, 39–40.

ENRIQUE GÓMEZ CARRILLO

1   For this somewhat arcane dispute, see Julio César Anzueto, *Enrique Gómez Carrillo: ¿En Dónde Deben Reposar Sus Restos?* (Enrique Gómez Carrillo: Where Should His Remains Repose?) (Guatemala City: Universidad de San Carlos de Guatemala, 1968).
2   Edelberto Torres, *Enrique Gómez Carrillo, el Cronista Errante* (Guatemala City: Librería Escolar, Guatemala, 1956), 9.
3   José Luis García Martín, introduction to *Treinta Años de mi Vida*, by Enrique Gómez Carrillo (Madrid: Renacimiento Biblioteca de la Memoria, 2011), 16.
4   Enrique Gómez Carrillo, *Le mystère de la vie et de la mort de Mata Hari* (Paris: Eugène Fasquelle, 1925).
5   Ibid., 194–95.
6   Ibid., 199.
7   Ibid., 200.
8   Paul Webster, *Consuelo de Saint-Exupéry: La Rose du petit prince* (Paris: Le Félin, 2002), 55.
9   Anzueto, op. cit., 59.
10 Torres, op. cit., 329.
11 García Martín, op. cit., 11.
12 Enrique Gómez Carrillo, *Manuel Estrada Cabrera* (Guatemala City: Siguere & Cia, 1898), 5.
13 Ibid., 6–7.
14 Carlos Wyld Ospina, *El Autócrata* (Guatemala City: Tipographía Sánchez & De Guise, 1929), 171.
15 Ibid, 171. For Gómez Carrillo's economic relations with Estrada Cabrera, see the same page.
16 Héctor Gálvez, *Conozca a Estrada Cabrera* (Guatemala City: Editorial Prensa Libr, 1976), appendix 3.
17 Wyld Ospina, op. cit., 107, 105, 104–05, 116.
18 Ibid., 121.
19 Torres, op. cit., 9.
20 Carlos Wyld Ospina, in the prologue to *Enrique Gómez Carrillo*, by Edelberto Torres, 16.
21 Torres, op. cit., 369.

22 Webster, op. cit., 58–70.

23 Wyld Ospina, op. cit., 18.

24 Enrique Gómez Carrillo, *La Rusia Actual* (Paris: Casa Editorial Garnier Hermanos, 1906), v–vi.

256

25 Ibid., 3.

26 Ibid., 3–4.

27 Ibid., 14.

28 Ibid., 168.

29 Ibid., 199.

30 Enrique Gómez Carrillo, *L'Ame japonaise* (Paris: E. Sansot, 1906), 7.

31 Ibid., 8.

32 Ibid., 12.

33 Ibid., 153–54.

34 Ibid., 176–84.

35 Ibid., 135–36.

36 Ibid., 138–39.

37 Ibid., 130–31.

38 Ibid., 214–15.

39 Ibid., 71.

40 Enrique Gómez Carrillo, *Psicología de la Moda Feminina* (Madrid: M. Pérez Villavicencio, 1907).

41 Enrique Gómez Carrillo, *Psychologie de la mode* (Paris: Garnier Frères, 1910).

42 Torres, op. cit., 9.

43 Gómez Carrillo, *Psicología de la Moda Feminina*, 27.

44 Gómez Carrillo, *Psychologie de la mode*, 44.

45 Ibid., 115–16.

46 Ibid., 166.

47 Gómez Carrillo, *Psicología de la Moda Feminina*, 16–17.

48 Enrique Gómez Carrillo, *Le Sourire sous la mitraillle* (Paris & Nancy: Berger-Levrault, 1916).

49 Ibid., 121.

50 Ibid., 30.

51 Ibid., 56.

52 Ibid., 71–72.

53 Ibid., 320.

54 Ibid., 323.

55 Ibid., 326.

56 Ibid., 318.

57 Ibid., 346.

58 Enrique Gómez Carrillo, *Treinta Años de Mi Vida*, 29.

CHARLES LOUDON

1 Charles Loudon, *A Practical Dissertation on the Waters of Leamington Spa; Including the History of the Springs, a New Analysis of Their Gaseous and Solid Contents, the Rules for Drinking the Waters, Bathing, Diet of the Patients, and Other Regimen* (Leamington Spa: Sharp & Fairfax, 1828), 50.

2 Frederick W. Price, *A Textbook of the Practice of Medicine*, 6th ed. (London: Oxford University Press, 1941), 1234–35.

3 A. L. Cochrane, *Effectiveness and Efficiency: Random Reflections on Health Services* (Oxford: The Nuffield Provincial Hospitals Trust, 1972), 8.

4 Ibid., 8–9.

5 See the first and third edition of Loudon's book, pages 2 and 14 respectively. The date of the third edition, 1831, was that of the decennial census, instituted in Britain in 1801.

6 Loudon, op. cit., 4.

7 Loudon, op. cit., 79–81.

8 J. T. Ward, *The Factory Movement 1830–1855* (London: Macmillan, 1962), 94–106.

9 *British Parliamentary Papers, Factories Inquiry Commission Second Report Together with Supplementary Report Part I Employment of Children in Factories with Minutes of Evidence and Reports of Medical and District Commissioners Industrial Revolution Children's Employment*, reprinted in the Irish University Press Series of British Parliamentary Papers, vol. 4 (Shannon, 1968), 1–23.

10 J. T. Ward, op. cit., 94–106. The quotations that follow come from the same source.

11 See above note.

12 Charles Loudon, "Medical Reports by Dr Loudon," in *Reports from Commissioners, Vol. 5: Factories: Ecclesiastical Inquiry* (London: The House of Commons, 1833): C.3., 24.

13 Francis Sharp, in Loudon, "Medical Reports by Dr Loudon," 12–14.

14 "Medical Reports by Dr Loudon," 1–23. All the quotations that follow are from the same source.

15 See above note.

16 See Charles Loudon's evidence in the *Second Report of the Factories Inquiry Commission*, published in the Irish University Press Series of British Parliamentary Papers, vol. 4 (Shannon, 1968).

17 T. R. Malthus, *An Essay on the Principle of Population*, 3rd ed. (London: J. Johnson, 1806), vol. I, 463.

18 Published by the Librairie Étrangère et Orientale de Girard Frères.

19 Karl Marx, *Economic and Philosophic Manuscripts of 1844*, tr. Martin

Milligan (Guildford, Connecticut: Prometheus Books, 1988), 32.

20 Charles Loudon, *Solution du problème de la population et de la subsistence, soumise à un médecin dans une série de lettres* (Paris: Librairie Étrangère et Orientale de Girard Frères, 1842), 328.

258

21 Charles Loudon, *The Equilibrium of Population and Sustenance Demonstrated, Showing on Physiological and Statistical Grounds the Means of Obviating the Fears of the late Mr Malthus* (Leamington Spa: John Fairfax, 1836).

22 Ibid., 6.

23 William Hazlitt, *The Spirit of the Age: or Contemporary Portraits*, 2nd ed. (London: Henry Colburn, 1825), 229.

24 Paul R. Ehrlich, *The Population Explosion* (London: Hutchinson, 1990), 39–40.

25 See, for example, Oliver Milman, *The Insect Crisis: The Fall of the Tiny Empires that Run the World* (London: Atlantic Books, 2022).

26 Charles Loudon to Thomas Doubleday, n.d., but probably 1842.

27 Loudon, *Equilibrium*, 311.

28 Ibid., 11.

29 Ibid., 14.

30 Ibid., 24.

31 Ibid., 67–69.

32 Ibid., 18–19.

33 Ibid., 95.

34 Ibid., 229.

35 Ibid., 229.

36 Ibid., 229.

37 Ibid., 229.

38 Ibid., 235.

39 Ibid., 250.

40 Ibid., 276–77.

41 Margracia Loudon, *Philanthropic Economy* (London: Edward Churton, 1835), 105.

42 Margracia Loudon, *Fortune-Hunting: A Novel* (London: Henry Colburn, 1832).

JULES CORNÉLY

1 Jean-Marc Stussi, "Georges Louis Warnecke," Facteurs de pianos en France, Histoire de pianos, https://www.lieveverbeeck.eu/Warnecke_Nancy.htm (accessed July 17, 2023).

2 Michel Cornely, Geneanet, https://gw.geneanet.org/supausa?n=cornely&oc=&p=michel (accessed July 17, 2023).

3 Jules Cornély, "Un Roman," *Le Gaulois*, May 30, 1893.

4   Ibid.

5   Jonathan Swift, *Travels into Severas Remote Nations of the World. By Lemuel Gulliver, first a Surgeon, and then a Captain of several Ships* (London: Benj. Motte), ch. 6.

6   Jules Cornély, *Le Czar et le Roi* (Paris: Le Clairon, 1884), 170.

7   Ibid., 239.

8   Ibid., 183.

9   Ibid., 187.

10   Ibid., 187.

11   Ibid., 85.

12   Ibid., 110–11.

13   Ibid., 111.

14   Ibid., 236.

15   Ibid., 236.

16   Ibid., 223, 236.

17   Ibid., 238.

18   Ibid., 222.

19   Jules Cornély, *Rome et le Jubilé de Leon XIII: Notes d'un Pèlerin* (Paris: Société Générale de Librairie Catholique, 1888), 1.

20   Ibid., 6–7.

21   Ibid., 8.

22   Ibid., 16.

23   Ibid., 28.

24   Ibid., 46.

25   Ibid., 249.

26   Arthur Meyer, "Une Démission," *Le Gaulois*, December 21, 1897.

27   Jules Cornély, *Notes sur l'affaire Dreyfus* (Édition du Figaro) (Paris: Société Française d'Éditions d'Art, n.d.), preface, i.

28   Ibid., 149.

29   Ibid., 92.

30   Ibid., 94.

31   Ibid., 76.

32   Ibid., 3.

33   Ibid., 3.

34   Guy Chapman, *The Dreyfus Case: A Reassessment* (London: Rupert Hart-Davis, 1955), 97.

35   Ibid., 97.

36   Cornély, *Notes sur l'affaire Dreyfus*, 557.

JEAN-RICHARD BLOCH

1   Louis Aragon, *Les plus belles pages de Jean-Richard Bloch presentées par Aragon* (Paris: La Bibliothèque française, 1948), preface.

2   Jean Albertini, *Aves-vous lu Jean-Richard Bloch?* (Chatillon sous Bagneux: Éditions sociales, 1981), 9.

3   Annie Angremy and Michel Trebitsch, editors, *Jean-Richard Bloch, ou L'écriture et l'action* (Paris: Bibliothèque nationale de France, 2002).

4   Ibid., 9.

5   Jean-Richard Bloch, "Lévy," in *Lévy* (Paris: Nouvelle Revue Française, 1912), 28.

6   Ibid., 32.

7   Ibid., 32.

8   Ibid., 33.

9   Ibid., 67.

10   Ibid., 51.

11   Ibid., 75.

12   Bloch, "Le Vieux des routes," in *Lévy*, 148–49.

13   Ibid., 154.

14   Wolfgang Klein, "'La volonté de 'la vie intelligente': Jean-Richard Bloch dans la presse française (1945–1947)" in *Jean-Richard Bloch, ou L'écriture et l'action*, ed. Angremy and Trebitsch, 275.

15   Ludmila Stern, "Journal du voyage en URSS de Marguerite ey Jean-Richard Bloch," in *Jean-Richard Bloch, ou L'écriture et l'action*, ed. Angremy and Trebitsch, 231–32.

16   Ibid., 231–32.

17   Jean-Richard Bloch, *Moscou–Paris* (Paris: Éditions "Raisons d'Être," 1947), 10.

18   Jean Cathala, *Sans fleur ni fusil* (Paris: Albin Michel, 1981), 313.

19   Ibid., 313–14.

20   Ibid., 314.

21   Jean Albertini, "Deux lettres inédites de Jean-Richard Bloch et Romain Rolland (7 and 10 octobre, 1936)," in *Retrouver Jean-Richard Bloch, Studia Romanica,* fasc. XVIII, 1994, quoted in Sophie Coeuré, "Jean-Richard Bloch intellectuel communiste, écrivain et témoin engagé, une autobiographie impossible?" in *Écritures autobiographiques: Entre confession et dissimulation*, ed. Anne-Rachel Hermetet and Jean-Marie Paul (Rennes: Presses Universitaires de Rennes), 297–313.

22   Nicole Racine, "Jean-Richard Bloch ou les épreuves de la fidélité," in *Jean-Richard Bloch, ou L'écriture et l'action*, ed. Angremy and Trebitsch, 262.

23   Bloch, *Moscou–Paris*, 49.

24   Ibid., 165–66.

25   Louis Aragon, "Staline et la France," *Les Lettres françaises*, March 12, 1953.

26   Jean-Richard Bloch, "Staline," *Europe*, December 1949, 41.

27   Louis Aragon, *Les hommes communistes*, vol. 2 (Paris: Gallimard, 1953).

28 Jean-Richard Bloch, *Offrande à la politique* (Paris: Les Éditions Rieder, 1933), 11.

29 Ibid., 22.

30 Ibid., 25.

31 Ibid., 27–28.

32 Ibid., 27–28.

33 Ibid., 79–80.

34 Ibid., 80.

35 Romain Rolland, introduction to — *& Co.*, by Jean-Richard Bloch, tr. C. K. Scott Moncrieff (London: Victor Gollancz, 1930), 8.

36 Jean-Richard Bloch, — *& Co.*, 105–06.

37 Jean-Richard Bloch, *Cacaouettes et bananes* (Paris: Gallimard, 1929). See Albert Londres, *Terre d'Ebène* (Paris: Albin Michel, 1929), and Andre Gide, *Voyage au Congo* (Paris: Gallimard, 1927).

ÉMILE SOUVESTRE

1   Eugène Lesbazeilles, "Notice sur la vie d'Émile Souvestre" (Notice of the Life of Émile Souvestre), in *Souvenirs d'un viellard: La dernière étape*, by Émile Souvestre (Paris: Michel Lévy frères, 1857), xxxiii–xxxiv.

2   David Steel, *Émile Souvestre, Un Breton des Lettres, 1806–1854* (Émile Souvestre, a Breton Man of Letters, 1806–1854) (Rennes: Presses Universitaires de Rennes, 2013), 13.

3   Ibid., 14.

4   Émile Souvestre, op. cit., 5.

5   Ibid., 88.

6   Ibid., 89.

7   Ibid., 106.

8   Ibid., 32–33.

9   Ibid., 33.

10 Ibid., 45.

11 Ibid., 47.

12 Ibid., 57.

13 Ibid., 57–58.

14 Ibid., 219.

15 Ibid., 14–15.

16 Ibid., 17.

17 Ibid., 50.

18 Ibid., 51.

19 Ibid., 52–53.

20 Ibid., 182–83.

21 Ibid., 26.

22 Ibid., 94–95.

23 Ibid., 96.

24 Ibid., 98.

25 Ibid., 99–100.

26 Émile Souvestre, *Un philosophe sous les toits: Journal d'un homme heu-reux*, 2nd ed. (Paris: Michel Lévy, 1851), 181.

27 Souvestre, *Souvenirs d'un viellard*, 7.

28 Souvestre, *Un philosophe sous les toits*, 76.

29 Ibid., 77.

30 Ibid., 77–78.

31 Ibid., 79.

32 Ibid., 84.

33 Ibid., 125.

34 Émile Souvestre, *Le monde tel qu'il sera* (Paris: W. Coquebert, 1846), 3–4.

35 Ibid., 15.

36 Ibid., 78.

37 Ibid., 79.

38 Ibid., 44–45.

PHOTOGRAPH CREDITS

Alice-René Brouillhet (1887–1960): Anthony Daniels
Eugène-Melchior de Vogüé (1848–1910): Pierre-Yves Beaudouin /
    Wikimedia Commons / CC BY-SA 3.0
François-Vincent Raspail (1796–1878): Kent Wang from London,
    United Kingdom, CC BY-SA 2.0, via Wikimedia Commons
Enrique Gómez Carrillo (1873–1927): Pierre-Yves Beaudouin /
    Wikimedia Commons / CC BY-SA 4.0
Charles Loudon (1801–1844): Pierre-Yves Beaudouin / Wikimedia
    Commons / CC BY-SA 4.0
Jules Cornély (1845–1907): Pierre-Yves Beaudouin / Wikimedia
    Commons / CC BY-SA 4.0
Jean-Richard Bloch (1884–1947): Pierre-Yves Beaudouin / Wikimedia
    Commons / CC BY-SA 4.0
Émile Souvestre (1806–1854): Coyau / Wikimedia Commons /
    CC BY-SA 3.0

A Note on the Type

Buried But Not Quite Dead has been set in Kingfisher, a family of types designed by Jeremy Tankard. Frustrated by the paucity of truly well-drawn fonts for book work, Tankard set out to create a series of types that would be suitable for a wide range of text settings. Informed by a number of elegant historical precedents – the highly regarded Doves type, Monotype Barbou, and Ehrhardt among them – yet beholden to no one type in particular, Kingfisher attains a balance of formality, detail, and color that is sometimes lacking in types derived or hybridized from historical forms. The italic, designed intentionally as a complement to the roman, has much in common with earlier explorations in sloped romans like the Perpetua and Joanna italics, yet moderates the awkward elements that mar types like Van Krimpen's Romulus italic. The resulting types, modern, crisp, and handsome, are ideal for the composition of text matter at a variety of sizes, and comfortable for extended reading.

SERIES DESIGN BY CARL W. SCARBROUGH